WTF, America? How the US Went Off the Rails and How to Get It Back on Track

D1622162

WTF, America? How the US Went Off the Rails and How to Get It Back on Track

● ● ●

John Atcheson

ISBN-13: 9780985071288
ISBN-10: 0985071281

Acknowledgments

No book truly worth reading has only one author, and *WTF, America?* is no exception. I would like to thank Joe Harrington, John Sherman, Mark Goldman, Jon Luft, Kari Palm, and Linda Giannelli Pratt for reading early versions of the book, and offering me the most valuable things a reviewer can give – honesty. I would also like to thank Jon Queally, managing editor of Common Dreams, for giving me the opportunity to reach – and hopefully influence – so many people. Twenty-eight thousand Facebook links for a single article makes me feel like we're succeeding. This book grew from the pieces published in Common Dreams.

Mark, I know much of what you found in this book was familiar to you from our lunch time rants. You make being a grumpy old man fun, and enlightening.

Joe, you continue to amaze me. Your comments and criticisms were detailed, insightful, and offered with care, kindness, and humor when humor was called for. It would be a much better book if I'd incorporated more of what you suggested.

John, our conversations and our email debates helped shape and hone my ideas. And your faithful readings of my columns – together with your honest reactions to them and this book – were invaluable.

Kari and Jon Luft, your willingness to plow through the manuscript in record time, and your insights are much appreciated.

And finally, Linda. Thanks for listening to me on those thousands of occasions when I think I've written something brilliant, congratulating me when you agree, and telling me I'm full of it when you don't. But most of all, thank you for making our life together one of the most fascinating journeys I could hope for.

WTF, AMERICA?
How the US Went Off the Rails and How to Get It Back on Track

The only sure bulwark of continuing liberty is a government
strong enough to protect the interests of the people, and
a people strong enough and well enough informed to
maintain its sovereign control over the government.

FRANKLIN D. ROOSEVELT

The citizen can bring our political and governmental
institutions back to life, make them responsive and
accountable, and keep them honest. No one else can.

JOHN GARDNER

As democracy is perfected, the office represents, more and more closely,
the inner soul of the people. We move toward a lofty ideal. On some great
and glorious day the plain folks of the land will reach their heart's desire
at last, and the White House will be adorned by a downright moron.

H. L. MENCKEN

Contents

Preface: Times Are Bad · xi

PART ONE: The Silent Coup—How the Oligarchy Used Lies, Deceptions, Money, and Myths to Take Over America · 1

Chapter 1   Throw Out the History Books; Forget the Fourth of July Fireworks; You Don't Live in a Democracy, Anymore · 3

Chapter 2   Funding the Coup · 9

Chapter 3   Muzzling the Press · · · · · · · · · · · · · · · · · · · 14

Chapter 4   The Myth of the Magic Markets · · · · · · · · · · · 25

Chapter 5   The Myth of the Bumbling Bureaucrat · · · · · · · · 40

Chapter 6   The Uncivil Society · · · · · · · · · · · · · · · · · · · 61

Chapter 7   Putting the Silver-Tongued Lizard in Charge · · · · · · · · 68

Chapter 8   How to Steal a Nomination · · · · · · · · · · · · · · · · 80

PART TWO: Drinking Sand · 91

Chapter 9   We Have Met the Enemy, and He Is Us · · · · · · · · · · · 93

Chapter 10   Dark Ages Redux: American Politics and the End of the Enlightenment · 102

Chapter 11   Scared Witless in the Home of the Brave · · · · · · · · · 110

Chapter 12   The Big Con—The Market Über Alles · · · · · · · · · · · 115

**PART THREE: Inheriting the Wind—The Sterile Seeds of
Greed** · **129**

Chapter 13   Neoliberalism and the Destruction of the Ecological
Commons · 131

Chapter 14   Economics and the Twin Horsemen of the New
Apocalypse · 135

Chapter 15   Home · 153

PART FOUR: Putting America Back on Track · · · · · · · · · · · · **177**

Chapter 16   A Revolution Is Coming · 179

Chapter 17   Mounting the Resistance—Administering Political
First Aid · 186

Chapter 18   Catch-22—Can't Change the Laws without Changing
the Culture; Can't Change the Culture without
Changing the Laws · 195

Chapter 19   A Blueprint for a Cultural Revolution · · · · · · · · · · · · · 200

Chapter 20   If It's Called Free Speech, Why Does It Cost So
Much? · 204

Chapter 21   Making Government Work Again · · · · · · · · · · · · · · 209

Chapter 22   Making the Media Serve the People, Not the
Plutocrats · 216

Chapter 23   Reforming Our Electoral Process · · · · · · · · · · · · · · · 225

Chapter 24   Funding the New Coup with "Viewers Like You" · · · · · 233

Chapter 25   Why the Establishment Will Tell You to Ignore
this Book And Why You Shouldn't Listen to Them · · · 240

Conclusion · 245

Notes· 249

Times Are Bad

● ● ●

Times are bad. Children no longer obey their
parents and everyone is writing a book.

ATTRIBUTED TO CICERO

LATE IN THE EVENING OF November 8 2016, the unthinkable was suddenly
transforming into the inevitable—America was about to elect a reality-
show buffoon as its president. By the next morning, he'd become our
own Dear Leader, and he did it by passing himself off as a populist. This
modern-day Midas, born on third base and backed by billions—soon to
appoint the richest set of plutocrats in our nation's history to his cabinet
and leadership positions—a pussy-grabbing, thrice-divorced, narcissist—
elected by conservative values-voters, the poor, and evangelists as a *popu-*
list? WTF, indeed.

Meanwhile, Hillary Clinton, a neoliberal, cast in the mold of the
Democratic Leadership Council (DLC)—"the inevitable, the shoe-in, the
most prepared candidate in history, etc, etc, etc"—went the same way as
JEB!, the establishment's other preferred candidate.

Many walked around that day in a daze, muttering, Trump?...Donald
J. Trump? Really?

Yes, really. He of the world's worst comb-over, backer of birther nonsense, a man devoid of any experience or knowledge about governance—this

obscene, latter-day carney barker—had just become president of the United States of America.

Meanwhile, the pundits, politicians, pollsters, and prognosticators—their foreheads red from head slaps, cheeks glowing crimson from embarrassment—went into hyper-drive to explain why the thing they'd described as impossible had just happened.

A few even tried their hand at explaining what we can do about it.

Almost none of them know the answer to either question. They're still focused on the 2016 election, dissecting tactics, examining polls, blaming emails or Russian hacks—all viewed through the lens of an outmoded left/right, Democrat/Republican political landscape that is evaporating in the face of a burgeoning revolution.

They were, and still are, completely unaware that this emerging revolution was occurring, let alone understanding that it was the inevitable response to a successful Silent Coup[1] four decades in the making, mounted by a cadre of conservative rich ideologues and corporations seeking to wrest power from the government for the purpose of enriching themselves. No, the Coup was not some shadowy conspiracy featuring clandestine meetings, passwords, secret handshakes, James Bond supervillains, Freemasons, or…gasp…even the Trilateral Commission. This Coup was more like a flock of vultures moving in tandem only because they were pursuing a shared vision of their own self-interest—which was to relentlessly fleece us to feather their own foul nests. But if it wasn't a coherent junta, it was fueled by money. Lots and lots of money. And it had a blueprint—the Powell memo.[2]

It was spectacularly successful: the top one-tenth of 1 percent of Americans now have as much wealth as the bottom 90 percent, democracy is all but dead in the Unites States, the press is a wholly owned subsidiary of the Oligarchy, and both parties dance to its tune.

The question of how this Coup and the revolt it inspired escaped the notice of the press, the political parties, academia, and political analysts of just about every stripe is the topic of this book, as is the outline of what we can do about it. As we will see in Part One, The Silent Coup: How the Oligarchy Used Lies, Deceptions, Money, and Myths to Take Over America, the uber rich and corporate America engineered it, and they skillfully took over both the political parties and the media.

The mainstream media had become a wholly-owned subsidiary of corporate America long before Trump appeared on the political scene, which explains in part why the existence of the Coup and the revolution that it inspired went virtually unreported.

But even the so-called liberal media outlets such as PBS, NPR, MSNBC, *The Rolling Stone*, *The Daily Kos*, *The Huffington Post*, and *Mother Jones*—which typically back Democratic Candidates—failed to understand that backing a status quo candidate like Clinton in the face of the emerging revolt was a form of political suicide. And certainly, the Democratic Party missed the signals. In fact, the Democratic National Committee (DNC) has voted in a chairman straight out of the party's DLC inspired, corporate centric wing, and it is fighting to keep corporate funding and neoliberalism at the core of the party's DNA. Lemmings have a better survival instinct than this.

But the explanation for why the political cognoscenti has been blind to—or at least silent about—what has been shaping politics over the last four decades goes deeper than money, power and greed.

Quite simply, the long-term forces shaping US and global politics are beyond the province of journalism, but are not yet the stuff of history.

The fact is, we seldom recognize history in the making except in hindsight. Journalists see their charge as reporting events as they unfold. Historians see theirs as assembling those events, once completed, into a larger context that makes sense when viewed through the clarifying lens of time. The landscape between these two disciplines is largely uninhabited, yet it is extraordinarily important, never more so than now. Viewed from this perspective, Trump is revealed as a symptom, not the problem. A virulent symptom, to be sure. A gut-wrenching, hugging-the-porcelain-goddess, dry-heaves-inducing symptom. But the real disease is far worse, and it lurks in the landscape between journalism and history.

But a few of us saw this revolution coming.[3]

Shortly before the election, Michael Moore was running around with his hair on fire, warning anyone who would listen that Trump would win. Thomas Frank, in *Listen Liberal*, explained how the Democratic Party had moved from the people's party to a Party of elites, by elites and for elites and warned of the consequences for mainstream candidates such as Hillary Clinton. While Frank acknowledged the role of money in this takeover, he chose to emphasize the less explored cause of this switch – the abandonment of the New Deal for the raw deal that was the product of a focus on the professional class, the entrepreneur, and the highly educated. The two forces—elitism and the influence of the moneyed interests—are not mutually exclusive; indeed, they are mutually reinforcing. But the full scope of the Coup and the tactics used has rarely been covered in its entirety, nor have its consequences or the solutions we must adopt to keep the money-leeches from bleeding us dry and the hate mongers from bleaching our souls.

That's where *WTF, America?* comes in. Backed up by extensive documentation, it describes how first the Republicans and later the Democrats—led by the Democratic Leadership Council—joined the Coup, and it demonstrates how this election was the inevitable outcome of these trends.

The existence of this Coup explains how we ended up with two such deeply flawed candidates—one a dangerous misogynistic megalomaniac, the other the personification of the status quo falsely posing as a progressive.

The distinguishing characteristic of this election was anger at the establishment. Trump won because he was able to pose as an outsider, and because he channeled that anger. And make no mistake, that anger was justified.

The political mainstream of both parties is either ignoring the extent to which they've alienated the people, or they don't care. Here's just one finding from a landmark study called the Smith Project that summarizes people's dim view of both political parties:[4]

Americans overwhelmingly agree (78%–15%) that both political parties are too beholden to special interests to create any meaningful change.

Here's another observation revealed by the Smith Project:

> American voters strongly believe that corruption and crony capitalism are among the most important issues facing our nation—almost equal to jobs and the economy. Political alienation has existed for decades, but it now envelops over three-fifths of all voters. *These are the numbers that precede a political upheaval.* (emphasis added)

Trump's Con: In the run-up to the election, much of the media were reinforcing Trump's claim to be an "outsider" and a "populist," and too many media outlets still are. But his transition team and his cabinet appointments and his policies reveal that his campaign was the biggest con since Ponzi developed his pyramid scheme. He is proving to be exactly what Republicans have wanted all along—a plutocrat intent on overturning the remnants of the New Deal, cutting taxes for the rich and corporations, further eviscerating government, rolling back regulations, and turning the country over to a privatized Oligarchy. The only difference is that Trump ran a better scam, and his appeal to hate, jingoism, xenophobia, misogyny, and the rest of the lizard-brained isms has been explicit, while the Republican Party's had been—until Trump—on the down-low.

Trump the populist? Hardly. His cabinet appointments are a collection of rich corporate foxes, assigned to guard the chicken coop, together with ultraconservative government-hating ideologues tapped with the task of governing. Just seven of Trump's appointments are worth more than $11 billion.[5]

Remember Trump excoriating the Goldman Sachs revolving door into senior government positions? Well, there are seven current or former

Goldman Sachs executives playing a prominent role in his new administration, including his secretary of treasury and his senior economic advisor.

Now, as I write this, Trump has succeeded in getting the collection of plutocratic puppies he's chosen to run the government confirmed by the Senate, he's put in place a Supreme Court Justice who brings corporate favoritism to new heights, and—with the help of Congressional Republicans—he's on his way to passing the most anti-populist piece of legislation the country has seen in decades, Trumpcare. Worse, he is withdrawing the US from the Paris Agreement -- an act that puts insanity in a race with ignorance.

How a plutocrat like Trump got elected as a populist, cries out for an explanation, particularly when you realize that the majority of Americans endorse liberal positions when viewed on an issue-by-issue basis, and the Democrats have an edge in the number of registered voters.

The Revolution to Come—Fascism or Freedom: Meanwhile, the Democratic Party, in thrall to neoliberalism, has been—and still seems intent on—embracing much of what we think of as "conservative": small government; austerity; free trade; deregulated markets; and capital conserving policies rather than the New Deal policies focused on protecting the interests of labor, the middle class, and the working class.

With no one speaking for and representing the middle-class and working-class Americans, we are seeing what is both an inevitable and epochal shift in people's attitude toward government—one that was, in fact, intentionally engineered by the moneyed interests managing the Coup—one that has undermined the basis of our democratic republic, one that has finally sparked a revolt by the 99 percent.

The issue before us is the nature of the inevitable revolution. It can represent the national id, unleashed by Trump and the Republicans—fueled by hate, greed, fear, jingoism, ignorance, and a lust for power. Or it can be the legacy of the movement Sanders captured—one rooted in hope, an equitably shared prosperity, and a government of, by, and for the people.

If the revolution is to be a rational and peaceful one, we have to examine and understand the roots of the Oligarch's Coup, and the roadblocks the establishment used to subvert, once again, the interests—and the will—of the people so that they can be removed peacefully. And that, in turn, requires that we understand the tactics used by the Coup that has taken the entire country—including the Democrats—into the hands of the Oligarchy over the past four decades. The alternative is the fascist, hate-filled chaos that looms over the horizon, visible in the rise of the Far Right as seen in Brexit, in Austria, the rise of a right-wing nationalist party in Germany, the Netherlands, the Five Star Party in Italy, and across the continent of Europe as well as in Trump's appeal here.

In this book, we will examine the roots of what brought Trump to power, but it is important to remember that Trump is merely a symptom of the disease infecting our national consciousness not the disease itself. In Part One, I explain how the Coup was pulled off, including the creation of the two great myths that dominate our political worldview; in Part Two, I examine how the Coup undermined the cultural commons—the Enlightenment basis of our democratic republic; in Part Three, we'll see the full price of the New Dark Ages and the existential threat it poses to our ecological commons; and in Part Four, we'll look at a blueprint for getting America back on track.

PART ONE: The Silent Coup— How the Oligarchy Used Lies, Deceptions, Money, and Myths to Take Over America

● ● ●

The greatest trick the Devil ever pulled was convincing the world he didn't exist.

ROGER "VERBAL" KINT,
FROM THE CULT-FILM CLASSIC *THE USUAL SUSPECTS*

CHAPTER 1

Throw Out the History Books; Forget the Fourth of July Fireworks; You Don't Live in a Democracy, Anymore

● ● ●

None are so hopelessly enslaved as those who falsely believe they are free.

JOHANN WOLFGANG VON GOETHE

THE SILENT COUP—THE GREATEST STORY **Never Told:** If you want to understand how and why a second-rate carney barker became our president, you need to understand what's happened within the last three to four decades. While we've chased trumped up threats and imagined slights overseas and here at home, our democracy has fallen. We have been taken over; defeated; our voices neutered; our freedoms trampled; our democracy vanquished.

No invading force accomplished this; no jackboots echoed across our republic; no alien flag was raised above our lands. Not a single shot was fired by our vaunted military to halt this takeover. No, this was a quiet coup, accomplished from within, and conducted in stealth.

In the cult film classic, *The Usual Suspects*, Roger "Verbal" Kint says, "The greatest trick the Devil ever pulled was convincing the world he didn't exist." Just so, has the Oligarchy taken over the United States.

Many of us continue with the delusion that we are free. We celebrate Independence Day. We vote. We express ourselves openly. We are not jailed for our opinions, at least not usually. We live where we want. We pursue the work we choose. We get our news from a "free" press. We engage in the pursuit of happiness.

And while all this seems true, we are not free. Our votes carry no weight. Our news is a hollow monoculture in which six corporations own 90 percent of the outlets with most of the rest controlled by elitists who can no longer relate to the average person, in which infotainment has replaced information, in which a modern-day version of bread and circuses keeps us distracted from the increasingly grim reality we are everyday immersed in. The jobs open to us are becoming increasingly exploitative. And the pursuit of happiness is marred by a lack of choice, increasingly desperate economic straits for the majority of us, and a feeling of impotence as we watch the American dream shrink before our eyes.

Consider[6]:

* When 91 percent wanted to strengthen rules on clean air and protection of drinking water, Congress—led by the Republican majority—proposed weakening them[7].
* When 90 percent wanted to protect public lands and parks, the Republicans proposed putting them on sale or otherwise privatizing them[8].
* When 74 percent of Americans favored ending subsidies to big oil, Congress retained most of them[9].
* At a time when the majority of citizens[10] favored allowing tax cuts for those earning over $250,000 to expire, the best Congress could do was to compromise on $400,000.
* When 70 percent of Americans favored staying in the Paris climate agreement, Trump dropped out[11];
* Some 80 percent of Americans favor shoring up social security even if it means higher taxes[12] and a similar number support retaining Medicare as is, but the Obama administration twice offered cuts to both programs as part of a "grand bargain" and the Republican budget and health care proposals routinely savage both programs.

* Or take this gem…more than 80 percent of Americans want to clamp down on Wall Street[13] but the best we could get was weak-sister legislation that doesn't even address too-big-to-fail or restore a Glass Steagall provision limiting the risks these big banks can take with your money. And even this slap-on-the-wrist legislation is being completely eviscerated as it is translated into regulations.
* After Orlando, 92 percent of the people[14] supported a bill expanding background checks to online purchases of guns, but Congress has been unable to pass it.
* And when 85 percent of citizens supported a bill barring people on the terrorist watch list from buying guns, Congress couldn't pass the it.

Dwell on these last two bits of political pornography for a moment: Congress denied the vast majority of the people's perfectly reasonable—in fact, barely minimal—desire to keep assault rifles and weapons out of the hands of potential mass murderers *because a few special interests opposed it.*

But it's not simply a list of specific issues where the Oligarchy defeats the will of the people. Their victory has been complete.

Even as we spent tens of trillions on defense, ostensibly to protect our freedom, we quietly relinquished it, not to an invasion from without, but to the Silent Coup by the rich and powerful from within. As Martin Gilens and Benjamin I. Page pointed out in their landmark study[15] on the influence of money and special interests in politics:

When the preferences of economic elites and the stands of organized interest groups are controlled for, ***the preferences of the average American appear to have only a minuscule, near-zero, statistically non-significant impact upon public policy***. (emphasis added)

They went on to note that "*… **the majority does not rule—at least not in the causal sense of actually determining policy outcomes**.*" (my emphasis).

Take a moment to consider this, too. We the people have no say and almost zero influence in our governance. Forget about the land of the free and the home of the brave—we've become the land of the duped and the home of the indentured.

The system which enabled this coup is the pay-to-play politics that Clinton and virtually all politicians subscribed to, until Sanders, and to a lesser extent, Trump, who regularly excoriates the elite establishment, even as his policy proposals and cabinet reward it.

The idea that we are not free isn't hyperbole; it can't be written off to the excess exuberance of the young, or the unrealistic reveries of ideologues that the establishment media would have you believe. It's data. It's reality. And it's the logical end-point of the pay-to-play PACster politics that reached its apogee with the Citizens United decision.

In 2014, it cost about $1.7 million to win a seat in the House, and $10.5 million to win a Senate seat according to a study by maplight.org[16]. *Daily News* reporter David Knowles spoke with Maplight president Daniel Newman for an article on a recent study they conducted, and Newman told him that much of this money came from corporations. He went on to say:

> most industries give money to members of Congress because it buys them access and influence. And now, with Citizens United, corporations can spend unlimited amounts of money on these races. The result is that members of Congress are fearful about voting against corporate interests because there's so much money at stake.

To which most Americans would reply, "Duh!"

Much of the rest of the money a candidate needs to run for Congress comes from über-rich individuals such as the Koch brothers, Sheldon Adelson, and George Soros. They too, have an agenda, and it isn't usually aligned with the interests or the wishes of the American people. Even liberal contributors like Soros, favor members of the establishment elite such as Clinton over "revolutionaries" like Sanders, who want to reform the pay-to-play system that gives conventional politicians, the über rich, and corporations such undue influence.

This is why we can't enact meaningful gun control legislation when the vast majority favor it; this is why we can't enact effective climate change policies when a majority of the citizens in both parties say they want to; this is why we let the people founder but bailed out the banks when they crashed the economy in 2008; this is why politicians from both parties still favor job-wrecking trade agreements when most citizens from both parties are against them; this is why the über rich and corporations can easily discharge debt and renege on promises to their employees using bankruptcy laws, but students and the poor cannot escape their debt; this is why we can't break up the too-big-to-fail banks or restore Glass-Steagall or pass a tax on securities trading; again, even though the majority of Americans favor all of these measures. This is why we are engaged in never-ending wars nobody wants and that nobody can explain or justify, at a cost of trillions of dollars that the people don't want to spend.

Quite simply, the United States is no longer a democratic republic; it is an Oligarchy.

The vast majority of the people—regardless of their political affiliation—understand this at some level. Their loss of power, influence, and wealth is palpable. The press, pundits, and politicians who comprise the elite establishment and the Oligarchy they serve are insulated from it or they are a part of it, and so they continue to navigate using an obsolete map across a left/right landscape that barely exists any longer.

The irony here is that while Americans are painfully aware that their elected officials, from the president down, are beholden to the rich and corporations, they keep reelecting them.

But if you want to understand what happened to JEB! or Marco or Hillary, this explains it. The people have figured out that these establishment candidates don't represent them, and they're dropping out.

Nowhere is this more evident than in the presidential vote in 2016. Despite the headlines about a large turnout, it's clear that many people weren't thrilled with their choice, and turnout was lower than anticipated.

In fact, in fourteen states, down ballot candidates received more votes than candidates for president.[17] That is, people voted for down-ballot candidates but left the top of the ticket blank. This was unprecedented. And it would have been the case in fifteen states, but Nevada allows voters to choose "none-of-the-above," an option 29,000 Nevadans chose rather than voting for Hillary or Trump.

CHAPTER 2

Funding the Coup

● ● ●

It's difficult to get a man [or a woman] *to understand something,*
when his [or her] *salary depends on him not understanding it.*

UPTON SINCLAIR

PEOPLE LOVE CONSPIRACIES. AS NOTED in the Preface, what I call the
Oligarch's Coup is not some secret organization that actually runs things
behind the scenes. Yet a disturbing number of people believe in precisely
this kind of shadowy entity, whether it's Freemasons, the New World
Order, the Trilateral Commission, or even water fluoridation as a commie plot. The Oligarch's Coup bears no resemblance to any of these faux
conspiracies.

Their Coup was more like a school of fish performing intricate moves
in tandem only because they were pursuing a shared vision of their own
self-interest. In the case of the Oligarchy, their interest was to suck the
wealth from the masses and leave their skeletal remains to bleach in the
sun.

It is likely that the startlingly effective transformation they caused
was a result of "increasing returns" and "path dependence"—a phenomenon that Brian Arthur[18] popularized in the 1980s and 1990s when he
applied principles of chaos theory to the study of economics. Essentially,
when a system is disturbed and set in flux—even by relatively small

forces—positive feedbacks can create extraordinary changes that, in hindsight, seem to have proceeded via orderly and systematized strategies. It is my contention that this principle explains the political and cultural changes of the astonishing scale we are seeing today. It also helps explain why the magnitude of the change has largely gone unnoticed.

But while this momentous shift may not have been part of a "vast conspiracy," the Oligarchy was there every step of the way to initiate, encourage, and take advantage of the changes as they occurred.

This is not to say it was not sophisticated, nor successful. It was. In fact, to the extent the Coup did mimic a strategic campaign, it was because there was at least a partial blueprint.

In a memo dated August 23, 1971, Lewis Powell, a corporate lawyer who would be appointed to the Supreme Court in two months, outlined a systematic approach to turning the country to the right and making it more business friendly. He focused on the long term, on institution building, and on influencing education at all levels, including what kind of textbooks should be allowed. He noted that most media outlets were owned by corporations, and thus, could be made to represent the perspective of corporate America. Powell's manifesto repeatedly used the terms "fair" and "balanced." Ring a bell?

The memo was solicited by the Chamber of Commerce, and Powell's general thesis was "… that the American economic system is under broad attack," and that what was good for business was good for America.

As Reclaim Democracy!—which describes itself as an organization devoted to "Restoring Citizen Authority over Corporations"—notes, Powell's memo "…influenced or inspired the creation of the Heritage Foundation, the Manhattan Institute, the Cato Institute, Citizens for a Sound Economy, Accuracy in Academe, and other powerful organizations."[19] As we shall see, these were the tip of a very large iceberg.

But if there was no spooky centralized authority—no secret quarterly meetings held to set up "the new world order"—there was money. Lots and lots of money.

A few rich families, operating behind the scenes and largely ignored by the press (particularly after corporations purchased most of it), achieved the Coup by doing precisely what Powell recommended and investing in the following six areas:

1. creating a conservative infrastructure to give far right extremism an intellectual basis beyond greed and self-interest, and to influence law and policy with a particular focus on academia—and the discipline of economics;
2. taking over the press;
3. glorifying the free market as the source of all things good—investing in the Myth of the Magic Markets;
4. discrediting government as a source of anything good—investing in the Myth of the Bumbling Bureaucrat;
5. perfecting propaganda and messaging—distracting, deceiving, dissembling, and lying to obscure the takeover; and
6. making it safe to buy politicians and elections.

Corporations joined them in this effort, and both reaped astounding returns, in terms of power and wealth.

The seeds of the coup emerged after the decisive defeat of conservative darling Barry Goldwater in 1964.

One of its early funders was Richard Mellon Scaife, who inherited about $500 million in 1965 to add to his war chest, and who enlarged it through investments and other trusts, ultimately becoming a billionaire, back when billionaires were rare.

Other über-wealthy individuals, including Adolph Coors, the Koch brothers (as well as their father, who helped fund the John Birch Society), Alice and Jim Walton, John Olin, Lynde and Harry Bradley, and Betsy DeVos also helped fund think tanks, foundations, and endowed university chairs designed to carry forward their assault on government and a mindless celebration of the free market.

Betsy DeVos, by the way, is Trump's secretary of education, and education was one of her major interests in her funding of the Coup. She's on record as wanting to make our schools more "Christian" and to privatize them. So much for Trump's outsider credentials.

But these wealthy individuals didn't simply dole out money personally. They also set up foundations to provide sustained, enduring, and continuing support designed to insert the conservative message into every facet of society including academia and the media. The combination of think tanks, as well as endowed chairs and fellowships at prestigious universities—including MIT, Stanford, University of Chicago, Princeton, Yale, Harvard, UVA, NYU, and Georgetown, to mention a few—allowed the rich to influence, and ultimately shape, the nation's policy agenda, give the cover of intellectual respectability to an ideology based on greed and self-interest, and create a cadre of leaders and upcoming leaders, in addition to creating "think tanks" that were de facto lobbyists for conservative political objectives.

Five of the biggest conservative foundations are the Lynde and Harry Bradley Foundation, the Koch Family Foundations (there are several actually), the John M. Olin Foundation, the Scaife Family Foundations (again, there are several), and the Adolph Coors Foundation. There are several very good reports detailing how much money these foundations give and what they give it for. One of the more concise summaries is "Buying a Movement: Right-Wing Foundations and American Politics."[20] SourceWatch is also an invaluable resource, as is the Foundation Directory.

Contributions to foundations not only allows the ultra-wealthy and corporations to establish grant programs that will outlive them, but since they are tax exempt, they allow the rich to channel money that would otherwise go to taxes and public programs into very specific activities that appeal to them or, perhaps more likely, laws, policies, and programs that benefit them more directly.

Of course, while they were spending on the war of ideas, the corporations and the rich were also purchasing candidates outright, a practice that accelerated after Citizens United.

Between lobbying, direct contributions to candidates, PACs, and foundation grants for various right-wing causes, corporations and the ultra-wealthy have spent many tens of billions of dollars on their successful Coup, if not more.

In the chapters which follow, we'll focus less on the funding of the coup, than on the key elements they employed to pull it off.

CHAPTER 3

Muzzling the Press

● ● ●

The crisis of modern democracy is a profound one. Free elections, a free press and an independent judiciary mean little when the free market has reduced them to commodities available on sale to the highest bidder.

ARUNDHATI ROY

THE FIRST THING ANY WOULD-BE despot needs to do is control the press. Conservatives and plutocrats accomplished this through four main mechanisms:

1. using foundation grants to influence press coverage, empower conservative voices, and effect change in the journalistic canon through contributions to academia and other influential organizations;
2. changing the laws and rules governing media and media ownership;
3. purchasing media outlets outright; and
4. crafting a sophisticated messaging campaign designed to influence, confuse, conceal, distract, and deceive.

A fifth mechanism was less intentional, but no less effective—absorbing the media into the elite political and economic establishment it was designed to cover.

Let's look at each in turn.

Buying Influence: A considerable part of the fortune that the ultra-wealthy conservatives put into their foundations was aimed at influencing the coverage of news, to make it bend to their preferences.

It's worth examining how a couple of foundations operated in this regard. The John M. Olin Foundation was charged with spending all of its assets within a generation of its founder's death, to avoid "mission drift"—that is, any movement away from its founder's far right dogma. By the time it shuttered its doors on November 29, 2005, the foundation had disbursed $370 million to right-wing organizations, and taking down the "liberal media" was an area of specific focus.

In 1977, William Simon, who was Nixon's secretary of treasury, took over as the executive director of the foundation. In 1980, he published *A Time for Action*, which was meant to be a scathing indictment of what the liberal consensus had done to America. Simon identified the core elements of the Liberal Establishment as "the media, the public interest groups and think tanks, the second and third echelons of the bureaucracy, and, increasingly, the courts."

As Bill Berkowitz wrote in BuzzFlash:

> Simon saw the news media as part of the enemy camp. He especially targeted journalists who, Simon charged, "… have been working overtime to deny liberty to others …"

Berkowitz went on to say that

> Simon and other wealthy benefactors were able to mobilize a number of right wing foundations, including the John M. Olin Foundation, the Lynde and Harry Bradley Foundation, the Koch brothers' foundations, the Smith Richardson Foundation, and the Scaife family foundations, and the transformation of the country's political landscape was under way.[21]

The grants these groups' foundations issued focused on influencing the curricula in economics, political science, and the humanities at major universities;

empowering conservative students and student leaders; and setting up and maintaining conservative newspapers and magazines on campuses.

As usual, conservative foundation grants were used strategically to create institutions and infrastructure that would lead to significant and enduring change,[22] rather than spending on projects and one-off demonstrations the way centrist and liberal foundation grant givers tend to do.

As Sally Covington, former head of the National Committee for Responsive Philanthropy noted, the institutions these funds went to (and still go to), have aggressive PR campaigns, complete with an array of media-savvy tools that get their slant on politics, economics, and government into the hands of the media and opinion leaders.

By the time Reagan completed his terms, the foundations had put the pieces in place in think tanks, journalism schools, and academia in general, to feed the conservative message to a press that was increasingly driven by market share, not ethics, and that was exploding in size and hungry for content.

As the media morphed into a profit center, their safest bet was to present both "sides" of an issue, and thus did Powell's "balance" begin to supplant such quaint, old-fashioned niceties as truth, accuracy, context, and objectivity. As we shall see, this meant that the press carried "both sides" of stories on climate change, trickle-down and supply-side economics, creationism, tax cuts, deficits, and any number of other issues long after the conservative slant on these issues had been clearly and incontrovertibly shown to be both counterfactual, and bad for most Americans.

Changing the Rules: But these investments could not pay off unless the rules and guidelines the Federal Communications Commission (FCC) had in place for governing programming were changed, or better yet, scrapped altogether. Prior to the 1980s, the FCC saw its mission as ensuring that Americans had access to a diversity of news sources and views throughout the United States.

One of the chief tools the FCC used to do this was the Fairness Doctrine—which was instituted in 1949 amid concerns about the three new networks holding a monopoly on reporting the news. The Doctrine required broadcasters to (1) cover controversial issues and (2) present a variety of perspectives on them.

Until Reagan, the government also maintained three critical positions on the press: first, that the airwaves were part of the public commons; second, that a license came with responsibilities to fulfill a public trust; and third, that the government had a right and a duty to assure that trust was honored. In a classic fox-guarding-the-chicken-coop move, Reagan appointed commissioners to the FCC who had been employed by the media companies they were charged with regulating.

Case in point, in 1981, very early in his first term, Reagan appointed Mark Fowler to chair the FCC. Fowler, who made his living representing telecommunication companies before his appointment, was a free-market ideologue of the first degree who once said, "The television is just another appliance...a toaster with pictures." Once approved, Fowler promptly went about the business of deregulating the media. By the time Reagan stepped down, the media had been converted from a public trust, to a commodity subject primarily to the whims of the free market. But as we were to learn, and as our founders knew, the press was far more important to a free society than...say...pork bellies. Here's a summary of some of the deregulation Fowler and Reagan oversaw at the FCC:

- extending television licenses from three years to five, in 1981 (since the FCC's main mechanism for assuring compliance hinged on licensing, this was vital to the industry);
- lifting limits on the number of stations any one company could own from seven to twelve between 1981 and 1985;
- in 1985, the FCC abolished guidelines on the minimal amount of time to be devoted to non-entertainment broadcasting, as well as limits on time devoted to advertising; and
- in 1987, the FCCA abolished the Fairness Doctrine.

Eliminating the Fairness Doctrine opened the way to philosophical monocultures like Fox News or MSNBC that reported the news with a distinct bias.

Deregulation—or marketization—of the FCC continued after Reagan's terms and even accelerated under Clinton. The Telecommunications Act of 1996 passed with the backing of the Clinton Administration contained several crucial provisions sought by telecommunications companies including

- lifting the cap on the number of radio stations a single company could own—which had already grown to forty. This opened the door to mega companies such as Clear Channel, which expanded ownership to over twelve hundred stations;
- lifting the cap on the number of local TV stations a company could own, and expanding the national share a company could have from 25 percent to 35 percent (it is effectively 39 percent today);
- giving licenses to broadcasters for free—eliminating a potential revenue stream of $70 billion (in 1995 dollars—it would generate nearly $108 billion in today's dollars);
- extending the life of broadcast licenses to eight years; and
- making it harder for citizens to challenge license renewals.

Once the limits on the size and reach of media conglomerates were lifted, and limits on time devoted to public goods broadcasting were eliminated, and content was no longer required to present differing perspectives, news became nothing more or less than a profit center. In essence, it had to compete with sitcoms, dramas, reality shows, and sports for airtime. Profit seeking—not the high-minded ethical canons and First Amendment philosophical theories such as the importance of a free press to a functioning democracy—became the driving force behind news content.

With deregulation, the barriers and costs of entry into the news market, together with the long tail economics of niche marketing, created an ever-increasing demand for news shows targeted at specific audiences. The result was a media that operated 24-7, with a huge appetite for stories and an addiction to sensationalism, controversy, and all too often, conspiracy.

Splintering audiences into ever-smaller affinity groups also directly undercut the notion of a "commonweal" which, as we will see in chapter 9, is critical to a functioning democracy.

Buying the Press Outright: News media not only became a profit center run by the amoral[23] tenets of the market place, but it also became a commodity to be bought and sold by the ultra-rich and corporations.

One prime example: as the Telecommunications Act of 1996 passed, yet another rich conservative with an agenda—Rupert Murdock—launched Fox News.

The Act also set off a stampede of consolidation. In 1983, for example, fifty companies controlled 90% of the media; today, six companies do. [24] with most of the mergers happening after the Act's passage. In essence, media became a property of Fortune 200 corporations.

With the vast majority of the media safely in the hands of the corporations, the conservatives' assault on government went mainstream, and the two great myths they would use to complete the coup went into hyper drive.

Think tanks and conservative politicians who had been aggressively trying to neutralize the "liberal media" since Reagan, intensified their campaign to discredit liberalism in general and liberal news in particular, as well as propagating the Myth of the Magic Markets and the Myth of the Bumbling Bureaucrat. In the next two chapters, we'll explore the power of these myths and how they were used to subvert the national political debate in a way that put progressivism at a competitive disadvantage.

Terms like "knee jerk liberal," "tax and spend liberal," and "liberal media" which had been around for decades were repeated in unison by conservative think tanks, interest groups, and the emerging conservative press. As the media consolidated and commercialized, what had been a small chorus erupted into a full-blown choir.

One of the early techniques they used was a process that Eric Alterman called "working the refs" in his landmark book *What Liberal Media? The Truth about Bias in the Media.*[25] For those who don't get sports analogies, working the refs refers to a practice common in sports, especially in home games and particularly in basketball, in which a coach expresses fury and invites scorn upon a ref early in the game when the ref calls a foul or otherwise favors the other team. At home games, it isn't hard to get the crowd to join in the effort.

The hope is to ramp up the transaction costs of making a call, causing the ref to think twice before making another one. The coaches who do this best mix in a little charm and "help" by pointing out fouls performed by the opposition that the ref missed. "Hey, that was a hack. You blind, Ref?"

In an article in the *Nation*, Alterman quotes Rich Bond, then chair of the Republican Party, in the run up to the 1992 elections:

> There is some strategy to it [bashing the "liberal" media]...If you watch any great coach, what they try to do is 'work the refs.' Maybe the ref will cut you a little slack on the next one.[26]

And it was having its intended effect. Bill Clinton complained about the so-called liberal media bashing him, while in their more candid moments, Republicans admitted they were treated fairly by the media. Alterman notes that even such a stalwart conservative as James Baker found media coverage to be fair, and Pat Buchannan—about as conservative as you can get—said he couldn't identify a single instance when press coverage had been unfair to him.

In short, the "liberal media bias," to the extent it ever existed, was disappearing rapidly by the 1990s, and virtually reversed by the turn of the century.

Indeed, by 2000, *balance* was replacing accuracy, context, facts, and truth, as journalism's pole star. Fox News's slogan, "fair and balanced" worked because the conservatives had created the illusion that press coverage was unfair and unbalanced.

In truth, balance is a poor compass that rarely leads to truth or contributes to accuracy. To take the analogy of balance to its logical end point, one could pile up a ton of bullshit on one side of the scale, and a ton of gold on the other and achieve balance. In fact, as the coverage of Bush's run up to Iraq would show, that's precisely what conservatives and neoconservatives began to do, and the mainstream media—increasingly driven by profits and audience share—meekly followed suit.

It's worth examining another period in our history, when the press failed in its First Amendment obligations. Sixty years ago, responding to the failure of the press to deal with Senator Joe McCarthy's bullying, Eric Sevareid said,

> Our rigid formulae of so-called objectivity…have given the lie the same prominence and impact that truth is given; they have elevated the influence of fools to that of wise men; the ignorant to the level of the learned; the evil to the level of the good.

Turning the press into an oligopoly allowed the evil, the ignorant, and fools to have equal standing with wise men, the learned, and the good. Having taken over the media, they wasted no time in fostering the myths they used to advance their own interests and neutralize government.

Messaging—Madison Avenue Comes to Politics: When it comes to rhetoric, conservatives have written the book on how to use language to confound, confuse, and mislead. In chapter 7, we will examine why the conservative's campaign worked so well; here we will simply describe it.

While conservatives have been extremely effective at deception, distortion, and dissembling, liberals haven't even been effective at communicating objective facts backed up by data. And god help them when they try to lie.

It's not that Democrats are any more honest than Republicans and conservatives, it's simply that they suck at lying.

Case in point: In 2008, in the heat of her race against Obama for the Democratic presidential nomination, when Hillary Clinton wanted to bump up her national security bonafides, and add some substance to her tenure as first lady, she recounted a tale of landing in Bosnia under sniper fire in 1996, and running with her head ducked down to a nearby armored vehicle.

When the comedian Sinbad, who had accompanied her on the trip, challenged her account, she doubled down, dismissing him as a "comedian." Even when she was forced to back off the lie, she still maintained that she was wearing a flak jacket, and that she was hustled across the tarmac as fast as protocol would allow.

Actual newsreels[27] showed her enjoying a lengthy greeting at the airstrip, with a long reception line of top military brass, an eight-year-old girl presenting her with flowers, and a longer line of young students, with whom she exchanged individual pleasantries, after which she and her daughter commenced on a leisurely stroll across the tarmac, still accompanied by the young students. There was no sign of any flak jackets.

Contrast this with the conservatives, who have maintained a three-decade scam built on lies such as "trickle-down" and "supply-side" economics or any of a hundred other oxymorons that seem to be harder to kill than a feline vampire zombie on steroids at midnight. It's enough to make Orwell's Big Brother look like a piker.

Conservatives have an extraordinary knack at message discipline. A stock bit from John Stewart often included Republicans using identical spoon-fed phrases[28] to explain away the fact that their policies were screwing the average American so that they could give corporations subsidies, and fat cats tax cuts.

Frank Luntz feeds the right wing "winning words" in memos, white papers, and weekly letters with advice about how to "frame" their issues. Here are a few classic examples:

* the Healthy Forest Initiative—a program that decreased public participation in public land use decisions while opening up public lands to timber interests;
* the Clear Skies Initiative—which essentially rolled back compliance time frames for key pollutants and watered down standards on others;
* wealth redistribution—instead of revoking generous tax cuts for the rich;

* government control over health choices—instead of "the public option";
* pro-life—despite the fact that most conservatives support endless wars, the death penalty, hardship budgets hurting the poor, and rolling back environmental regulations that save hundreds of thousands of lives each year;
* the Help America Vote Act—which required states to review and purge voters from their registries, generally making it harder to vote;
* right-to-work laws—established to prevent or reverse unions—perhaps better labelled "right to work for peanuts";
* the Patriot Act—an act that overturns many of the things the patriots fought to earn or protect—our Fourth Amendment protections, for example.

And it's not restricted to government. There's a plethora of foundations and PACs with names that are at best deceptive, at worst, contradictions in terms. For example, there's the American's for Prosperity, an organization that fosters policies and candidates that primarily represent the interests of the 1 percent, while impoverishing the rest of us.

While Reagan was adept at this kind of doublespeak, it took Bush Jr. to make it a central policy practice. As Ron Susskind reported in the *New York Times Magazine*, here's what a Bush administration official (generally believed to be Karl Rove) said to him:

The aide said that guys like me were "in what we call the reality-based community," which he defined as people who "believe that solutions emerge from your judicious study of discernible reality." I nodded and murmured something about enlightenment principles and empiricism. He cut me off. "That's not the way the world really works anymore." He continued "We're an empire now, and when we act, we create our own reality. And while you're studying that reality—judiciously, as you will—we'll act again, creating other new realities, which you can study too, and that's how things will sort out. We're history's actors...and you, all of you, will be left to just study what we do."[29]

This approach resembles a military psyops campaign conducted against an enemy, more than simply an unethical PR campaign. And the grotesque deceptions throughout Bush's two terms bear this out.

Look at the record. Budget periods cut from ten years to five to hide exploding deficits. Elaborate Mission Accomplished-style propaganda backdrops at every public event. Orwellian names like "Clear Skies," and "Healthy Forests" designed to hide real intentions. Fake news stories filmed at government expense and released to an all too incurious media. Paid journalists and columnists writing fawning stories for profit without revealing their conflict of interest. Bogus paid White House correspondents throwing softball questions under assumed names. Staged "town-hall meetings" with prescreened crowds and prescreened questions—questions like, "Mr. President, did you know my wife and I pray for you every night?" Whew. That's a toughie. And even with the hand-selected audiences, strong-armed stooges roamed the crowd intent on silencing, rousting, or arresting any stray dissenters who somehow made it past the crumbled remains of the First Amendment that blocked the entrances to these tax-supported events.

Bush's administration even went so far as to try to reclassify fast-food jobs as manufacturing jobs in The President's Economic Report to disguise the disappearance of the US manufacturing sector. Didn't catch that one? Not surprising, the Elite Establishment Media (EEM) barely mentioned it.

But while Bush raised propaganda to a black art, the practice goes on among both conservatives and neoliberals, with the ultimate purpose being the rebranding of government, and the elevation of the free market. They've redefined government *from* being the way we come together to assure the common good, *to* being our common enemy.

Meanwhile, they've simultaneously elevated corporations and the free market—which are by design, meant to exploit us and extract the maximum amount of money from us—to being our ally and savior.

CHAPTER 4

The Myth of the Magic Markets

● ● ●

In the Soviet Union, capitalism triumphed over communism.
In this country, capitalism triumphed over democracy.

FRAN LEBOWITZ

As THE RICH BEGAN FUNDING the Oligarchy's propaganda machine, Milton Friedman—a Nobel Prize winning economist from the University of Chicago—was creating the intellectual scaffolding upon which they could hang their self-serving policies and programs. Beginning in 1962, with a series of essays culminating in a widely read book entitled *Capitalism and Freedom*, Friedman pushed the notion that capitalism and freedom were inextricably linked, and advocated limited government, less regulation, and wide-open markets.

Others were perverting Adam Smith's "invisible hand" to justify the same kind of wild-west economy in which anything goes and the notion that the capitalist crucible not only was the highest expression of truth, justice, and the American way, but was also *good for all of us.*[30] Being selfish, according to these folks, benefited society at large; indeed, it did so better when it was the accidental by-product of economic activity than when we intentionally tried to use government programs to do good.

And thus, the Myth of the Magic Markets (MMM) was born. The Conservative Cabal used it and, as we will see in chapter 5, the Myth of the

Bumbling Bureaucrat (MBB) to undermine and overturn the New Deal. Before they were through, both parties, the media, pundits, much of academia, and even the majority of the people had swallowed this intellectual pigswill.

Beginning with Reagan, a steady drumbeat of *trickle down, supply side,* and *job creators* tripped off the tongues of Republicans in a chorus of conformity, and they were soon joined by the Democrats—at first because they were afraid to confront the popular juggernaut of tax cutters, but by the 1990s they'd joined the Coup. Under this school of…well…thought… putting in place policies that benefitted the über rich was just peachy, because it was the wealthy who made the investments that created the jobs we all needed. So the more they got, the better off we all were.

It gets worse. Many influential folks on the right took their economic policy from Ayn Rand—a second-rate novelist who wrote adolescent paeans to unbridled selfishness, and the rugged individualists who had the…er… integrity to practice it. Here again, any regulations or mores meant to promote the public good actually defeated it, since it was the Marlboro Men of the world who created wealth, not the namby-pamby do-gooders. Not too surprisingly, many of these later day Marlboro Men (and women) actually profited from the public policies they want to deny to others in the name of the public good. In short, they were—and are—self-serving hypocrites.

A couple of examples. There's Michelle Bachman who was a dedicated government basher and opponent of social spending of all kinds, whose husband benefited handsomely from Medicaid funds.[31]

But my favorite has to be Paul Ryan, who regularly proposes budgets that cut taxes on the rich and the corporations to the bone, while cutting any kind of support to the poor or middle class lest they be "coddled" to the point where they have no incentive to work. This is all done, by the way, because the rich and corporations are the "engines" of growth and the creators of jobs, while the poor and middle-class recipients of government favors like unemployment benefits are just lazy no-gooders who won't get off their asses.

Ryan got where he is today because of the very public programs his budgets would eviscerate or eliminate. He was a beneficiary of Social Security as a teenager after his father died; he used this to fund his education at a low cost *public* university—before tax cuts forced tuitions to rise to the point where this would have been impossible, and he has worked in the public sector his entire life.

What makes Ryan's hypocrisy truly astounding is not only that he espouses Randian über independence for others that he himself never had to practice, but his budgets spare the ultrarich and corporations from such crippling mutations of self-reliance. Moreover, the budgets he proposes routinely explode the deficit while he rails against deficits.[32] Indeed, he proposes his deficit-exploding budgets as austerity measures, and the corporate-owned press doesn't blink an eye. Austerity, as we will see in the next chapter, is closely tied with the MBB.

Another Ayn Rand acolyte, one who contributed to the 2008 economic collapse, was former Federal Reserve chief Alan Greenspan, who wrote articles for Rand's *The Objectivist Newsletter*, contributed essays to her book *Capitalism: The Unknown Ideal*, and was a member of her "collective," a group of extreme conservatives who met regularly to bad mouth government and glorify markets. Greenspan's easy-money, low-interest, hands-off approach while chairing the Fed was based on the notion that markets know best, and a rejection of Keynesian—or any other kind of interference. It's widely recognized that his policies were instrumental in allowing the bubbles that led to the Great Recession.

Even Greenspan himself admitted as much in testimony before the House Oversight and Government Reform Committee on October 3, 2008, as the economy collapsed around him. Here's how *Mother Jones* correspondent David Corn, in the article "Alan Shrugged," reported on Greenspan's reply when Democrats on the committee suggested his reliance on the libertarian notion that markets know best contributed directly to the ongoing crash [33]:

You know...that's precisely the reason I was shocked, because I have been going for 40 years or more with very considerable evidence that it was working exceptionally well. While Greenspan did defend his various decisions, he admitted that his faith in the ability of free and loosely-regulated markets to produce the best outcomes had been shaken: "I made a mistake in presuming that the self-interests of organizations, specifically banks and others, were such as that they were best capable of protecting their own shareholders and their equity in the firms."

While many in the Oligarchy were true believers in the MMM, many others just saw it as a rationalization that allowed them to justify cutting government regulations and government itself. Government, by the way, is the only force capable of constraining corporate power, so the MMM provided the excuse to keep it on the sidelines. As we will see in the next chapter, when the MMM was used in conjunction with the MBB, it became a powerful argument for gutting, cutting, and otherwise disabling government at all levels.

All of these believers and fabricators of the MMM share four things in common:

1. They support the notion that markets will produce all good things by pure serendipity.
2. They identify government's highest and best function as just getting the hell out of the way.
3. They were—and are—heavily promoted by the conservative mafia and the infrastructure they funded in think tanks, universities, the media, and both political parties.
4. They benefit the Oligarchy at the expense of the people.

One of the remarkable things about the MMM is how persistently it has survived, despite overwhelming evidence that it simply doesn't work.

It turns out, we have a lot of data on that. Laissez-faire policies have been the basis of US economic strategy off and on throughout our history, but it reached its zenith in the late nineteenth century, again in the 1920s, and finally, in the period after Reagan until—well, now.

The reality is, laissez-faire, free-market policies have failed miserably every time they've been tried. They have a nasty habit of causing grotesque income inequalities, huge market volatility, and severe financial collapses. In fact, the Great Recession of 2008 should have been strike three for the free marketeers.

Strike one was the Panic of 1893 and the depression which followed it. The depression was preceded by a long period of laissez-faire policies, and the extreme income inequality that accompanies such policies. For example, from 1860 to 1900, the wealthiest 2 percent of American households owned more than a third of the nation's wealth, while the top 10 percent owned roughly three-fourths of it.[34] The bottom 40 percent had no wealth at all. In terms of property, the wealthiest 1 percent owned 51 percent, while the bottom 44 percent claimed 1.1 percent.

Strike two was the Great Depression of the 1930s. This, too, was preceded by a decade of market über-alles policies and profound income and wealth disparity.

The 1920s saw a return to a laissez-faire market economy; the top tax rate was lowered to 25 percent and the stock market began its spectacular rise, proving once again that there is no correlation between the stock market and general welfare.

Deregulation in the 1920s allowed for heavy concentration of large corporations. About twelve hundred mergers swallowed up more than six thousand previously independent companies; by 1929, only two hundred corporations controlled over half of all American industry.[35]

Meanwhile, wealth and income—once again—became concentrated in the hands of the very few, and income disparity approached its highest point in our history.[36]

Sound familiar?

And of course, strike three was the Bush recession of 2008 and the weak recovery that followed it, which again was preceded by three decades of increasing income and wealth disparity fueled by deregulation. By Obama's second term, here's what the Oligarchy had accomplished.[37]

* Analysis by economists Saez, Zucman, and Piketty found that since 1980, the average income for the top 10 percent grew three times faster than for the rest of us—a scant .07 percent.
* In the same time period, the average income for the top 1 percent grew four times as fast as for the 99 percent.
* The top 10 percent now take home half of all income earned in the United States.

And it's getting worse—since 2009, 58 percent of all income growth has gone to the top 10 percent.

When it comes to net wealth, the divide is even starker. The twenty richest people in the country now have as much wealth as the bottom 50 percent of Americans.

It's not just the rich who reap the rewards of political payola. The payoff for corporations has been nothing less than extraordinary. While gauging the return industry gets from lobbying and investing in corporate-friendly politicians and policies is an inexact science, we do know the payoffs are astonishing.

Two studies show the return on this investment to be beyond the wildest dreams of even the best speculator. One found the ROI on lobbying to be 22,000 percent.[38] That is, for every dollar spent on lobbying, the companies received $220 in tax benefits. Another, more recent and comprehensive study examining the two hundred most politically active companies found that they got an astounding 76,000 percent return on their federal lobbying and campaign investments.[39]

So the MMM may be hypocritical; it's certainly counterfactual; and it's definitely destructive—but none of that matters when the folks who are shaping political thought for fun and profit are profiting so handsomely.

There's an unholy or very unvirtuous cycle going on here. The Oligarchy has skillfully invested in creating the belief that funneling money up to the rarified atmosphere of the ultrarich and big corporations is good for us, then bribed our lawmakers to pass laws that do it. Both parties can do so comfortably under cover of the MMM.

And the press—which as we saw in chapter 3 was first neutered, then purchased outright—all too often repeats the mantra of the MMM without question. Indeed, until the Occupy Movement raised it, one of the best-kept secrets in America was the degree to which the 99 percent were getting fleeced, while the 1 percent prospered.

It should have been obvious all along that in a consumer economy, when the majority of the wealth goes to a very few, the economy suffers. You simply can't run a successful *consumer* economy when *the vast majority of consumers* don't have enough money to buy anything. After all, Paris Hilton can buy only so many yachts; Corporate CEOs can purchase only so many jetliners—even with their special jet tax credits; and Wall Street traders can buy only so many Bugattis. But middle- and working-class Americans need to spend all or most of their money on food, lodging, and other necessities, so when they get a larger share of the economic pie, it penetrates into the broader economy and stimulates economic growth. The *real* job creators are the middle- and lower-class consumers, who fuel demand for goods and services and spend nearly all their money to get them, not the rich and corporations who hoard money or ship it overseas.

And hoard it they have. The fact of the matter is, the "job creators" didn't invest in job-creating expansions, and the wealth didn't trickle down.

For example, between 2008 and 2012, American corporations increased their cash holdings by an astounding 15 percent a year.[40] David Cay Johnston found that in 2012, corporations were sitting on $14.6 trillion in liquid assets and cash, $6.7 trillion of it in cash.[41] Where did all this money come from? Well, a lot of it came from a provision in the 1986 Tax Reform Act, passed in the frenzy of trickle down hysteria ignited by the fat-cat funding of conservative think tanks fostering the MMM. The provision, by the way, allowed companies to defer taxes on money parked overseas.

As Johnston said, "When liquid assets grow six times faster than revenues, it tells you that companies are hoarding cash, not investing or spending."

So much for job creation. So much for trickle down. Yet despite the evidence, by the 1990s, both parties embraced the MMM. The DLC Democrats under Bill Clinton completed the deregulation of Wall Street, eliminating Glass-Steagall, removing constraints on futures trading (this allowed financial interests with no stake in the markets to speculate in commodities, leading to higher volatility and market manipulation), easing capital requirements for swaps...the list is lengthy and ignominious.

With markets elevated to mythical status, the Oligarchy wasted no time in cashing in, and tax breaks for the rich and corporate welfare exploded, while social safety net expenditures for the disadvantaged dwindled. Following are some examples of fiscal policies and corporate welfare that siphons money from middle-class and low-income Americans into the hands of the über wealthy and corporations in the name of magic markets, supply side, and trickle down.

Capital Gains and Dividends: Rich folks make the majority of their money in the form of dividends and capital gains, which are taxed at 15–20 percent. Over a ten-year period, this costs the US treasury $1.3 trillion, or an average of $130 billion a year.[42]

Carried Interest: Hedge fund managers avoid at least $2.1 billion in taxes a year. This sweet deal—not available to the ninety-nine percenters, by the way—allows hedge fund managers, private equity firms, and venture capitalists to take what amounts to ordinary wages and have them taxed as if they were capital gains. So instead of being taxed at 39.5 percent, it's taxed at 20 percent. Ayn Rand would be proud. Thomas Jefferson, not so much. This amount—$2.1 billion—is roughly equivalent to the entire budget for the Administration on Aging – that is until Trump cut it. Wouldn't want to deprive millionaire and billionaire hedge fund managers of their windfall just to help a lot of old geezers.

Bank Bailouts: Then there's the $700 billion bank bailout—to rescue banks from problems they themselves created. Yes, it got paid back; and yes, we had to do *something*. But the reason this money was little more than white collar welfare was because the banks got to do what they wanted to with it. It could have come with strings—we could have insisted that they write down mortgages to market value or allowed refinancing at lower interest rates or longer amortization periods. We could even have given the money directly to stressed homeowners, instead of the banksters who caused the problem. Any of these approaches would have prevented defaults, slowed—or even reversed—the precipitous declines in real estate values, and given low- and middle-income consumers some ability to consume, which, as we have seen, is the real "job creator." And we most certainly could have insisted that banks loan out the money to small businesses and homebuyers.

But we did nothing like that. Instead, we allowed the banks to play a high stakes game of pump-and-dump—complete with flash trading—with our money. Instead of loans designed to jump-start the economy, we got risky investments underwritten with our tax money that paid off mostly the Wall Street elite.

And as Matt Taibbi reported in *Secret Lies of the Bailout*, the public story on the bailout is one of the biggest cons ever pulled.[43] It wasn't a one-time payout. In reality, it continued and still continues, under such names as TALF, PPIP, and TLGP, and some were larger than the TARP. Worse, in some cases, banks paid back their original loans with government money from other ultralow interest loans. An audit in 2011 revealed that the size of the bailout was dwarfed by $7.7 trillion in emergency low-interest loans handed out to Wall Street—loans which weren't going to be disclosed until Bloomberg went to court to be allowed to report on it.

Talk about welfare. Talk about your welfare kings and queens. It doesn't get any more obscenely selfish and opportunistic than this.

$9 Trillion in Low- and No-Interest Loans from the Fed: At the end of the day, the Fed loaned out a total of about $9 trillion at below market rates to banks—some of it as low as 0.5 percent?[44] Here again, this money disappeared into the money vaults of the select few, rather than benefiting the common good.

And here again, we could have insisted that public money be used to serve the public good. But instead, it was given as white-collar welfare—a freebie to the real welfare kings and queens—the financial sector and the fat cats they serve.

As we've seen, to the extent conservatives acknowledge these facts, they justify it with a neo-Reaganomics logic that the wealthy and the corporations who receive this largess are the "job creators." But here's the deal. As long as the middle class is in debt and feeling insecure, no company in its right mind will invest in expansions or any other type of job creation. Why on earth would they? If people can't afford to buy your service or product now, how will making more of your product or expanding your capacity to provide your service or product make them do it? And as economists can tell you, Paris Hilton, Mitt Romney, or Donald Trump and other millionaires can only buy so many yachts, so many second, third, fourth, or fifth homes. They simply don't have the numbers to lead to an economic recovery.

Robbing from the Poor to Pay the Rich: It's not enough for the Oligarchy to take the lion's share of new income and wealth from the working poor and middle class, they've also been working to actively prevent people from getting their share.

There are the laws discouraging unionization and collective bargaining; there's the cutting of funds for education, unemployment, and jobs programs; there's the stagnating minimum wage, and, of course, their tax proposals actually punish the poor, while rewarding the rich.

Monopolies and Oligopolies, Oh My: As we will see in the next chapter, the MBB, the Oligarchy has actively undermined the role of government in society. One of their most effective tactics has been the call for a "small government." The appeal strikes at the heart of what many feel is one of the core principles underpinning our system of government—one beloved by our founders.

But if one examines the conservative's embrace of small government, it's easy to see that it is neither Jeffersonian, nor sincere. It's all about power. Bottom line: small government is just a proxy for a weak government—one that can't effectively counter the power of the über rich and corporations.

Doubt that? Consider this: the size of government increased under Reagan and Bush—the self-proclaimed champions of small government—but decreased under Clinton and stayed essentially the same under Obama. Here are the numbers: under Reagan, government increased in number of employees by 237,000, and under George W. Bush it grew by 54,000. Meanwhile, government employment went down by 381,000 under Clinton, and will probably be about 30,000 less under Obama at the end of his last term (the latest data on federal jobs lags by two years, so Obama's final numbers are estimates). Moreover, Obama used several wage freezes to cut the growth in the cost of employing the federal workforce, something Republican president rarely did.

The same is true if you look at the growth in the budget, year to year and term to term. Bush and Reagan exploded the growth in federal spending and deficits, Clinton cut the growth in spending and the deficit, and Obama—even after an expensive bailout and a stimulus package—ended up with a lower deficit than Bush ran by the end of his term.

But both conservatives and neoliberals embrace the notion of a small government. Remember, it was Clinton who declared the era of big government to be over. And regardless of the rhetoric, both conservatives and neoliberals have allowed corporations to merge and couple with all the abandon of a bacchanalian orgy.

Bottom line? When Republicans or neoliberals praise small government, hold onto your wallet—your pocket is about to get picked in three ways. First, spending is likely go up to fund corporate welfare; second tax cuts for the rich will cause cuts in middle-class and low-income benefits; and third, corporations—freed from those nasty regulations—will steal you blind, expose you to toxic chemicals, sell you shoddy or dangerous foods or products, force you to work in treacherous or unhealthy conditions, depress your wages, increase prices, and otherwise run rough-shod over your well-being.

Oh, but the magic of competition makes companies compete for our dollar, and they can't afford to be irresponsible, right? Not so much.

There's unlikely to be much relief from the magic elixir of competition—for the simple reason that there isn't much competition anymore. Having convinced folks that regulation is bad, the Oligarchy is in the midst of a frenzy of mergers that is giving a few large conglomerates control of many of the major market sectors.

Derrick Thompson, in a recent article in the *Atlantic*, lays out some of the grim statistics that illustrate the trend. As Thompson writes,

> To comprehend the scope of corporate consolidation, imagine a day in the life of a typical American and ask: How long does it take for her to interact with a market that *isn't* nearly monopolized? She wakes up to browse the Internet, access to which is sold through a local monopoly. She stocks up on food at a superstore such as Walmart, which owns a quarter of the grocery market. If she gets indigestion, she might go to a pharmacy, likely owned by one of three companies controlling 99 percent of that market. If she's stressed and wants to relax outside the shadow of an oligopoly, she'll have to stay away from ebooks, music, and beer; two companies control more than half of all sales in each of these markets. There is no escape—literally. She can try boarding an airplane, but four corporations control 80 percent of the seats on domestic flights.[45]

We've already noted the consolidation of the media, 90 percent of which is now controlled by just six corporations. And of course, there's the inconvenient fact that the "too-big-to-fail" banks that were a major cause of the 2008 Great Recession are now bigger and fewer.

As Nobel-prize winning economist Joseph Stiglitz points out, there are two schools of thought about "what determines the distribution of income and how the economy functions."[46] As Stiglitz notes, one school emanates from nineteenth-century economists and Adam Smith's faith in the invisible hand and focuses on the sheer wonderfulness of competitive markets (my words, not Dr. Stiglitz's). It is, in many respects, the school of thought that has dominated US economic policy since Reagan, and it underlies much of the dogma that feeds the MMM. It has been embraced by both the neoliberals and the conservatives.

As Stiglitz notes, "The other, cognisant of how Smith's brand of liberalism leads to rapid concentration of wealth and income, takes as its starting point unfettered markets' tendency toward monopoly." This school of thought emphasizes the role of power in the economy, and more broadly in society. It's worth noting that only this school provides an adequate explanation for the abuses rampant in our society.

The neoclassical economists who celebrate competition also favor laissez-faire policies—that is little regulation of the economy, small governments (and weak, too), and limited or no intervention in the workings of the free market. Those who focus on market power and monopolies, on the other hand, favor a stronger government that intervenes in the market to prevent monopolies and to assure a level playing field for all the players in the market.

While politicians have been celebrating the miracles of Smith's "invisible hand," it's been robbing us blind. Not only do monopolies exercise considerable political power with all the attendant dangers posed by a deregulated society—tainted food, polluted waters, climate change, unsafe working conditions, dangerous products, information monocultures in which lies and truths are treated with equal respect, and shoddy services—but they also exercise market power which depresses wages and increases the price of goods, services, and products. In fact, the rise of monopolies is one the most powerful—and unrecognized—sources of the explosion in income inequality that has been infecting our nation since the embrace of the neoclassical economics around Reagan's reign of error.

It is also directly responsible for one of the most annoying aspects of modern society—the decline of service. Think of the endless hours we spend listening to our menu options, which have always *just changed*. Think of the plethora of companies asking you to press 1, press 2, press 3, press 4 or 5 or 6 or more, shortly before you hear the dreaded click followed by "If you'd like to make a call, please hang up," while you scream hopelessly into the implacable mouthpiece, "I just want to speak to a godammed human."

But you can't. Why? Market power. You've got nowhere else to go. Or at best, you've got a choice between a few companies all of which value you as a commodity, not a person. And that's true whether you're an employee or a customer. Adam Smith's invisible hand is slapping us all across our ignorant faces, while we vote for the people who have given it the power to do so.

The Tragedy of the MMM: Let's review what the MMM has accomplished:

Earlier, we listed the grim statistics uncovered by Seaz et. al., but it's easy to let your eyes glaze over when numbers are tossed about like dice. But the invaluable David Cay Johnston has given us a graphical picture of just how obscene this wealth grab has been. I'd include it as a figure, but I can't and you'll see why in a moment. As Johnston says,

> In 2011 the average AGI [adjusted gross income] of the vast majority fell to $30,437 per taxpayer, its lowest level since 1966 when measured in 2011 dollars. The vast majority averaged a mere $59 more in 2011 than in 1966. For the top 10 percent, by the same measures, average income rose by $116,071 to $254,864, an increase of 84 percent over 1966.
>
> Plot those numbers on a chart, with one inch for $59, and the top 10 percent's line would extend more than 163 feet.
>
> Now compare the vast majority's $59 with the top 1 percent, and that line extends for 884 feet. The top 1 percent of the top 1 percent, whose 2011 average income of $23.7 million was $18.4 million more per taxpayer than in 1966, **would require a line nearly five miles high.** (emphasis added)

Holey hockey stick, Batman. They're robbing us blind, and we don't even know it.

Globally, the situation is equally bad. Fed by the neoliberal economic agenda and reinforced by corporate-friendly trade agreements, inequality has skyrocketed. As Oxfam's, <u>*Broken at the Top*</u>[47] reported recently:

> The gap between rich and poor is reaching new extremes. The richest 1% have accumulated more wealth than the rest of the world put together.
>
> Meanwhile, the wealth owned **by the bottom half of humanity** has fallen by a trillion dollars in the past five years.
>
> **Just 8 individuals now have the same wealth as 3.6 billion people**—half of humanity. In 2010, we thought it was unjust when 388 individuals controlled half of all wealth.

The real tragedy, though, may be that even though the people are fed up with the Oligarchy's theft of our collective wealth, the narrative of the Magic Market still dominates both parties, most of the press, academia, and much of the public policy infrastructure. Which shouldn't be surprising given that it's all been bought and paid for by the Oligarchy.

In the next chapter, we'll examine the other great myth—the MBB—which compliments and reinforces the MMM.

CHAPTER 5

The Myth of the Bumbling Bureaucrat

● ● ●

The most terrifying words in the English language are:
I'm from the government and I'm here to help.

RONALD REAGAN

Better the occasional faults of a government that lives
in a spirit of charity than the consistent omissions of a
government frozen in the ice of its own indifference.

FRANKLIN D. ROOSEVELT

IF THE OLIGARCHY'S COUP WAS to succeed, they had to do more than simply elevate markets to magical status, they had to also tear down government in general and regulations in particular.

The Oligarchy's Challenge—Erasing Forty Years of Success: This would be no simple matter. New Deal policies had delivered the longest, most sustained, and most equitably shared period of prosperity in US history, and it was done in no small part by regulations that kept the banks and Wall Street from making risky bets with other people's money; assuring that they retained enough capital to cover their bets; insuring people against loss in the event banks went belly up; fostering unions; maintaining a fair minimum wage and by preventing the rise of monopolies and oligopolies. In short, by actively intervening in the not-so-magical markets to keep things transparent, fair, safe, and equitable for the average American.

Government had also put in place a social safety net that was not only effective, but, as we will see, far more efficient at accomplishing important, socially critical tasks than anything the vaunted Magic Market could do. The safety net also modulated the radical swings that often accompany market economies, thus dampening the boom-bust cycle.

As the Oligarch's Coup was being launched, the government was in the midst of another popular success: tackling an emerging environmental disaster, complete with rivers so polluted that some caught fire, massive black clouds over many of our major cities, unregulated dumps containing hazardous wastes that were not tracked or documented, and a nearly indiscriminate use of toxics in agriculture and commerce. Not only did they tame the worst of these problems, but they did it without the widespread economic devastation predicted by purveyors of the MMM.[48]

Meanwhile, the social safety net established under the New Deal and expanded under the Great Society, kept consumer demand viable when unemployment ticked up, serving to dampen extremes and the effect of economic downturns.

Social Security, the flagship of this social safety net, was and is a popular program that delivered checks to millions of people every month—by Obama's presidency, some 58 million people were receiving monthly checks. And the overhead for administering Social Security remained at or below 4 percent—far lower than the 20 percent[49] overhead for private sector attempts at providing similar services in countries like Chile.

Similarly, Medicaid and Medicare were delivering a higher quality of care, both in terms of health outcomes and customer satisfaction, at much lower overheads than private sector insurance. Specifically, Medicare and Medicaid maintain an overhead of roughly 2 percent, while private sector health insurance averaged about 17 percent prior to the passage of Obamacare and comes in at between 12 percent and 14 percent now.[50] Of course that means we should repeal Obamacare, right?

The same was true when Congress sought to privatize student loans—the private sector ended up costing far more than the federally administered grants and loans.

In fact, privatization, the Holy Grail for many of the shrink-the-government types in the Oligarchy, as well as elitist neoliberals, rarely saves money over the much-maligned big government programs run by the not-so-inept government worker. In a study examining the costs of privatizing government functions, the Project on Government Oversight (POGO) found that it cost more to contract out functions in thirty-three out of the thirty-five job classifications they examined than it would to keep them in government. On net, POGO found that contracting out services to the private sector cost twice as much as doing the function in-house with government workers.[51]

So much for the Bumbling Bureaucrat. So much for Magic Markets.

Not only did the Oligarchy want to get government "off its back"—which is to say to eliminate its role in providing for public welfare and in assuring fair, transparent, and responsible practices for labor, the environment, and the financial sector—but it also wanted to turn what had been legitimate and highly successful government investments in these areas into privatized profit centers, even if it cost the people more. To paraphrase Country Joe and the Fish, "there's plenty of good money to be made by supplyin' the army the tools of its trade" or any other public function. That's why companies who run privatized prisons are such great campaign contributors. That's why we're in perpetual wars. That's why cities are selling off toll roads, parking meters, schools, and anything else where there's a buck to be made.[52] That's why we pay three times as much for drugs than citizens of Great Britain do.[53]

But the big Kahuna of privatization, the thing that the Oligarchy and its supporters hunger and thirst after is Social Security—imagine the hundreds of billions—if not trillions—of dollars to be made if some significant part of this money were handed over to Wall Street.

And as with the MMM, the right-wing Coup and their neoliberal enablers didn't let facts get in the way of their story.

Still, with so much evidence showing that most functions are run better and cheaper by government, and that government had been instrumental in creating and sustaining the longest-lasting and most equitably shared prosperity in US history, you'd think it would be hard to make the MBB stick.

But you'd be wrong. Here's how they accomplished it.

First, they had to create and sell failure.

Step One—Launch a Massive PR Campaign: By 1980, disillusionment with government was on the rise, and it had been growing since the end of the Vietnam War. OPEC's embargoes, a skyrocketing inflation rate, and our inability to successfully deal with the Iran hostage crisis, was feeding the dissatisfaction. It seemed government couldn't do anything right anymore.

Onto this stage, walked Ronald Reagan. In his first inaugural address, he said, "Government is not the solution to our problem; government is the problem," and the assault began in earnest.

For decades prior to Reagan, Republicans targeted New Deal policies, particularly Social Security, in a stealth attack. Reagan took it head on.

After years of epithets, repeated like mantras (or Madison Avenue campaigns)—"tax and spend liberals," "government is the problem," "faceless bureaucrats"—on and on it goes…the anti-government crowd began to gain traction. As we saw in chapter 3, they were aided and abetted by a compliant press that was increasingly owned by a few powerful corporations. And by the end of the 1980s, the Democratic Party was rapidly becoming a tool of the Oligarchy as Clinton and the DLC took over the party and adopted a neoliberal agenda that was essentially similar to the Oligarchy's.

Reagan—or rather his speechwriters—were particularly adept at developing sound bites. Here are a few choice quotes from Reagan:

* Government's view of the economy could be summed up in a few short phrases: If it moves, tax it. If it keeps moving, regulate it. And if it stops moving, subsidize it.

- The government is like a baby's alimentary canal: a happy appetite at one end and no responsibility at the other.
- Republicans believe every day is the Fourth of July, but the Democrats believe every day is April 15.
- Government always finds a need for whatever money it gets.

By the time Reagan left office, government had become a punch line. Long after it became politically impossible to stereotype racial and ethnic groups (with the possible exception of Muslims) it was—and is—quite acceptable to characterize government workers as shiftless, lazy, and incompetent, and government programs as ineffective, wasteful, and bloated.

Once government had been discredited, it became easier to cut funding, and once that was accomplished, government began to underperform in actuality—not simply in myth. Which bring us to step two.

Step Two—Starve the Beast: The conservatives' strategy involved not only discrediting government, but starving it. In the words of Grover Norquist, "I simply want to reduce [government] to the size where I can drag it into the bathroom and drown it in the bathtub." Norquist's organization, Americans for Tax Reform, is a nonprofit that is funded by the Donor's Trust, which receives funds from the likes of Koch, Olin, Bradley, and DeVos among other ultrarich, ultraconservatives.

Sound familiar?

ATR's main activity is to extract a pledge from all Republicans (and whatever Democrats they can intimidate) vowing not to increase taxes. Until 2014, signing it was a prerequisite for running as a Republican, and it still is in many districts.

"Starve the beast" works particularly well when you combine it with massive deficits and huge government debt. One of the truly remarkable accomplishments of the conservatives was to run up record-breaking deficits and debt, while championing austerity. Again, facts reveal the full measure of their hypocrisy. We'll run through them in a moment, but first, it's worth noting that the establishment media and the Democrats watched in silence as this Kabuki dance played out.

Reagan and Bush each racked up more debt than any other president prior to Obama, who had to cope with the biggest recession since 1930.[54] Reagan increased the debt by 186 percent, while George Bush raised it by 101 percent.[55] Together, the two created as much debt as all other presidents combined up to that time.

Bush used two unfunded wars, a giant giveaway to big pharma, and two huge tax cuts, mostly for the ultrawealthy, to generate his debt. Reagan's contribution was largely a result of the failure of the benefits of tax cuts promised by the MMM to materialize, together with obscene spending on defense.

What's fascinating is that Congress, the establishment press, pundits, and other assorted elites were essentially silent on these massive run-ups of our national debt. Interestingly, as soon as Obama was elected, the debts and deficits became a national emergency, used to justify austerity budgets, government shutdowns, and all manner of panic. The Tea Party types, who'd been silent as Bush and Reagan spent like a pair of drunken sailors on shore leave, suddenly appeared out of the closet when Obama took over. Of course, it didn't hurt that the Koch brothers and other prominent conservative funders basically created them by funneling money into the deadly brew of ignorance, fear, jingoism and greed.

Apparently, debts and deficits were a serious problem only when someone was trying to have the government do something useful, like provide a stimulus in the face of a crippling recession (brought on by a belief in the MMM), or to pass a health-care bill that might benefit people (even if it was a giant giveaway to the medical insurance industry). Yup, gotta keep the MBB alive. No solutions here, please.

But either way, if government programs get defunded, they don't work as well, or at all, and the MBB gains credence.

Step Three—Distract, Deceive, Dissemble: In many ways, the United States' defense policy marks the beachhead of the forces of the Oligarchy, the area where they refined their weapons—fear, jingoism, faux patriotism, xenophobia, hate, and greed—to unleash our national id and harness the destructive force of our lizard brain to neutralize reason and critical thinking.

The fruits of this strategy are obvious, if not well known. We see it in the fact that we have troops stationed in over 150 nations; we see it in the over six hundred bases in more than 70 countries overseas, placed there in order to "project power"—all done in the name of protecting our freedom.

We see it in the way Hillary Clinton brandished the "threat" of Russia and China, which—combined—spend less than a fifth[56] of what the United States spends on its military. We see it in Trump's claim that the military is "in shambles." And, of course, we see it in the response to the prospect of Russian hacking of the DNC and their alleged attempts to influence the election in favor of Trump. A logical response would be to beef up our cyber security, not throw an additional hundred billion into traditional defense spending. But if the product is fear, then solutions don't really help.

The real reason for this wretched excess, of course, is about distraction in the service of money and power, not national security.

Eisenhower said it best, nearly sixty years ago:

> In the councils of government, we must guard against the acquisition of unwarranted influence, whether sought or unsought, by the military industrial complex. The potential for the disastrous rise of misplaced power exists and will persist.

In an age where we have no enemies who pose existential threats to our freedom and sovereignty, we are exaggerating the threat of terrorism[57] so that we can keep the money flowing. Indeed, while terrorists are essentially stateless, most of the trillions we spend on defense still go to cold war weaponry designed to fight wars against other nation-states. And we wage such wars despite all the evidence showing it does not work. Indeed, we are pursuing strategies that increase both the number of terrorists and threat they pose, in the name of reducing the terrorist threat.[58] That would seem stupid if you didn't understand the real motives are to make money, and keep the citizens distracted.

Talk about undue influence—a complete takeover is more accurate. With troops in nearly 80 percent of the world's nations and an annual defense budget that is just under $600 billion, *consuming more than half of all discretionary spending in the United States*, there's little left for domestic programs[59]. Again, there is no clear articulation of how—or whether—any of this makes us safer, and there is a great deal of evidence suggesting it makes us less safe. Meanwhile, the vast military industrial complex is doing quite well, thank you.

Indeed, the fact that we had to establish a new Homeland Security Department after 9/11 is prima facie evidence that the *Department of Defense* and the trillions we'd spent on it, hadn't done a good job of actually *defending* us. In fact, it would be more accurate to call it the Department of Offense, because its bloated budget supports a bloated mission that centers on "projecting power and winning," rather than on actually *defending* us here at home.

Exactly against whom this power needed to be projected and why has never been adequately addressed, and the justification has shifted over time, although protecting access to Middle East oil was frequently cited. Even now that our production of domestic crude makes Middle East oil less important to us than it has been since the 1950s, the Middle East plays a disproportionate role in our national security policy. Oh, and the increase in oil production in shales here at home was made possible by advances in drilling technology pioneered in our national labs – you know, those bumbling bureaucrats.

In fact, all available evidence shows that the most effective strategies for combatting terrorism—the threat du jour—rely on good intelligence, effective police work, and selective use of special ops.

The fact that instead of using these relatively less-expensive policies proven to work, we use terrorism as an excuse to fund massive investments in expensive weaponry designed to invade and occupy other nations, justified by an arrogant and belligerent neocon foreign policy based on "American exceptionalism," should be proof enough that we've fallen into Eisenhower's trap.

Hell, if you want further evidence, look at how Congress routinely funds weapons even the defense department says it doesn't want. Look at the size of our "defense" budgets, which are completely out of line with the rest of the world and with our own security needs.

Justifying it has become a cottage industry based on fear and manufacturing inflated threats, which goes as far back as 1958 when then Senator John F. Kennedy warned of the nonexistent "missile gap."

In what is, perhaps, one of the greatest political sleights of hand in history, the Oligarchy applied this formula of fear, jingoism, hate, and greed in the service of distraction to the rest of our governance and took over the country.

Recall the various faux issues that have defined many of the political "debates" of the past forty years. For example, consider the Democratic debate in Philadelphia in April of 2008. At a time when the United States was still engaged in a war in Iraq (a war that was started using fear, deception, distraction, and dissembling) and showing early signs of a cataclysmic market collapse (because we'd been believers in the MMM), much of the debate concerned such weighty issues as whether Obama should wear a flag lapel pin.[60] Here's what George Mitchell had to say after the debate in a piece in the *Huffington Post*:

> Wars in Iraq and Afghanistan, the health care and mortgage crises, the overall state of the economy and dozens of other pressing issues had to wait for their few moments in the sun as Obama was pressed to explain his recent "bitter" gaffe and relationship with Rev. Wright (seemingly a dead issue) ***and not wearing a flag pin***. (emphasis added)

This plays both ways. Recall in 2004, when John Kerry went "hunting"— apparently with the intent of showing what a regular guy he was—or his infamous windsurfing skit—this time with the intent of showing how healthy he was, apparently—all this meaningless symbolism while he was being savaged by the Karl Rove swift boat liars. The press covered the swift boat campaign in the typical "he-said, she-said" nod to balance, but they were all over Kerry's ludicrous attempt to use empty BS symbolism to paint a picture of the candidate he thought people wanted to see. Then of course there was Obama's equally infamous attempt to pass himself off as bubba the bowler, which almost derailed this skilled split-the-difference orator.

Perhaps no one misused the symbolism tactic as often and as poorly as Hillary Clinton. Almost every word out of her mouth was carefully scripted to evoke an image—usually one that was completely at odds with her character, or contradicting a position she held a few months before.

The reason Democrats fail so miserably at this tactic is because they haven't invested in creating a brand. As we will see in chapter 7, conservatives have a readily identifiable brand that accommodates their distraction nicely. Progressives? Not so much. As a result, their attempts at distractions stand out like the proverbial turd in the punch bowl.

As a result, the national political debate here in the land of the free and the home of the not so brave has been dominated by fear, deception, and distraction. Take Bush's ill-fated rush to war in Iraq. First there was the specter of WMDs to raise fear. No proof, mind you, and a great deal of proof that we were being lied to. The Senate Intelligence Committee's Phase II Report concluded—in 2008—found that the Bush Administration "repeatedly presented intelligence as fact when in reality it was unsubstantiated, contradicted, or even non-existent."

The fact is, as early as 2002, anyone reading the *Knight Ridder* coverage of Bush's pre-Iraq propaganda knew as much. Curveball, mushroom clouds, yellow cake from Niger, anodized aluminum tubes as centrifuges for uranium enrichment—all were debunked or questioned by our own intelligence, as well as German, Italian, and British intelligence long before the Iraq invasion. The Bush administration ignored these warnings while concocting lies, spins, and distortions.

And the EEM simply repeated each "sides'" statements, like some mute stenographer. No analysis, no context, no commitment to accuracy, truth, or reality. Ahhh, but it was oh, so, "balanced"…so off to war we went.

But it's not just fear and lies. It's distraction. There's the infamous "lapel pin controversy," of course, or whether someone should sit in the oval office without...gasp...a suit and tie. I don't know about you, but give me blue jeans and a brain over an Armani and an empty head any day.

Then there's gays and gay marriage, immigrants, gay immigrants, gay African American immigrants, gay African American Muslim immigrants, or the various attempts to create Sharia; the war on Christmas, creationism vs. evolution...or birther nonsense; or does the president "hate America" or...oh, you get the idea. No matter how ridiculous, outlandish, or irrelevant the issue, the EEM reports it as if it were of equal weight with say...the existential threat of climate change, or the fact that most of the middle class has evaporated before our eyes—both of which they essentially ignored until the Occupy Movement and the XL pipeline protests made them impossible to ignore any longer.

It is this reliance on fear and distraction and the EEM's willingness to cover it all, no matter how absurd, that has enabled the Coup, and more specifically, allowed the Oligarchy to dismantle the government and make it underfunded, ineffective, and unpopular.

Fear, it turns out, trumps reason every time. Fear messages are handled differently by the human mind—they are processed in a more primitive portion of our brain, and they form more powerful memories in a much shorter time than messages based on reason do. Same with hate, greed, envy, and bigotry. They are stepchildren of both our personal and our national id. Countering primitive limbic responses requires relentless cognitive challenges based on reason. But of course, with very few exceptions, the voices of both the press and the Democratic establishment were essentially muted by their dependence on the rich corporations.

So it didn't matter that countries that tried austerity budgets after the Great Recession of 2008 suffered double-dip recessions, while those which used stimulus measures regained prosperity sooner. Conservatives demanded austerity budgets, and the media covered the ensuing "debate" about austerity as if there was no data—as if it were a "he-said, she-said" argument with no clear answer.

And of course, Democrats, indentured to the plutocracy, raised only the weakest of objections, and rather than taking on the austerity argument, they practiced a reckless brand of preemptive capitulation[61] which would have effectively cut social security payouts among other atrocities.

It's important to note that Democrats were prepared to carry out this giveaway without arguing for the effectiveness of government programs; without noting the devastation that austerity budgets were causing in Europe in real time, or had here at home in the past; without noting that government borrowing could be done at virtually no cost, because interest rates were effectively zero.

Such was the power of the MBB, the PR campaign that fostered it, and the press that amplified it, that few in government had the courage to confront it, even though the proof was available, easy to understand, and even easier to explain. Of course, if your party represents the Oligarchy, you have no interest in actually rebutting these myths—a few mumbled objections you can point to on the campaign trail and you're good to go.

But damn…how about those lapel pins?

So it didn't matter that the Recovery Act created or preserved some 3.5 million jobs; that's just facts, and we don't need no stinkin' facts…

And it didn't matter that the exploding interest rates and the plummeting dollar conservatives said would come from running deficits never showed up. Again, just facts, and we don't need no stinkin' facts.

And it didn't matter that terrorism was not and is not an existential threat[62] while climate change is—just be afraid and keep on fracking. Anything but questioning the MBB or the MMM…

Step Four—Putting it All Together—Arsonists Posing as Firemen: Across the board, conservatives have been sabotaging government by a variety of measures, then pointing to the resulting—and inevitable—governmental failures to reinforce their Ayn Rand fantasy of government as inept and the private sector as the solution to all our problems. I call this process Arsonists Posing as Firemen.

All the time this was occurring, the Democrats stood back and mumbled lame protestations under their breath, being careful not to anger the corporatists and fat cats at whose trough they fed. And the press? Pulleez. They *are* the corporatists.

None of this is new, as far as a generally accepted meme, but what's gone largely unnoticed is how conservatives actually *generate* the *specific* problems they shout themselves into a frothing frenzy about.

Let's look at five recent examples, and one they're still trying to engineer.

Benghazi Two-step: While hypocrites like Darrell Issa held show hearings trying to create the illusion of malfeasance, guess who rejected budget requests for defending our embassies and consuls overseas? Why yes. The Republicans. And guess who warned them this would have consequences. The Obama administration. And yet, when the inevitable happens, who do Republicans blame? You guessed it—government.

Witness the basic two-step: sprinkle gasoline on our embassies, strike match, erupt in faux outrage and spread blame.

And the establishment Democrats, playing their part in the Oligarchy's Kabuki dance, don't point out the rank hypocrisy, nor does the press. Gotta be balanced, ya know.

Veterans on Waiting Lists: People like Boehner and McConnell and assorted other blowhards were full of righteous indignation and blame about veterans on waiting lists and attempts to hide the wait by the Veterans Administration (VA).

Well, guess whose fault the waiting lists are? You got it: the self-righteous "defenders of our troops" have been systematically and single handedly lowballing the budgets for the VA for over a decade now, by voting down attempts to increase the VA's budget. And of course, establishment Democrats did little to point this out. Don't want to anger your sugar daddy.

So this little two-step goes something like this: (1) start a war under false pretenses and in complete ignorance of historical tensions in Iraq stretching back for centuries and send completely unprepared and ill-equipped troops over to wage that war (remember hillbilly armor?), increasing the demand for Veteran's health care by up to $2 trillion; and (2) then consistently reject proposed increases in the agency's budget necessitated by their war. Geez, do you think that might cause a waiting list?

Why anyone listened to these asshats is a complete mystery, as is the Democrat's abject silence, and the press's near universal failure to cover it.

It's worth noting that Bernie Sanders spearheaded the successful effort to get the VA more money, and it's interesting to examine the press's portrayal of his effort.

For example, the *New York Times* and several other media outlets characterized Sanders's tireless—and ultimately successful—attempt to increase the VA's budget and get better care for Veterans as a failure.[63] How could that be? The story claims Sander's faith in government caused him to be slow to act, even though one of their chief sources for the story reveals their contention to be false:

> "Bernie initially came out like this was a Republican attack and was extremely defensive about it," said Dr. Sam Foote, one of the primary whistle-blowers who revealed the delays at the Veterans' hospital in Phoenix. He said Mr. Sanders's "impulse is to stick up for the little guy—and the V.A. serves a lot of little guys."
>
> "But he is no dummy," Dr. Foote said. "He quickly realized the V.A. was lying, and he turned right around and was all over them."

The real story here, of course, is that Sanders understood the Arsonist Posing as Firemen routine that Republicans and the shrink the government crowd were playing, and wasn't having any of it. For example, earlier in the story, *The* Times quotes Sanders as saying:

> "There is, right now, as we speak, a concerted effort to undermine the V.A...You have folks out there now—Koch brothers and others—who want to radically change the nature of society, and either make major cuts in all of these institutions, or maybe do away with them entirely."

To read the entire story—which has only one source suggesting Sanders was slow to pick up on the problem—is to see how tortuous the reporters' reasoning had to be to spin this accomplishment into a negative. It smacks of desperation and an almost blind faith in the ultimate truth of the Myths distorting our national dialogue.

But wait, it gets worse.

IRS Beach Blanket Bingo: Meanwhile, the "targeting" of conservative groups by the IRS seemed to be a desperate attempt by an underfunded IRS branch trying to keep up with an explosion in potential abuses of the tax-exempt status under the 501(c)(4) provision. This section of the IRS code restricts political action, and the number of requests to qualify under this provision, as well as groups operating as such—mostly by conservative groups—were exploding. Faced with budget cuts, the IRS branch office sought to use search terms to find the groups who might be abusing the provision. Since most of the growth in requests to qualify as a 501(c)(4) organization came from conservative groups, that's where they focused, and the search terms they used reflected that.

Get it? Cut budgets. Make global accusations based on one small branch of the IRS attempting to do its job without adequate resources. Erupt in faux outrage. Repeat. And Repeat. And keep repeating, as long as the grossly malfeasant media covers it, and the Democrats' only response was…well, not much.

Spread accelerants, strike match, call in credulous or complicit media.

Gutting the Post Office: With the possible exception of the social security system, nothing gives lie to the Ayn Rand delusions of the Republicans and neoliberals about government ineptitude like the post office. Six days a week, a person shows up at your house with mail, reliably. This has been going on since the Constitution was passed, and it has even survived challenges like e-mail to continue to this day. If government incompetence was going to be marketed, then clearly this system had to be discredited or better yet, destroyed.

What to do? Why, require the post office to forward fund health-care benefits for seventy-five years—in other words, to fund benefits for "employees" who haven't even been born yet, and do it in fewer than ten years. That's what the Bill favored by the Bush administration and passed by Congress in 2006 required. And of course, it was signed into law. Could FedEx or any corporation operate successfully with this kind of model? Of course not.

So once again, we see conservatives and their pale doppelgängers—the neoliberals—manufacturing failure, then standing back and using that failure as evidence that their laissez-faire fantasy of government ineptness and market über alles is true, while the press and media politely avert their gaze.

Sprinkle gasoline...oh, you get it. Question is, why doesn't the press? Or what's left of the real Democrats. Well, I guess we know why the Democrats don't see it...their view is blocked by piles of corporate cash.

When is the Budget Deficit not a Problem? Well, for Republicans—who have been screaming about the deficit problem since even before Saint Ronnie raised it (literally and figuratively) thirty years ago—the opportunity to get an additional $300 billion or more a year in tax revenue doesn't seem too important, especially if it means raising the budget of the IRS so they can afford enough investigators to recover it. Of course, much of that missing revenue would have to come from the über-rich or corporations. Oh, and if you were to add legal tax dodges—again mostly benefiting the rich and the corporations—the total lost revenue is in the trillions.

If budget deficits were the hoary-headed, nation-wrecking monster conservatives say they are, you'd think they'd cast a few millions toward collecting these trillions of dollars.

And by the way, you'd think Democrats would actually highlight this hypocrisy.

But of course, you'd be wrong.

Apparently, the deficit is only a problem if it leads to cutting and gutting government, not if it means making it work.

Coming soon...Hog-tying the Social Security Administration: If the post office is the most visible government program, Social Security and Medicare are the most successful and beloved. Every month, almost fifty-eight million people receive retirement and disability benefits. The system is reliable, and there are some thirteen hundred field offices, making it easy to apply, resolve problems, and update information.

The trust fund is fully funded for the next three decades, and a few simple and politically popular fixes would fund it essentially for as far as we can forecast. One of them involves extending the payroll tax to income over the current cap of $117,000, which, by itself would just about cover all anticipated needs. To be clear here, if you make a billion dollars, you pay the same amount of payroll tax as someone making $117,000—actually much less since most of your income isn't counted as income (see section on corporate and fat-cat welfare above).

As we have seen, social security has an overhead of less than anything the private sector can touch, as well as favorability ratings higher than just about any private-sector function you can name.

What's a poor government hater to do? Why, fabricate stories of insolvency, and when that doesn't work, try to starve their budget, close the local offices because there's not enough money, wait for the inevitable dissatisfaction, then privatize, privatize, privatize.[64]

All together now...spread the gasoline around...strike match...point fingers...feed the Oligarchy.

Democrats—The Plutocrats' Puppies Posing as Progressives: It's worth examining the establishment Democrat's role in this effort to fabricate the MMM and the MBB. After all, most of the insanity was actively pushed by the Republican Party. Or so it would seem.

The fact is, while Republicans shaped national opinion polls, Democrats were driven by them. Republicans navigated using a long-range map and a sense of strategic direction; Democrats steered the national ship of state using their hood ornament. Cowardice is one explanation for why. Complicity with, and reliance on, the Oligarchy is another. Bottom line: once Democrats embraced neoliberalism under Bill Clinton, there was little difference between the parties when it came to fiscal and trade policies.

In a word, the Democrat's response was silence. Or at best, barely audible protestations while they held their hands out hoping for spare change from the Oligarchy.

By the time Bill Clinton ran, Democrats still spoke the language of egalitarian rhetoric, but the DLC centrists and center right had firm control of the party. Clinton's political genius enabled him to sound progressive and populist, while pushing one of the most conservative economic and social agendas of any Democrat in over a century.

As Thomas Frank noted in an interview with Mark Carlin published via Truthout:

> Clinton had five major achievements as president: NAFTA, the Crime Bill of 1994, welfare reform, the deregulation of banks and telecoms, and the balanced budget. All of them—every single one—were longstanding Republican objectives.[65]

The Telecommunications Act of 1996, in particular, was a free marketeer's wet dream. Not only did it give away airwaves for free, but it also removed any remaining meaningful constraints on the media designed to assure that it met its First Amendment responsibilities.

The rest of the party pretty much mirrored Clinton's approach. While purporting to be the champions of the people, they paid homage to the Magic Markets, and they declined to defend government or to suggest it was capable of anything good, for the most part. A critique of Bill Clinton's first two years in office written by Bernie Sanders back in 1995 published by *In These Times*,[66] sounds much like the debates between Sanders and Hillary Clinton we heard during the primaries.

Barak Obama mouthed stirring speeches advocating the vital role government could play in a civil society and generally espousing progressive policies—but only around elections. In between, he was strictly a centrist, and until his final two years, he practiced a perplexing policy of preemptive capitulation every time the Republicans threatened to hold their breath until they turned blue. He famously offered a "grand bargain" that would have compromised social security and the rest of the social safety net, rather than risk defending it. Given his rhetorical skills, he could have used his presidency as a bully pulpit and given meaning to his slogan of "Hope and Change."

The Clinton/Sanders debates were a proxy for the positions of the entire establishment wing of the Democratic Party. Which is to say, an elite center-right corporatist establishment, against a large cohort of progressives who, until Sanders, were all but ignored.

This position is perplexing because, as we saw in chapter 1, the majority of Americans hold progressive positions on most issues, and polling shows they have for decades. How hard would it have been for the majority of the party to advocate gun control laws (favored by 90 percent of Americans), or stricter regulations on Wall Street (favored by 80 percent of Americans), or to cut subsidies to big oil (favored by 74 percent of Americans), or to defend social security (which 80 percent of Americans say they'd be willing to pay more taxes to do)…this list could go on and on.

More to the point, why didn't Democrats take the overwhelming evidence showing that trickle down, deregulation, "job creators," and the rest of the empty rhetoric used to justify the MMM was an empty shell?

Given all the historical evidence, how hard would it have been to suggest that the solution to bad government—to the extent it even existed—is good government, not no government?

If the historical data wasn't enough, they could have simply pointed to the two states—Kansas and Louisiana—that embraced the MMM and the MBB and cut taxes for the wealthy while gutting social programs. The MMM, just to remind you, said that the economy would prosper, jobs would increase, and tax revenue would go up if taxes and government regulations were cut—particularly those applying to corporations and rich folks. What actually happened in both cases is that their economies tanked, job growth fell well below the national average, and tax receipts plummeted.[67] Kansas had to close schools early in 2015 because it couldn't afford to keep them open, and it kicked disabled people off Medicaid. Louisiana turned a $1 billion surplus into a projected $1.6 billion deficit. And Kansas Governor Brownback's "grand supply-side experiment" with tax cuts ended up with a Republican legislature passing emergency repeals of his tax cuts over his veto, after the state nearly went bankrupt, it's economy tanked, and none of the jobs promised materialized.[68] As the Business Insider put it, Brownback's experiment failed "on its own terms."

For that matter, they could have pointed to California, where Democrats obtained a sufficient majority to run the state.[69] Governor Jerry Brown promptly raised taxes, and since, the state created two million new jobs and racked up a huge surplus, while the economy grew far faster than states which followed conventional wisdom.

The point is, refuting the Republican's favorite myths would have been easy, and it would have paid political dividends. In fact, there's real evidence that failing to do so has hurt the party.

For example, back in the 1960s,[70] half of all potential voters in the United States identified as Democrats. Currently, 29 percent do. If one tracks the losses, it appears that the more the party moved to the center and beyond, the more the people abandoned the party.

Democratic leaders have been moving to the center (and often well beyond to the right of center) ostensibly to capture the independent swing voters. In reality, swing voters have always been a small portion of the independent voter bloc. Since 1960 they've comprised at most only 15 percent of self-identified independents, and currently they make up about 5 percent of independents (about 42 percent of people identify as independents). It turns out, more independents favor progressive positions on most issues which suggests the growth in independents comes, at least in part, from disaffected progressives leaving the Democratic Party. As we will see in chapter 7, many people who hold progressive positions on an issue-by-issue basis don't necessarily consider themselves progressive, so it would take some effort and education to win these independents over. The fact that the establishment elite advocate chasing the mythical centrist swing voters, rather than winning over progressives, suggests they are either ignorant, or they're being disingenuous.

By the 2014 midterms, the harm caused to the Democrats by their unwillingness to stand for anything reached its zenith. The media, the pollsters, and both parties were completely blindsided by the scale of the

Republican domination at the polls. Oh, folks were predicting the usual gains an opposition party typically gets in the midterms, but nothing like what happened. Many of the inside-the-beltway pundits interpreted this as yet more evidence of their favorite delusion: that the United States is a right-of-center country politically.

Of course, it is no such thing, as polls have been showing for some time now.[71]

The fact is, the real winner in 2014 was "none of the above." With Democrats running from Obamacare and anything else Republicans happened to be attacking—which was just about everything short of bat-shit crazy right-wing lunacy—the progressive majority had no choice and they shunned the elections like they were Ebola transmission centers. In fact, 2014 set a record for the lowest turnout (36.2 percent) since World War II—and the only reason that was lower than 2014 was that a sizable portion of voting-age males was overseas and unable to vote.

Democrats practice a better brand of rhetoric, and they're not as lunatic as the Republicans have become on social issues, but the fact is, they're no less a wholly owned subsidiary of the Oligarchy than the Republicans, and the people have gotten wise to it.

With the press in the pocket of the Oligarchy, it took a people's movement to expose the reality behind the carefully constructed facade of the Democratic Party as the People's Party. That's what the Occupy Movement in the run up to the 2012 elections accomplished—it put inequality on the public's radar. It took someone like Sanders to give this nascent movement a political voice. And it will take us, we the people, to complete the revolution in the next few years.

In the chapter that follows, we'll examine how the elite establishment hijacked the civil institutions that normally serve as a counterweight to the interests of corporations and the ultrarich, enabling them to win the primary battle.

CHAPTER 6

The Uncivil Society

● ● ●

Quis custodiet ipsos custodes? Who will watch the watchers?

Juvenal, Satires

The final piece of the puzzle for understanding the Coup comes from the fact that the civil institutions we used to rely on to be watchdogs and counterweights to political, economic, and corporate power have been taken over by the elite establishment.

Just as our constitution established checks and balances to constrain the power of any one branch of government, we've developed institutions to perform the same task on a society-wide basis. Time was when religion performed that function. Today, religion is more a captive of politics than a shaper of it.

By the late seventeenth century, the press emerged as a powerful check against government malfeasance or abuse of power. But as we've seen, the EEM—which still serves as the primary source of news for most Americans—is now a wholly owned subsidiary of corporations. An evolving alternative—what some have termed the Fifth Estate—is the confluence of information technology and the use of social media to expose, often in real time, the secrets of the powerful elite, but as yet, they don't rival more conventional news sources, except perhaps among the young. And of course, the Internet allows people to "shop" for a place that reinforces their bias, and thus, it has the potential to be divisive, deceptive, and a source of misinformation.

But the jury is out on whether the Fifth Estate will function as one of the guardians of a civil society, or a threat to it. There's evidence that the system will be self-policing, as we see the seeds of efforts to identify and neuter fake news.[72]

Interestingly, on the one hand, the young—who get much of their information from the Internet—have been a major force in the revolt against the Oligarchy and have proved instrumental in Sanders's success. On the other hand, Trump used social media to bypass the elites, and spread his appeal across America like manure on a fallow field.

By the twentieth century, unions, not-for-profit interest groups, and citizen activists became a force for a more civil society. Well before the 2016 primaries, as we will see, these institutions were headed by the establishment elites who often had little in common with the rank and file they purportedly represented.

Thomas Frank, in *Listen, Liberal or Whatever Happened to the Party of the People* notes how the Democratic Party got taken over by a cohort of the accomplished—mostly highly educated, and many graduates of elite Ivy League schools who came to believe not only that their own success was warranted by their hard work and brilliance, but also that the trials and tribulations of the less fortunate were also earned—perhaps by their lack of work and ability. Frank suggests that Democrats chose to appeal to the professional class at the expense of working-class Americans, and he maintains that this shift preceded the role of money in politics. But money was already buying access as far back as Reagan, and it continued through both of Clinton's terms at both the Congressional and presidential level.

As I noted earlier, this book emphasizes the role of money and corporate power in the Coup, but Frank's theory of elitism can exist side by side with the notion of an economic Coup: indeed, they are mutually reinforcing. Both Silicon Valley and Wall Street are loaded with graduates of elite schools, both have a larger share of wealth, these wealthy individuals contribute generously to Democrats, and Democratic politicians routinely tap members of both communities to serve as senior members of their administrations, as well as for campaign funds.

This same cadre of the elite took over many of the civil institutions and even some unions, bringing with them the identical belief in their own rightness and their innate high regard for their own talents and abilities and the talents and abilities of those who were like them.

As a result, Hillary Clinton—the elite establishment's choice—racked up endorsements from large unions and other groups that used to represent the interests of the people they served.

In essence, the elites who ran these groups were intimate with the Oligarchy and sympathetic to their interests. It's as if they were all living in a gated community together, and national policy was being shaped by the neighborhood architectural committee that ran that community. You and I don't live there, and the rank-and-file membership of the organizations they supposedly represented didn't have the code to the gate and rarely mingled with this elite establishment.

A close look at a few of these endorsements shows how their leaders bypassed the interests and desires of their members. The elitist's stampede for Hillary began as early as *November of 2015*, well before she began her lurch to the left, when she still held positions that were anathema to the interests of the organizations that endorsed her.

Exhibit A—The Service Employees International Union: SEIU endorsed Hillary Clinton in November of 2015. This, despite the fact that Hillary had not and never did endorse one of their chief demands, a fifteen-dollar-an-hour federal minimum wage, something Sanders had supported since before the campaign started.

There was a backlash among the rank and file, many of whom remember when Bernie Sanders stood with them in tough times, and who knew that Clinton did not back the union's highest priority.

Exhibit B—The League of Conservation Voters Endorsement of Clinton: When the LCV endorsed Hillary Clinton over Bernie Sanders, it ignited a firestorm among environmentalists. Not too surprising, given their respective records.

It's worth taking a closer look at the LCV endorsement to see what it reveals. Let's start with the facts[73]:

- Hillary Clinton's lifetime LCV score is 82. Bernie Sanders's is 95. Even her 82 seems bloated when you examine her scorecard[74] compared to Bernie's[75].
- The LCV's response—that they were factoring in electability—is patently and obviously false, considering Sanders beat Republicans by as much or more than Clinton[76] in polls at the time of the endorsement.
- Hillary's positions of record on the environmental issues of the day shifted dramatically in the few months preceding the LCV's endorsement; indeed, the LCV cited her opposition to the XL pipeline as justification for their endorsement, without noting she historically signaled support for the XL, while Sanders had always opposed it.
- The LCV's board chair is Carol Browner, who was appointed by Bill Clinton to head the EPA.
- Among major contributors to the LCV, big banks and people from the finance industry dominate—including past officers of Goldman-Sachs.
- This is the earliest endorsement in the history of the LCV.

This last bullet is a clue to what's really going on. There was no reason to rush this endorsement, unless they wanted to tip the scales one way or another, and certainly there was no reason to tip it toward the candidate with the *lower* lifetime score—aka Clinton. The most plausible explanation for this action is that the DLC branch of the Democratic Party—essentially the Oligarch's wing—was moving as expeditiously as possible to put one of their own in power; mission, membership and environment be damned.

The rank-and-file greens reacted explosively, and rightly so. In the days following the announcement, the rating on LCV's Facebook page plummeted from over 4 to 2.3, and the comments on the endorsement were universally—and strongly—negative.

Beyond the LCV Endorsement—The Power Elite vs. the People: This same phenomena—those in power going against the people they claim to serve—can be seen with unions, where Hillary collected early endorsements despite her long history of supporting job-killing trade agreements and her opposition to a fifteen-dollar minimum wage. Again, let's look at the facts:

* Hillary has been a strong proponent of trade agreements in general and the TPP in particular, until Sanders made it a political liability.
* Sanders has opposed them throughout his career.
* Clinton opposed a national minimum wage of fifteen dollars per hour, while Sanders supported it.
* Over the years, Clinton has received much of her campaign contributions from Wall Street and big banks who have encouraged overseas investment in manufacturing and offshoring of American corporations.
* Sanders got his campaign money from the people.

So, the evidence shows that Sanders had been far more supportive of the issues and positions labor cares about than Clinton, for far longer. But by November of 2015, early in the primaries, Hillary had received endorsements from the American Federation of Teachers (AFT), the National Education Association (NEA) and the American Federation of State, County and Municipal Employees, the International Association of Machinists and Aerospace Workers (IAM) in addition to the SEIU, while Sanders had picked up only two.

Clinton continued to rack up union endorsements throughout the primaries at rates higher than Sanders, often angering and alienating rank-and-file members.

As with the LCV endorsement, the reaction of the rank and file in these unions to the endorsements was swift, broad based, and negative.

Take the IAM for example, where members complained bitterly about the endorsement, with some claiming that support for Sanders dominated the union.[77]

The NEA and FTE endorsements created the same <u>outrage</u> among the rank and file, with many dissenters expressing strong support for Sanders.

So, why did these institutions, charged with representing the interests of their members, endorse the candidate who least shared their organization's objectives? Here again, the answer lies in what the senior officials said. IAM president Randi Weingarten defended her union's endorsement of Clinton, saying, "If you want to shape something, you get in before the primaries."[78]

Now let's parse this statement out.

For starters, the union's first responsibility should be its member's interests. How did "shaping" the primaries to benefit Clinton do that?

Answer: it didn't, for two reasons.

First, the only possible justification for "shaping" the primaries was if one candidate was so superior in terms of representing union interests, you wanted to do everything you could to push the nomination his or her way. Viewed from what the union itself listed as their primary objectives, Hillary was the weakest candidate, so toss out that reason.

Second, since her nomination offered no clear advantage to labor—in fact, given her historical positions it would likely result in a less sympathetic voice in the White House—the Unions' best strategy (after endorsing the strongest candidate—Sanders) would have been to wait as long as possible before endorsing a candidate and use the time to extract promises from them.

The same is true of the major environmental organizations, as the major national ones lined up behind Clinton.[79]

Even the Watchdogs Have Been Co-opted: As we noted earlier, civil institutions functioned as a third arm of society distinct from government and business, and were capable of holding both accountable. The press, unions, NGOs, religious organizations—in theory, at least—worked to hold both business and government accountable.

As we saw in chapter 3, thanks in no small part to Reagan and Bill Clinton, we began losing the press thirty years ago. Today, they are little more than a wholly owned subsidiary of the Oligarchy. Our increasingly secular society means that religion follows politics rather than shaping it.

And now, it's clear that NGOs and unions have been absorbed into the elite establishment Borg as both parties become pawns to moneyed interests.

So, not only has our government and political process been bought, but the senior members of the NGO and union community have become enmeshed in the game of money and power that is destroying our democracy.

In short, someone tossed the watchdogs a steak, and they're off in the corner, gnawing on their prize and plotting ways to get more.

It Will Take a Revolution to Reclaim Our Country: Trump's victory was a direct result of people understanding that the Democratic Party had been taken over by fat cats, plutocrats, and elitists.

Unions and environmental organizations were born in picket lines and protest marches. They earned their place in society by wading through tear gas and even bullets to speak truth to power, to bear witness for the rights of the people and the planet.

This time, the elite establishment of the Democratic Party won the battle for their support, and as a result, the party fielded a neoliberal centrist and a Washington insider at a time when the electorate was looking for a progressive outsider. In 2018 and 2020 the rank and file of these organizations must do more than complain about their leadership. It's time for them to lay the groundwork for leading us in the revolution that Sanders started, and the first step in that process is to get the party elite out of their own management.

CHAPTER 7

Putting the Silver-Tongued Lizard in Charge

● ● ●

Political language...is designed to make lies sound truthful and murder respectable, and to give an appearance of solidity to pure wind.

GEORGE ORWELL

It's easier to fool people than to convince them they've been fooled.

MARK TWAIN

BY NOW, ANY READER WITH a healthy dose of skepticism will have a question or two about my thesis. If the majority of the American people do, in fact, hold progressive views on virtually every issue that is important to them, then why do center-right and right-wing candidates win so often?[80]

And win they do.

Prior to this election, the commentariat had been predicting the death of the Republican Party for at least a decade. To hear them tell it, it was a simple matter of demographics. The young are far more liberal than the general population and soon whites will no longer be a majority—just a matter of time, they said.

Meanwhile, Republicans control both Houses of Congress, and presidential elections are typically close. In fact, since 1980, the nation has had three conservative Republican presidents and one middle-of-the road

Democrat, and one who was conservative in deed, if not in language. And now there's Trump.

And of course, in 2016 the conservatives swept the table—not only did Trump win the presidency, but they held onto both houses of Congress, and made further inroads in the states, winning governorships and legislatures in record numbers.

Part of this is structural. The electoral college gives a higher weight and greater representation to voters in states with smaller populations, many of whom are rural and conservative. Beyond that, the Republican Party—aided and abetted by corporations and rich funders from the Oligarchy—targeted some key down-ballot races at the state level in 2010[81] with an eye toward increasing gerrymandering to decrease Democratic seats and increase Republican seats after the 2010 census. They were spectacularly successful, as evidenced by the fact that even though Democrats received 1.4 million more votes than Republicans in House races in 2012, Republicans emerged with a thirty-three-seat majority.

At the state level, the situation is even more skewed. Republicans control both legislatures and the governorship in twenty-five states, while Democrats control all three institutions in just six states.[82] Nebraska, which has a unicameral, nonpartisan legislature, isn't counted in this total.

Republicans control both legislative bodies in thirty-two states, while Democrats do so in just thirteen.[83] And they're picking up momentum. In 1978, Democrats controlled both legislative branches in thirty-one states, while Republicans had majorities in only eleven.

Currently thirty-four states have a Republican governor, while only fifteen are headed by a Democrat, and one—Alaska—is headed by an independent.

The numbers and the trends suggest that it is the Democratic Party that is on life-support, not the Republicans.

This begs the question of why there is an enormous disconnect between what people want on an issue-by-issue basis, and what our government chooses to do, and why we continue to pick people who won't do our bidding. Yet, as we saw in chapter 1, the disconnect is undeniable. The people overwhelmingly favor progressive positions on matters ranging from economics and fiscal policy, to gun control, to social tolerance, to environmental policies, to education, to defense and foreign policy—on almost every topic you can name, people choose positions that are left of center.

Yet when you ask Americans to self-identify as liberal, moderate, or conservative, most will call themselves conservative. For example, in one of the most recent polls on the topic, Gallup found that 37 percent of Americans self-identified as conservative; 35 percent called themselves moderates; and only 24 percent considered themselves to be liberal.[84] Earlier polls showed even higher numbers of conservatives, but the disparity persists.

Similarly, we hold the current crop of politicians and officeholders in the lowest regard, but continue to elect them. For example, in the last five years, with the exception of one year, approval rates for Congress have been below 20 percent, dipping as low as 9 percent in 2013, while *disapproval* rates have exceeded 70 percent in all but one year, going as high as 86 percent of Americans on several occasions. Yet we overwhelmingly vote for incumbents. Essentially, Americans seem to be saying "throw the bastards out," except my bastard. He or she is OK.

If you need further proof that America is left-of-center, progressive ballot measures did well in 2016, just as they did in 2014.

This all points to one of the most unrecognized conundrums in US politics: how an electorate that is overwhelmingly progressive on an issue-by-issue basis considers itself to be conservative, and more to the point, why right-wing and center-right candidates consistently win at all levels of government when almost no one is happy with what they stand for.

Equally baffling is why this disconnect—one of the most important political issues we face—is so rarely discussed.

You won't see or hear this mystery covered in the EEM. You won't see it explored by think tanks or pundits. It's rarely studied by academics. Neither party addresses it. With the exception of Thomas Frank—and a few less mainstream political writers—it's largely ignored, as if it were some egregious social faux pas to even acknowledge it—the proverbial elephant in our national living room, which no one mentions.

In fact, the disconnect is worse than these numbers would suggest, since the Democratic Party is now right-of-center on most issues, and most people who vote for them perceive them to be to the left.

So what gives? Why do so many people with predominantly liberal views consider themselves to be conservative or moderate?

The twin myths dominating our political discourse go a long way to explaining the disconnect.

And, of course, as we've seen, it serves the Oligarchy's purpose to ignore it, and they've actively intervened in the social commons to essentially take over the parties, the media, and the institutions that are used to police both.

But taking over institutions is one thing—taking over the hearts and minds of the people is quite another. How were they able to do it?

To answer this, we'll have to take a few side trips, starting with Madison Avenue and going back to ancient Greece with a possible stop-off at Stratford-upon-Avon.

Branding and the Demonization of "Liberal": The astute reader will detect some overlap in this discussion and the one in chapter 3 on bringing Madison Avenue to politics. The more discerning reader will understand why I'm repeating some things. The most discerning reader will note the important differences in these discussions.

The *Business Dictionary* defines branding as

> the process involved in creating a unique name and image for a product in the consumer's mind, mainly through advertising campaigns with a consistent theme. Branding aims to establish a significant and differentiated presence in the market that attracts and retains loyal customers.

Notice what is *not* mentioned in this definition. The differentiation of the product or service need not have any basis in truth, accuracy, reality, or substance.

In politics, branding is used as much to vilify the opposition as to foster your own brand, and the right wing has been quite adept at it. The key ingredients of a successful branding campaign are repetition, repetition, and repetition. Oh, and repetition. There are other considerations: use simple words, use figures of speech, and metaphorical language.

Branding is frequently designed to sell the attribute, not the product. Coke doesn't sell cheap flavored sugar water, they were selling "opening happiness" for years, and now they sell "taste the feeling." Everyone in their commercials is young, hip and having much more fun than you and I.

Omega doesn't sell watches—they sell "chronometers" that are a "perfection of mechanical devices." With cheap digital watches able to keep time as well or better than these "perfect mechanical devices" how could they compete? Well, how about trying to convince you that owning one of their watches ushers you into a select and elite group, setting you apart from the riffraff? In essence, they convert a watch to a talisman—no different than the bone through the nose sported by witch doctors, thought to confer magical properties.

Old Spice doesn't sell a moderately nice-smelling aftershave; it sells "The man you could smell like." And he is decidedly not like you and me... but heck, slap a little aftershave on and well...everything could change, especially us, apparently.

In short, the brand is directed at convincing you that you can become a different person or enter a different realm simply by buying whatever geegaw, gadget, or service they're slapping their logo on.

In the same way, conservatives don't sell tax cuts for the rich, ineffective government, perpetual wars, corporate hegemony, and constraints on personal choice; rather, they sell "trickle down," "deregulation," "strong Defense and national security" (always with a capitol D, and always having more to do with offense). Similarly, they sell "family values," not restrictions on whom you may sleep with, who you may—and may not—marry, what sexual practices you may engage in, whether you may choose to die on your own terms, etc.

And they do it using the best lessons of rhetoric, a field that is virtually unstudied today.

As Joseph Romm, author of *Language Intelligence: Lessons in Persuasion from Jesus, Shakespeare, Lincoln and Lady Gaga*[85] notes, most of us are taught to use big words, avoid repetition and be as literal as possible—using facts, numbers, and details. This runs counter to two thousand years of evidence showing that the right way to persuade is to use short words and common words, repeat yourself again and again, and then again, and speak in figurative and metaphorical language.

But I repeat myself.

One important emphasis conservatives have made when using Dr. Romm's rhetorical formula is to target the limbic lizard brain in us all with messages grounded in fear, hate, anger, greed, jingoism, jealousy, or bigotry.

These simple techniques go a long way toward explaining how conservatives have successfully branded both their "product" as desirable and good and the liberal "product" as something between mindless and evil, why it worked, *and why liberals (aka progressives) have been unsuccessful in countering the conservative rhetorical juggernaut.*

Let's look at some of the names conservatives have used in their branding of liberals and leftists:

* Knee-jerk liberal;
* Bleeding-heart liberal;
* Tax-and-spend liberal;
* The Democrat Party (not the Democratic Party) used as a pejorative;
* Soft on crime;
* Limousine liberal;
* Latte-sipping liberals;
* Pinkos...

This list could go on and on. Each of these has been repeated until they are burned into our collective national brain. Even liberals eschew the word liberal and have since the 1960s.

Note the use of simple words, alliteration, and metaphor.

Now try to think of an equivalent list of pejoratives used by liberals to describe conservatives. Couldn't do it, could you?

These are just name-calling, you say? Turns out, sticks and stones may not be the only thing that can hurt you. Conservatives have also been adept at short, quotable phrases that stick in your mind with as much tenacity as one of those commercial jingles. Those over a certain age have no doubt found themselves humming the dreaded "double your pleasure" Double Mint tune and unable to get it out of their heads. Just so with many of the conservative's favorite memes.

No surprise here, but these phrases—and the advertising jingles—use figures of speech to make them memorable.

As Romm points out, the rules of rhetoric were codified by the Greeks a couple of thousand years ago. They emerged in part, because in plays and speeches, long passages had to be remembered, and since written copies of anything were rare and expensive, language had to be memorable.

Reagan was a master at this. For example, here's some of his short quotes that are still remembered thirty or more years later:

"Government is not the solution to our problems; government is the problem."

"As government expands, liberty contracts."

"The most terrifying words in the English language are, 'I'm from the Government and I'm here to help.' "

"It isn't so much that liberals are ignorant. It's that they know so many things that aren't so."

"Government does not solve problems; it subsidizes them."

The constant assault on government and liberalism through the skillful use of language explains why so few of us identify as liberals, and why so many of us accept the MBB. That, and the fact that there was no rebuttal. But it's hard to defend government when you're on the take from people who want to eviscerate it.

Conversely, conservatives have been extraordinarily effective at building their own brand.

Quick, think about what conservatism stands for. As Kevin Drum put it,

> Every American over the age of ten knows what the GOP and the conservative movement stand for. Sing it with me now: low taxes, small government, strong defense, traditional families. See? You know the tune, and the harmony line, too…Everybody knows what the conservative brand stands for, because the conservative leadership has spent four decades nurturing a consistent brand identity for themselves.[86]

OK, now try to come up with a description of what it means to be a liberal, or a progressive, for that matter (humming the Jeopardy theme, now…still humming…time's winding down…buzzer sounds). *Oh, I'm sorry…we do have a lovely parting gift for you…*

The chances are, even if you consider yourself a liberal, you couldn't come up with a quick and easy summary—worse, it's likely that some of those conservative memes crept into your head as you considered this question.

At best, you might have listed some general principles couched in logic with detailed examples of policies that supported the principles. Snooze alert. No one cares.

As George Lakoff has often noted, humans perceive in frames, not in specifics. We deal with attributes, not analytics. And liberals always talk in terms of reason, logic, and facts, while conservatives speak figuratively in the language of values. Progressives spout statistics and specific policies; conservatives talk in terms of family values, patriotism, motherhood, and apple pie. Oh, and fear and loathing, with a heavy dose of God—that's their God, of course—the Jesus loves you (but not *them*) God.

This juxtaposition of Christianity—a religion rooted in love, tolerance, and forgiveness—with fear, hate, and jingoism explains why conservatives love the Old Testament, Revelations, and the misogynistic, misanthropic writings of Paul, but eschew the Gospels.

Conservative language is actually less about moral and ethical stances than it is about creating an "us" and a "them," and it's typically designed to appeal to our limbic lizard.

Their value statements are tribal, not timeless. For example, the afore-mentioned lapel pin "controversy," or whether or not someone wears... gasp...jeans in the oval office, or claiming to be pro-life while supporting

- psychotic positions on gun regulation that result in more than thirty thousand deaths per year;
- the death penalty;
- wars of choice killing millions;
- repeal of Obamacare—killing hundreds of thousands;
- cuts to life-saving environmental and social regulations killing hundreds of thousands;
- appeals to irrational fear, blame, and hate toward Mexican immigrants at a time when net immigration is negative and statistics show that immigrants commit fewer crimes of any kind than natives; and
- fear of Muslim Americans establishing Sharia law in the United States, when they comprise about 1 percent of the population—all the while advocating what amounts to a Christian Sharia in which *their* religious beliefs are intertwined in some perverted way with the secular Enlightenment-age basis of our government.

There's method to this madness. Conservative politicians can't run on their positions—which most Americans oppose—so they have to distract, deceive, and delude, or otherwise appeal to something other than reason. And nothing does that like appeals to the limbic lizard, particularly with conservatives.

Thus, we have conservatives functioning as merchants of death on an issue-by-issue basis, while claiming the mantle of pro-life. And you'll rarely see the full hypocrisy of this challenged in the EEM, and it is rarely refuted by the Democrats.

It's Hardwired: In an extraordinarily comprehensive summary of sixteen peer-reviewed studies on the differences in brain structure and function between conservatives and liberals, we get a sense of what motivates each group.[87] Conservatives are more orderly and crave order, they are less tolerant of change, they are less likely to change their minds when offered information that contradicts their worldview, they respond more strongly to fear and negative stimuli than do liberals, and they are more focused on avoiding negative outcomes than pursuing positive ones. In addition, the right amygdala—which processes deep, emotional memories—is physically larger in conservatives than liberals.

Lest you dismiss these kinds of studies as the biases of pointy-headed liberal intellectuals, the "conservative brain" confers a number of advantages beyond being more orderly. Studies suggest they sleep better, trust their peers more, and they are far more organized than liberals, who not only tolerate chaos, but seem to generate it.

When the conservative tendencies toward order, fear avoidance, enhanced responses to fear, and other intensely emotional stimuli are combined with the more *generally* applicable phenomena of memory formation and learning shared by all humans, it becomes obvious why conservative messaging works so well, even for liberals.

Specifically, memory formation is stronger and more immediate when the experiences are emotional, whether positive or negative. And this holds true for both liberals and conservatives. Put another way, it's easier to remember your first kiss or your first serious fight than it is to remember a calculus proof, or the names and sequence of US presidents. This is because there are two pathways for forming memories (there are actually more, but they can be loosely aggregated into these two). The two are called the affective and cognitive, with the affective involving deep emotional experiences and the cognitive less emotional learning centered on reasoning. Fear and other deeply felt emotions go through both the amygdala and the hippocampus, while cognitive experiences are processed by the hippocampus alone.

The more primitive amygdala mediated memory is an adaptive inheritance found in early life-forms and passed on by natural selection. Being able to remember and recognize threats helped avoid them, and this attribute is present in all vertebrates. In humans, it bypasses reason, for a reason. If early humans had replaced or inactivated the lizard-memory, and instead had to spend time contemplating whether that saber-toothed tiger over there posed a threat, their chances of having progeny would have gone down. And we wouldn't be here.

So what? Well, as a baseline, appeals engaging deep emotions tend to create stronger memories that are more easily formed and more easily retrieved than appeals based on reason, whether one is conservative or liberal.

So, while conservative messaging works particularly well with the "conservative brain," it may also register more immediately and with more intensity on both liberals and conservatives.

No wonder people don't think of themselves as liberals, regardless of the individual—and reason-based—positions they hold. Conservatives speak in frames of reference that are more easily accepted, use more effective language, and often engage a deeper, more powerful memory and learning mechanism that is hardwired into our brains.

Unfortunately for liberals/progressives, people don't often vote on specifics or statistics—rather, they vote on values, and they define themselves by values.

One of the reasons "progressive" has resonated more with people than the dreaded "liberal" is because it has been resurrected and used at a time when conservatism was being branded by a people's movement—Occupy Wall Street—which not only identified income inequality as a political issue, but also imbued it with a frame that was value based: Greed and injustice vs. equity and a fair distribution of wealth. It is a sign of just how much the DLC branch of the Democratic Party—which is to say the vast majority of it since Bill Clinton—has sold out to the Oligarchy that they didn't use these far more effective means of labelling themselves and their opposition. The country was ready, the message was ripe, the political advantages obvious. But the fact is, DLC Democrats couldn't adopt Occupy's more effective framing because they didn't share their progressive values.

At any rate, the conservatives' use of language to appeal to the limbic, to construct values-based frames—and branding—explains why people who overwhelmingly hold liberal positions on an issue-by-issue basis often don't vote in ways that are consistent with those positions, why they may not identify as liberal, and it also explains why the Coup proceeded so effortlessly.

To quote fictional President Alan Shepard, who was locked in a race with conservative Bob Rumson in Aaron Sorkin's film *The American President*,

> Whatever your problem, I promise you, Bob Rumson is not the least bit interested in solving it. He is interested in two things and two things only: making you afraid of it and telling you who's to blame for it. That, ladies and gentlemen, is how you win elections. You gather a group of middle-aged, middle-class, middle-income voters who remember with longing an easier time, and you talk to them about family and American values and character.

If only our candidates could muster even a tenth of the insight and courage of Sorkin's fictional characters we'd be far less likely to get conned.

But if you own the press, control the civil institutions that used to be watchdogs, buy candidates outright, and use more effective rhetorical tools, it's pretty easy to pull that off, as we'll see in chapter 8.

CHAPTER 8

How to Steal a Nomination

● ● ●

A society without the means to detect lies and theft
soon squanders its liberty and freedom.

CHRIS HEDGES

UP UNTIL NOW, WE'VE EXAMINED how the Oligarchy conducted their Coup and why it worked. Here we'll focus specifically on how the elite establishment worked to keep Sanders from getting the nomination, and why it didn't work with Trump.

We've talked about how both parties subscribe to the twin myths and how those myths are used to delude the people. We've also examined the conversion of journalism from a profession with an ethical canon, to a mere commodity that is bought and sold as if it were no more important to our democracy than pork bellies, and how the media have become a wholly owned subsidiary of the Oligarchy.

And we've seen how the civil institutions that used to function as watchdogs, were turned into lapdogs.

Finally, we examined the use of rhetorical devices to short circuit reason and appeal to our ancient lizard in the limbic system.

It's worth examining how these forces were combined in the 2016 primary race to result in the nomination of two of the most distrusted and disliked candidates ever to run for the presidency[88], and ultimately, how the most disliked one won.

There's been a lot of head scratching on the part of pundits, media, and politicians about what happened in this election cycle, and how to account for Trump's takeover of the Republican Party and Sander's near takeover of the Democrats, and how—in the name of all that's rational—someone like Trump triumphed.

There's also been a tendency to lump Sanders and Trump together, as two sides of the same coin, representing the disgruntled, the disaffected, and the fringes of both parties. As we will see, this is half-right.

Trump—a Natural Rhetorician: Republicans—shocked that their silent dog whistle politics of hate, racism, jingoism, and militarism has turned loud and rowdy and explicit—are still trying desperately to understand what happened to JEB! And Marco. Particularly JEB!, who had the money, the backing of the establishment elite, and name recognition.

But Trump is easily explained. It is precisely this three-decades-long reliance on dog-whistle politics that made Trump or someone like him nearly inevitable. In essence, the party's reliance on these forces for over three decades eliminated anything like a moderate or a true conservative, leaving only the angry, the hateful, and the fearful. And with conservative policies creating income disparity, hate, divisiveness, blame and anger on a stealth basis, there was no shortage of these embittered voters. More to the point, they were often justified in their alienation.

And Trump, for all his faults—and they are legion—is adept at exploiting these emotions and speaking in the language of the lizard: simple words, often directed at a "them," and couched in the language of hate and designed to inspire fear and blame, spoken over and over again. Once he brought these forces out of the closet, none of the candidates pretending to be less extreme or trying to achieve the same appeal through coded language and secret handshakes had a chance in hell of defeating him. It's no accident that Ted Cruz was the last man standing before Trump's fear and hate-filled express wiped him off the stage. Cruz used dog whistles and coded language, but he was also not averse to more explicit appeals to the lizard within us.

By 2016, Republicans had authored their own version of *Lord of the Flies* or *Dr. Jekyll and Mr. Hyde*, and no one espousing moderation in any way, shape, or form could make it through the gauntlet that was their primary.

Finally, the media, sensing a man-bites-dog headline, gave Trump some $2 billion in free coverage before the primaries even began. And many were loath to challenge or question his cascade of lies. Even after the primaries were over and the general election race was heating up, Matt Lauer gave him a pass on what amounted to serial lies about his position on Iraq.

Even though fewer than a quarter of the people identify as Republican, they are all in the same tribe, united and passionate, excited to have someone explicitly endorse ideas they've long felt but rarely heard espoused. The rest of the clown car was doomed, once Trump unveiled his act, and revealed the hateful heart and soul of a party gone bad.

So, OK, that's how he got the nomination. But how did he win? Here again, the answer is simple. The Democratic Party—in thrall to the Oligarchy and embracing neoliberalism—sabotaged Sanders and ran the only candidate who could lose to Trump.

Hillary Clinton—The Oligarchy's Pyrrhic Victory: But why, if Trump's challenge succeeded, did Sanders's fail?

Unlike Trump, Sanders challenged the Oligarch's Coup with the politics of equality and inclusion told in the context of facts and reality. So while both Trump and Sanders were perceived as coming from outside the elite establishment stable, the resemblance ends there.

So why was Hillary Clinton, the establishment's chosen one, able to hold on and defeat Sanders?

For starters, the Democratic Party still lives in Davos-land, a place where it remains possible to believe—or at least pretend—that serving the ultra-rich and corporations while purporting to represent the people at the same time is anything but a conflict of interest. Thus, Hillary succeeded—with a massive assist from the EEM—to campaign as "a progressive who gets things done," even though she wasn't progressive and got very little done as a senator and who, as secretary of state, advocated a neocon foreign policy that was closer to Bush than it was to anything like a progressive position.[89]

It's worth examining this label of a "progressive who gets things done." It was one of her favorite lines and it got picked up by her many surrogates in the press. The fact is, it never stood up to scrutiny. For example, she only sponsored three Bills that became law during her eight- year tenure. One established an historic site in New York, another renamed a Post Office, and the third named a portion of a highway in New York after Timothy J. Russert.

How about her claim of being able to work with Republicans? Politifact, which normally finds at least a little truth in just about any statement, rated her claim that "…every piece of legislation, just about, that I ever introduced had a Republican co-sponsor" as flat out false.[90]

Ms. Clinton also didn't rank as particularly progressive, according to GovTrack.us, a non-partisan organization which has been keeping stats on legislators for several decades.[91] And while she introduced a lot of Bills, she had a very low rate of getting them to become law, relative to the average Senator over the years.

Bottom line: She didn't get a whole hell of a lot done, and she wasn't particularly progressive.

Incidentally, Sanders also sponsored three bills during the same period that became law. Two were largely ceremonial, much like those Clinton sponsored. The third Bill added $17 billion to the Veterans Health care system, gave the Administrator of the Veteran's administration broad powers to fix a broken system, and extended educational benefits to veterans and their dependents. In short, it was consequential. And Bernie got it done with bi-partisan support. Finally, GovTrack rates Sanders as one of the most progressive members of Congress.

So much for a "progressive who got things done," and so much for dismissing Sanders as a dreamer – something much of the EEM did routinely.

Then of course, there is the clear and incontrovertible evidence that the Democratic Party itself was working against Sanders and for Clinton behind the scenes. Under their own charter, the DNC is supposed to be neutral with regard to the candidates running for office. But hacked DNC e-mails released in June show a clear pattern of favoritism toward Clinton, with actions ranging from plotting ways to undermine Sanders and his campaign, to directing resources meant to support down-ballot candidates to Clinton's campaign.[92] The favoritism was evident before the first vote was cast, and it continued even after the e-mails exposing it were released.

This support reveals the power of the Democratic establishment and its commitment to the Oligarchy. Despite the fact that Sanders offered the prospect of dramatically expanding the party's base by attracting new comers and dropouts and that Clinton was likely to dampen turnout, such was the power of the establishment's hold on the party that they chose to favor the candidate who benefited the Oligarchy, rather than the one who benefited the party.

Even more amazing was the support of superdelegates for the candidate most likely to lose to Trump.

The Democratic Party's journey to this sorry place is a little less obvious than the Republican's, but no less disheartening. It began with the rise of the DLC and the rejection of the New Deal and culminated in a commitment to corporatism and elitism. It was and is, a clear example of the victory of a lust for power over a love of principle.

Long before the nominating process for the 2016 presidential candidate began, the interests of PACs trumped the interest of people and the corporatized DLC-type democrat was firmly in control of the party.

Democrats had in place rules that favored establishment candidates as well as rules which placed numerous impediments and hurdles to newcomers and outsiders. The most obvious of these are the use of superdelegates, which gives the party a huge say in who the nominee will be, and closed primaries, which keep outsiders...well...out.

The effect of this is to make the primaries increasingly undemocratic. With the Democratic Party's share of potential voters falling from a high of 50 percent in the 1960s, down to just 29 percent now, closed primaries exclude an ever-increasing number of voters from participating in the nomination of their president. Even "open" primaries often have unfathomable administrative requirements that make it difficult for independents and voters who aren't part of the establishment wing of the party to vote. And that skews the nominating process to the right.

Superdelegates, closed primaries, and arcane rules that make it difficult for independents or new voters to participate in supposedly open primaries certainly played a significant role in allowing Hillary to win.

The role of the EEM was equally decisive and particularly pernicious. If one candidate is continually portrayed as the winner and the other is essentially ignored, the media's embrace of the "winner" becomes a self-fulfilling prophecy, and the media stops simply reporting the news and becomes the architect of it. Time was this would have been seen for what it is—a complete abrogation of journalistic ethics, but those times are gone. Now, the corporate-owned media supports the corporate-backed candidate, professional ethics be damned.

There's no shortage of evidence for this. For example, the *New York Times*' own public editor suggested that a quick rewrite of a favorable online article about Sanders's legislative accomplishments to make it appear less favorable was inappropriate.[93] And Krugman's jihad against Sanders—in which he abandoned fact and long-held positions in order to be critical of him and supportive of Clinton—is boosterism at its worst.

In contrast to Trump, the establishment media largely ignored Sanders for the first half of the race,[94] then marginalized or ridiculed him over the second half. For example, the Tyndall Report, which tracks nightly news coverage by ABC, CBS, and NBC—still the largest source of news for most Americans with more than twenty-four million viewers combined—found that in 2015, Hillary Clinton received 121 minutes of coverage, while Sanders got just 20 minutes.

As the *New York Times* columnist Charles M. Blow noted, Sanders's coverage was scarce, and much of what he got was negative or dismissive.[95]

Analysis by the GDLT project shows that the cable news stations, including programs such as *The Daily Show* on Comedy Central, barely mentioned him for nearly a year after he announced his candidacy.[96]

This noncoverage extended beyond the cable networks. As mediaQuant—an outfit that tracks media coverage in all media (including social media) and then imputes a value to that coverage—noted, by mid-March, Trump got just under $2 billion in free coverage, Clinton about

$742 million, and Sanders got less than half that. And much of Sanders's coverage was in social media, and much of what did appear in the EEM was negative. For example, at about the time mediaQuant was doing its analysis, the *Washington Post* ran sixteen negative stories about Sanders in just sixteen hours[97]...one an hour. Talk about a jihad. Bottom line, the extent to which Sanders got ignored, slammed, or slighted by the elite media is a matter of record, not the opinion of disgruntled followers.

This blackout of the Sanders campaign was not warranted by the record-breaking crowds he was generating or by the polling showing that he was rapidly gaining on Clinton in Iowa, and ahead of her in New Hampshire. Clearly, something dramatic was happening and just as clearly, the EEM didn't want you to know about it.

The fact that Sanders managed to break through this de facto blackout and reach voters directly is a testament to the power of his message, the anger that is infecting both the Left and the Right, and the thirst people have for an authentic voice that represents them.

Donna Brazile, a Democratic Party fixture, CNN commentator, and then vice chair of the DNC was found to have fed debate questions to Clinton's campaign, and she apparently worked to discredit Sanders with the African American community.

If we examine the two biggest electoral prizes—New York and California which combined have nearly a third of the 2,382 delegates needed to win the Democratic nomination—the role of the party, the elite media, and how they interact to preordain outcomes becomes obvious.

Let's start with party rules.

In the New York primary, independents who'd failed to register as Democrats more than six months before the voting took place couldn't vote. This was well before many had even heard of Bernie Sanders. As a result, millions of potential voters[98]—the vast majority of them independents—were denied the opportunity to vote in New York. Given that Sanders was winning the independent vote overwhelmingly,[99] it's safe to say, Sanders could have—and likely would have—carried New York if the rules had not prevented independents from voting. Clinton won the primary by a little fewer than three hundred thousand votes, and some three million independents were excluded from voting in the primary.

Had Sanders won New York, it would have altered the narrative which followed. Instead of widespread stories about Clinton's "inevitability"—which even with the New York results simply wasn't true—the media would have been forced to admit and report on just how close this race was. But the media narrative after New York essentially declared the race over, which gave Clinton a decided edge, not warranted by her relative popularity among voters at large.

But instead, the headlines after the New York primary were nearly universal in suggesting that Sanders had no chance to win. The numbers didn't support this—Sanders needed 1,117 more delegates to win, and there were 2,186 delegates remaining and he was surging, until New York.

And the margin separating the two was grossly exaggerated in the media, because most insisted on adding in 712 superdelegates to Clinton's total. Again, saturating the media with "Bernie has no chance" messages while exaggerating her lead dampened support from independents and those who'd dropped out of the whole election process, but were coming back in to vote for Bernie.

The dropouts, in fact, comprised the largest block of voters and had for three decades.

The 2014 election set a record for the lowest turnout in more than seventy years, for example, with just over 36 percent of eligible voters bothering to show up. It wouldn't be inaccurate to say that in every election since Reagan, "none of the above" was the winner. The real story in the 2016 nomination process was the return of many of those "none-of-the-above" voters, but the media underplayed it, to the extent they covered it at all.

Thus, leading up to the all-important western states, the media were gathered against Sanders in a confederacy of dunces, to paraphrase Jonathon Swift.

Despite the stacked deck, in California—the ultimate electoral prize—polls were showing Sanders rapidly catching up and most saw the race as close to even in the days before the voting. Even after California's popular governor, Gerry Brown, endorsed Clinton, the "none-of-the-above" Sanders voters continued to register. The number of new registrants was setting records in nearly every precinct, and in just the six weeks prior to the primary 650,000 new voters signed on to the rolls, and 76 percent were Democrats[100]. The evidence suggests they were not signing up to vote for Hillary.

Going into California and the June 7 primaries, there were fewer than three hundred delegates separating the two candidates for the nomination (excluding superdelegates). With nine hundred delegates left in the mix, Sanders was still well in the race.

In fact, a USC Dornsife/*Los Angeles Times* poll released on the evening of June 2, gave Sanders a one-point lead over Clinton among eligible voters less than a week before the primary.[101] It should be noted that Clinton still held a small, but rapidly shrinking, lead among those deemed to be "likely voters."

Dan Schnur, director of USC's Jesse M. Unruh Institute of Politics, which partnered with the *L.A. Times* to conduct the poll said, "If Clinton manages to hold him off and win the primary, it would be as a result of a low turnout that tilts the electorate in her direction."[102] Schnur is one of the most knowledgeable observers of California politics in the country.

All the evidence suggested Sanders was poised to pull off another come-from-behind victory similar to his Michigan win. Had that happened, it would have been extremely hard for the superdelegates to justify backing Hillary.

But on June 6, the day before the California primary, the Associated Press led with the following story: **HILLARY CLINTON CLINCHES DEMOCRATIC NOMINATION.** Within minutes, almost the entire media establishment repeated the story on their on-line outlets, and led with similar headlines in the evening news.

Of course, the story wasn't true. AP's count included a straw poll of super delegates, and they wouldn't actually vote until July. There was nothing binding the super delegates to Clinton, and it's not all that uncommon for them to switch votes well into the primary season. Indeed, Hillary herself saw her commanding lead in super delegates completely erode in 2008.

But those kinds of subtleties were largely ignored or buried in the gazillionth paragraph, and the overwhelming impression given by the overwhelming majority of the press and media was that the race was over.

As a result, what was poised to be a record-breaking turnout in California ended up at only 47.72 percent of the eligible voters, well behind 2008's showing.

Basically, the AP story and the treatment the rest of the press gave it was journalistic malpractice of the highest—or perhaps lowest—order. Neal Gabler, in an article that was critical of the media's treatment of Sanders generally, called the timing of AP's story "suspicious."[103] And it was.

But even after essentially suppressing Sanders's votes, the media misreported Clinton's margin of victory in California, which was used by the press and her campaign to bolster her claim on the super delegates.

Specifically, it was widely reported that Clinton beat Sanders by 13–14 percent of the vote immediately after the primary. But voters who wanted to switch parties were given provisional ballots which would be counted after the preliminary results were announced and the actual margin of victory would not have been known until mid-July. What was knowable is that most of the provisional ballots went to Sanders supporters who were switching their affiliation from "no preference" to Democratic. Any honest appraisal of how close the race was should have acknowledged that Clinton's margin would shrink drastically, but again, these kinds of subtleties were either ignored or placed in the gazillionth paragraph.

Sure enough, when the actual margin came in at only about 7 percent (despite the vote-chilling declaration that the race was over), it went virtually unreported. So what? Well, many folks continued to justify the superdelegates' support of Hillary Clinton *at a time when she performed far worse than Sanders against Trump* by her "big" win in California and her "big win" wasn't so big. Throw in the fact that it was guaranteed by press malfeasance in the manner in which they reported the superdelegates' role and timing in the election, and the fix was clearly in.

Dan Schnur's suggestion that a relatively lower voter turnout was the only way Clinton could hold off Sanders's surge, was exactly what the AP story and the media's coverage of it guaranteed.

Bottom line: The premature announcement of Clinton "clinching" the nomination the day before the California primary reduced the number of Sanders supporters going to the polls, her win wasn't all that big in the end, and Sanders still enjoyed a double-digit lead over Trump, while at the time, Clinton was even or behind Trump in the polls.

With the coverage by the EEM of the California primary, the press's reporting finally became overtly what it had been all along—an exercise in creating a self-fulfilling prophecy—not an exercise in the practice of journalism. And the party's rules, aided by the media oligopoly, all but guaranteed the *selection* of their "inevitable" candidate—not the *election* of the candidate holding the views that were most consistent with the vast majority of the Democrats.[104]

In the end, excluding independents from voting in primaries, combined with media malfeasance, resulted in the Democrats running the candidate who would be weaker in the actual elections—where independents can vote—ultimately assuring Trump's victory.

Next, in Part Two, we will examine how the changes allowed by "we the people" played a role in enabling this theft; in Part Three, we will look at how profoundly these changes endanger us; and in Part Four, we will identify laws, tools, practices, and policies that will make it far more difficult for the Oligarchy to steal our elections and purchase our candidates—not to mention our souls.

PART TWO: Drinking Sand

● ● ●

People want leadership, Mr. President, and in the absence of genuine leadership, they'll listen to anyone who steps up to the microphone. They want leadership. They're so thirsty for it they'll crawl through the desert toward a mirage, and when they discover there's no water, they'll drink the sand.

FROM THE FILM *THE AMERICAN PRESIDENT*
SCREENPLAY BY AARON SORKIN

CHAPTER 9

We Have Met the Enemy, and He Is Us

● ● ●

*America will never be destroyed from the outside. If we falter and
lose our freedoms, it will be because we destroyed ourselves.*

ABRAHAM LINCOLN

A nation of sheep will beget a government of wolves.

EDWARD R. MURROW

PART ONE REVEALED THE TACTICS and techniques the Oligarchy used to
accomplish their Coup. As we noted in chapter 2, although the Powell
Memo provided a general blueprint or manifesto for the right-wing and
business interests to increase their political and cultural influence, the
Coup was not a conspiracy involving shadowy entities operating in collu-
sion behind closed doors.

Nevertheless, they were extraordinarily successful in taking over the
political parties, the media, key parts of the academic community, the
national security infrastructure, and the civil institutions that dominate
our political system and define our government. But they did more than
simply change our institutions; they fundamentally changed the way
Americans perceived themselves and their relationship to each other and
to the government, and finally towards the planet we live upon.

Because in the end, no Coup can be successful unless the people allow it. In Part Two we will examine the role we the people had in enabling it—this is about who *we were*, who *we've become*, what *we value* as a culture, as a people, and more importantly, *how* the techniques outlined in Part One not only changed our institutions, but also changed our national character.

Freedom and Culture: Americans tend to believe that freedom is embedded in the documents our founders developed; it's not. Rather, it derives from the collective cultural commitment to freedom that, until recently, was a part of our national DNA, and it is rooted firmly in ideas that come from the Enlightenment.

The Constitution was built on two key principles developed by Enlightenment thinkers Thomas Hobbes, John Locke, and Jean Jacques Rousseau. The first is the simple concept that the governed and those who would govern essentially entered into a social contract: an agreement about how we would apportion and share power. The second is the belief that we organized governments to assure the "commonweal," that is, the general welfare of the people. Inherent in both concepts is the notion of "we the people," and it implies a sense of shared identity and mutual responsibility. Madison and Jefferson have acknowledged Locke's influence on both the Declaration of Independence and the Constitution.[105]

Both of these principles were, in turn, grounded in another Enlightenment idea: the Baconian commitment to inductive empiricism— a system of inquiry in which knowledge was derived from observation, data collection, experimentation, and formation of hypotheses, which were tested and revised to fit reality—as opposed to a system in which the answers were assumed a priori, and facts were arranged to support them.

For centuries prior to Bacon, such modes of knowing—reasoning to a presumed result—ruled. After the Enlightenment, we abandoned them, adopted the scientific method, and it ignited a sustained technological revolution that increased human welfare exponentially for the next several centuries. Now, we are abandoning the scientific method and reentering the Dark Ages in which answers are preordained, science and scientists are held in contempt, and demagogues and necromancers rule.

Quaint notions like the social contract and the legitimacy of government established by the governed to assure the commonweal are vanishing among the vapors of hate, blame, fear, and ignorance.

At any rate, without a commitment to these Enlightenment principles, the documents we cherish are merely fragile pieces of parchment with no authority and no weight.

Beyond the Parchment: It's interesting to note that many totalitarian countries have constitutions that contain guarantees of freedom fully equivalent to those found in our own. For example, here's an excerpt from The People's Republic of China's constitution:

Article 34

All citizens of the People's Republic of China who have reached the age of 18 have the right to vote and stand for election, regardless of ethnic status, race, sex, occupation, family background, religious belief, education, property status or length of residence, except persons deprived of political rights according to law.

Article 35

Citizens of the People's Republic of China enjoy freedom of speech, of the press, of assembly, of association, of procession and of demonstration.

Tiananmen Square, notwithstanding.

Or take this excerpt from Russia's constitution:

Article 19

1. *All people shall be equal before the law and in the court of law.*
2. *The state shall guarantee the equality of rights and liberties regardless of sex, race, nationality, language, origin, property or employment status, residence, attitude to religion, convictions, membership of public associations or any other circumstance. Any restrictions of the rights of citizens on social, racial, national, linguistic or religious grounds shall be forbidden.*

3. *Man and woman shall have equal rights and liberties and equal opportunities for their pursuit.*

The point is, many nations have laws in place guaranteeing the rights and freedoms of their citizens, even ones in which citizens have few freedoms and fewer rights. They have elections and people vote, but the choices are limited and the political landscape is like a monoculture, their options restricted—at best—to choices in which Tweedledee and Tweedledum run against each other, with little in the way of real or substantive difference between them. At worst, there's only a single party. Either way, they have little influence on what their government chooses to do after the election.

Wait. Doesn't that sound familiar?

Remember Paige and Gilen's analysis on how much impact the average American voter has on politics and policy? Just to refresh your memory, here's what they concluded: *the preferences of the average American appear to have only a minuscule, near-zero, statistically nonsignificant impact upon public policy.*

Two things separate a true democracy from a paper democracy. The first is they have the institutions in place to make it work; the second is that the people have the experience of freedom and the vigilance to protect it. In short, there is a culture that nurtures freedom, and without it, no amount of parchment can confer it. Similarly, when it is present, no army can deny it.

The difference is delicate, as delicate as the paper outlining the freedoms we take for granted.

Here in the United States, until recently, we've stumbled toward freedom and held tyranny at bay for over 225 years—not with the simple pieces of parchment, but with a culture that nourished and fed the thirst for freedom, and a belief in a "we the people" and the commonwealth (or commonweal).

Yes, the Constitution, in its original form, was a less-than-perfect document. It condoned slavery and excluded women from voting; it included a Senate and electoral college designed to give the rich and elite greater control over governance (much like the Democratic Party's use of super delegates, closed primaries, and arcane rules does now). But until recently, we rode the tide of history, moving steadily in the direction of greater freedom and wider participation. But within the last three to four decades, we the people increasingly swallowed what amounts to a medieval worldview in which tribalism, superstition, and myth triumphed over the Enlightenment principles that underpin our democracy.

The Constitution was ratified on June 21, 1788. It was only five pages long, written on paper so thin you can almost see through it, possessing no power except the integrity of those who signed it and the authority of the ideas embedded in it.

On December 15, 1791, the states ratified the Bill of Rights, the first ten amendments to the Constitution. Another sheet of paper-thin parchment—it extended individual freedoms and further limited government's power over the people. Here again, the parchment had no authority except the legitimacy derived from a commitment to the Enlightenment ideals that shaped it.

Over the years, African Americans were granted full citizenship; women were enfranchised; government's power was further constrained.

Wars were fought, nominally to protect these freedoms; men and women died, were wounded, and disabled in the name of guarding these rights from threats. Yes, many wars were fought for reasons of imperial or economic hegemony, not defense of the freedoms inherent in our system of government, but some were, and it formed the rationale—if not the rationalization—for nearly all our wars.

But for nearly two centuries, the overarching story of this nation of immigrants was one of increasing inclusion, although it was by no means as high-minded as our history books tell it. Indeed, elements of the struggle between those who sought to widen the "we" and those who sought to constrain it have been with us since before the revolution.

The Children of Light and the Children of Darkness: An interesting take on our historical dialectic comes from Reinhold Niebuhr's *The Children of Light and the Children of Darkness* published in 1944. If you strip away the religious baggage, Niebuhr essentially says America's political history can be understood by the tension between the overly optimistic (the children of light) and the extremely cynical (the children of darkness). Optimistic liberals focus on the common good and general welfare, while the cynics emphasize self-interest, often using it to pit us against each other.

It is a struggle between the rugged individualist and the communal socialist—between an Ayn Randian Marlboro Man, and a hippy, liberal, commie.

Niebuhr's taxonomy does a better job than most of capturing the manipulative and exploitative elements at work today in our political world in both parties. The tension he describes is directly hardwired into our national heritage and flows from disagreements among the authors of the parchment papers our founders authored, and it has been with us from the beginning.

For example, writing in the *Atlantic*, Ben Heineman Jr. noted:

> ...the two-party system emerged out of the competing visions, and personal hatreds, of the Federalists led by Hamilton and the Republicans led by Jefferson and Madison. Indeed, the fundamental issues of America's first decade and the source of its vicious political divisiveness—the balance between federal and state power, the tension between government action and personal liberty, and the ambiguities in the Constitution on these and other crucial issues—remain a powerful source of contention today.[106]

By 1796, after George Washington stepped down following two terms, the country had divided itself along party lines, with the Federalists, led by John Adams, being the party of order, merchants, creditors, commerce, and business, and the Democratic-Republicans (not the same party as today's GOP or the Democratic Party) led by Jefferson, favoring extending the rights of the revolution to the common man, more agrarian interests, and more egalitarian policies. Here's how one partisan newspaper reported the division:

> According to one Republican-minded New York newspaper, the Federalists were "aristocrats, endeavoring to lay the foundations

of monarchical government, and Republicans [were] the real supporters of independence, friends to equal rights, and warm advocates of free elective government.[107]

As for vitriol and dirty politics, the founders more than matched anything you might see today. When Jefferson and Adams faced off in 1800,
the insults and slurs were off the charts. For example, here's a sample as
reported in *Mentalfloss Magazine* by Professor Kerwin Swint, author of
Mudslingers: The 25 Dirtiest Political Campaigns of all Time:

> Jefferson's camp accused President Adams of having a "hideous
> hermaphroditical character, which has neither the force and firm-
> ness of a man, nor the gentleness and sensibility of a woman."
> In return, Adams' men called Vice President Jefferson "a mean-
> spirited, low-lived fellow, the son of a half-breed Indian squaw,
> sired by a Virginia mulatto father." As the slurs piled on, Adams
> was labeled a fool, a hypocrite, a criminal, and a tyrant, while
> Jefferson was branded a weakling, an atheist, a libertine, and a
> coward. Even Martha Washington succumbed to the propaganda,
> telling a clergyman that Jefferson was "one of the most detestable
> of mankind."[108]

Personal attacks? States' rights and the tension between government
action and individual liberty? Sounds a lot like the political arguments we
hear today, doesn't it? And this kind of discourse continued through most
of the nineteenth century, with brief detours toward greater civility.

After the Civil War, the modern Republican and Democratic parties
emerged, although each took a turn as children of the light. Prior to the
turn of the century, a populist movement emerged from the Democratic
Party, and in the early twentieth century, a progressive party emerged
from within the Republican Party.

The point is that partisanship and party politics have been with us
since the second presidential election, and they have not always—or even

generally—been a positive force, and no one party has a claim on being progressive or adhering to the Enlightenment principles that our country is based on. Party ideals and values changed with the times, with parties shedding "core values" as easily as you and I might remove a topcoat.

But despite the party politics and partisanship, for most of our history, Americans held onto the notion of "we the people," and a commonweal. And for most of our history, we expanded who constituted the "we," and believed that government was a necessary guarantor of our commonweal.

Now? Not so much.

Of course, our nation has greeted each wave of immigrants with the same xenophobic reaction we see now among Trump and his supporters. Jews were—and still are—the object of prejudice, and Muslims, Middle Easterners, and Latin Americans are the new Italians, Poles, and Irish.

African Americans, the LGBTQ community, and anyone else deemed to be different have always experienced prejudice and bias. And half our population—women—were second-class citizens with no vote until August 26, 1920, when the Nineteenth Amendment was passed. But here too, the longer arc of our history has bent toward a larger "we"—toward inclusion.

Until recently.

It's always hard to define a shift when you are in the midst of one, but it seems to me, that throughout our history, a belief in a "we," and a sense that it is government's legitimate purpose to assure a commonweal, and a commitment to the scientific method—three Enlightenment values we used to share—leavened the hate and prejudice, and ultimately overcame them.

No more.

Now that we as a society are abandoning these as polestars, there is a danger that we have, indeed, returned to the Dark Ages where prejudice, hate, bigotry, and the ignorance they feed on are not only condoned, but valued, and rather than an expanding "we," we're experiencing a more rapid disintegration of society and an explosion of "thems" and "others," instead. Together with the disintegrating forces of the commercial world fostered as part of the MMM, these combine to make assimilation of the "other" more difficult, and less likely now. Indeed, they are multiplying the them's and narrowing the we's exponentially. The explosion in media outlets fostered by turning journalism into a commodity enables ever-smaller groups to get "their" news—as opposed to a more objective news—and it's served up in predigested bites of bias.

In the chapters that follow, we will examine this drift into the Dark Ages, and how the great American fear machine and the marketization of America changed us and compromised any notion of "we the people."

CHAPTER 10

Dark Ages Redux: American Politics and the End of the Enlightenment

● ● ●

Sapere aude! (dare to know)…"Have courage to use your own reason!"—that is the motto of enlightenment.

IMMANUEL KANT

IN THIS CHAPTER WE WILL examine the effects of abandoning the Enlightenment on our country and culture.

We are witnessing an epochal shift in our sociopolitical world in real time. We are de-evolving, hurtling headlong into a past that was defined by serfs and lords; by necromancy and superstition; by policies based on fiat, not facts.

As noted, much of what has made the modern world in general, and the United States in particular, a free and prosperous society comes directly from insights that arose during the Enlightenment.

Too bad we're chucking it all out and returning to the Dark Ages.

Literally.

Now, we seek to operate by revealed truths, not reality. Decrees from on high are offered up as reality by politicians on behalf of the Oligarchy. The press dutifully presents these revealed truths in a "balanced" presentation, and what passes for progressives in our political monoculture stays mostly silent—or unreported—in the face of head-splitting inanity.

For example, North Carolina lawmakers recently passed legislation against sea level rise[109]. A day later, the Virginia legislature required that references to global warming, climate change, and *sea level rise* be excised[110] from a proposed study on *sea level rise*. A few years ago, the Texas Department of Environmental Quality, which had commissioned a study on the effects of rising sea levels on Galveston Bay, cut all references to sea level rise—the main point of the study.

Florida's Department of Environmental Protection has been banned from using the words "climate change" or "global warming."[111] Florida, by the way, is the state that will be most impacted by climate change. Wait. Impacted? No. Way beyond impacted—10 percent of its land area will literally be gone by 2100, and most of its cities will be unlivable due to storm surges and crippling heat well before then. Florida has already experienced about 1 foot of sea-level rise, and it will likely exceed 3 feet by 2050 and 6 feet by 2100. But it doesn't stop there. Seas will continue to rise for more than twenty thousand years, and even if we meet the cuts in carbon emissions called for in the Paris Agreement, ultimately sea levels could reach 170 feet above current levels.[112] At that point, Florida becomes a series of about forty small islands, dotting the southern Atlantic.

Meanwhile, the Texas Republican Party *opposed* an effort to require critical thinking in the state's educational curriculum.

And now we have Trump, with a cabinet of antiscience whack jobs who would be laughed off the public forum in most developed countries.

As Stephen Colbert so aptly put it: "if your science gives you results you don't like, pass a law saying that the result is illegal. Problem solved."

Except it isn't. Wishing reality away, doesn't make it go away. Pretending that the unreal is real doesn't make it real.

And the descent into the Dark Ages is marked by more than global warming. Take austerity budgets. As we have seen, there is an extensive historical record showing that implementing austerity measures in an economic slowdown is counterproductive. And this data is backed up by the experience in Europe, where their flirtation with austerity measures have been disastrous, and in our own states, where those who adopted the preordained answers of austerity budgets and deregulation have suffered severe economic collapse, while those who increased taxes and regulations prospered (see chapter 5, "The Myth of the Bumbling Bureaucrat").

So the data is telling us austerity during a jobs crisis hasn't worked in the past and isn't working now. What do conservatives want to do?

Pass an austerity budget, of course. And Trump's Budget proposal is no different.

Welcome to the Dark Ages.

The litany of ignorance goes on and on. Teach Creationism. Teach the "controversy" on climate science and intelligent design. Declare deregulation—which was a primary cause of the 2008 economic collapse—to be the solution to it. Preach trickle-down economics, even after it has failed every time it's been adopted, even as we watch wealth rocket up the income brackets.

What's next? Give the flat-earthers a say. Oh hell, why stop there. Let's put earth back in the center of the solar system where it belongs. And if you're a Democrat, don't take these issues head on, because it might hurt your campaign finances. Hell, chances are, you're a neoliberal DLC Democrat who embraces most of this voodoo, anyway. If you're part of the EEM, don't you dare mock these beliefs as the idiocy they are—not balanced, you know, and above all else, you must be balanced.

We don't need no stinkin' science. We don't need no pesky reality. We just gotta pass a few laws and declare things to be the way we want them to be, facts be damned. You know, keep your government hands off my Medicare.

Reason, empiricism, and scholarship are the punch line to right-wing jokes and jihads. In 2012, Rick Santorum captured the Tea Party's hostility to these Enlightenment virtues when he likened college education to indoctrination. Thankfully, Santorum is now irrelevant, but the embrace of ignorance he advocated lives on in characters like Trump, who, despite the EEM's treatment of him as an outsider, adheres closely to the formula of all fear, all the time, for the purpose of short-circuiting reason. Remember "Only I can make you safe?" And while Trump conducts his masquerade as a man of the people at the top of his voice, and screams over and over again what a mistake the Iraq war was (a position he's been on both sides of, as and when it's convenient) he proposes the same-ol, same-ol tax-cuts-for-the rich, trickle-down, shrink-the-big-bad-government, deregulate, it's-scary-out-there, rhetoric as the rest of the Republicans, with a cabinet that is truly straight out of the Dark Ages—or the Oligarchy.

But if this kind of ignorance is allowed to run rampant, it's because we the people have become ignorant *and we don't care*. And of course, the Democrats are as guilty by their absence, as the Republicans are by their presence.

In fact, there's a remarkable overlap between the Democratic neoliberals' dogma—tax cuts are good, privatization is better, deregulation is great, and trade agreements and the free movement of capital are wonderful—and the Republican's destructive economic myths—supply side-job creators, trickle-down economics, and deregulation. The thing is, these ideas have never worked, but they've been harder to kill than a zombie vampire black cat in a coal mine at midnight. Nine lives? That's for pikers. These myths have survived so many run-ins with reality it's beyond astounding.

Democratic neoliberalism and Republican orthodoxy have literally ripped money and wealth out of the hands of low-income and middle-class Americans and given it to the über rich.

The reason these destructive myths survive is because they're rarely confronted, and that's because the neoliberal Democrats essentially buy into the conservative's myths. Oh, the rhetoric is different, particularly around election time. And the parties differ on social issues. But at the end of the day, Democrats' embrace of neoliberalism, with its laissez-faire, market über-alles policies, closely mirrors conservative dogma.

Which goes a long way to explaining the horrific phenomena of President Trump.

Absent a pushback, the Oligarch's juggernaut rolls on. And it doesn't help that Americans are getting more ignorant by the minute.

Check out this YouTube video on how Westerners in general and Americans in particular are reenacting *Idiocracy*.[113] Evidence shows that IQs are dropping and our brains are actually shrinking.

How much have we abandoned the Enlightenment? Here's some statistics revealing our ignorance:

* 20 percent of Americans believe the sun revolves around the earth.
* 29 percent couldn't point to the Pacific Ocean on a map.
* 25 percent couldn't identify what country the United States gained its independence from.
* Only 51 percent knew where New York was.
* When asked what year 9/11 took place, 30 percent didn't know.
* Only 25 percent knew how long a Senator's term was, and only 20 percent knew how many Senators there were.
* Only one in 1,000 knew what freedoms the First Amendment protected, but 22 percent could name all the members of the Simpson Family.
* An astonishing 51 percent reject evolution, according to a CBS News poll, while only 15 percent believe humans evolved without divine intervention.
* Only 26 percent of Americans can name all three branches of government, and 31 percent can't name a single one...

The saddest thing about this list is that it could go on and on. I could literally fill page after page with examples like these. Then there's the infamous signs from the tea-partiers ("Keep your government hands off my Medicare," "Get a brain moran" and "Obama is a Muslin" are among my favorites).

These reflect ignorance—the state of not knowing something—as opposed to stupidity, but the result is indistinguishable. Whereas, once ignorance was something to be ashamed of, today it is nearly celebrated. And meanwhile the scientific method and critical thinking as a means of acquiring knowledge and insight are in full retreat, as balance and relativism replace truth and relativity.

Even our colleges fail to challenge and inform, as they succumb to the massive media blitz that has infected our discourse and our experiences, in a modern-day version of bread and circuses.

For example, Michael Snyder listed twenty stupid courses offered in US colleges in recent years; here are some examples:[114]

* What if Harry Potter Is Real?
* Lady Gaga and the Sociology of Fame;
* Philosophy and Star Trek;
* Learning from YouTube;
* How to Watch Television; and
* Oh, Look, a Chicken!

Is it any wonder that a know-nothing like Trump can emerge as a candidate and win when this is the nature of the preparation for citizenship we have? Is it any wonder that Hillary Clinton can go from a right-of-center pay-to-play politician to a "progressive who gets things done" and back to a center-right politician in the space of nine months and nearly get away with it?

Is it any wonder that Clinton lost when the best she could offer was "not as crazy as him?" At the end of the day, we need real progressives who are willing to counter regressive bullshit with a stance based on progressive values, or the bullshit will stand, and people like Trump will win.

Trump won because once again, Democrats ran a candidate who wouldn't stand up for and with middle- and low-income Americans against the Oligarchy.

Clinton was a classic split-the-middle Democrat. Consider climate change. She pushed renewable energy but backed fracking, refused to put a price on carbon, while calling for exploration and production of fossil fuels on public lands and claiming to be tough on climate change.

The "terrible math" revealed by Bill McKibben tells us we have to leave the vast majority of the oil we've found so far in the ground—but Americans are not equipped to understand that finding and exploiting new oil will doom the planet, the people, and the species we share it with to changes that are literally unimaginable. And so, Hillary was the candidate who got to claim "she's serious" about climate change, despite favoring more exploration and development of new fossil fuels.

But if you go off the climate cliff, does it really matter whether you're travelling at one hundred or at fifty miles per hour at the time? The sad truth is, the policies of both candidates were driving us over the cliff's edge—but only one was giving lip service to being concerned about it. The only reason Clinton's woefully inadequate (and fossil-fuel friendly) policies don't seem suicidal is because Trump denies the existence of climate change, while Clinton accepts the science, but not the necessary policy response. Come to think of it, both of these stands are antiscience and anti-Enlightenment in their own ways.

But it's not just fossil fuel interests. Hillary Clinton's e-mails reveal that she has two faces when it comes to Wall Street and the big banks, and corporations in general. And Trump? Basically, he embraces an incoherent blend of populist policies and conservative truisms that have proven untrue and which border on crazy. And yet a sizable portion of the people and the press respond to this sad state of affairs as if it were normal. In reality, people should be marching on the headquarters of both parties, and the EEM's head offices, filled with righteous anger and carrying torches and pitchforks.

Meanwhile, corporations are now accorded the rights of citizenship. Power, once again, is meted out by birthright and bankroll, not inalienable right. By possession of wealth, not by justice or equity or merit. Facts and data are ignored or shaped to fit the wishes of the prevailing economic powers, and the quaint notion of scientific method is tossed on history's waste pile. And we the people are too ignorant and too distracted with fear, commercial fluff, or superficial myths to know the difference.

So what?

Well, the United States now has the same income inequality as Cameroon, Uganda, and Rwanda[115], and we're trapped in this pathetic state—income mobility in the United States lags behind most other developed nations.

In short, Horatio Alger is dead, long live Exxon.

We are, indeed, at an epochal threshold. We can continue to discard the Enlightenment values which enabled both an untold increase in material wealth and a system of government which turned serfs into citizens. A system which—for all its flaws—often managed to protect the rights of the many, against the predatory power of the few.

Or we can continue our abject surrender to myths, magical thinking, and self-delusion and the medieval nation-state those forces are resurrecting.

Republicans and poor whites may be leading this retreat from reason, but they operate in an unholy alliance with the Oligarchy, its media, and the neoliberal arm of the Democratic Party. And until Occupy and Bernie Sanders, we the people were mute observers of our own disenfranchisement. Unless the embers they ignited are fanned into life once again, the fire they stoked will go out, and the Oligarchy will continue its self-destructive rush to oblivion.

CHAPTER 11

Scared Witless in the Home of the Brave

● ● ●

If you want to control someone, all you have
to do is to make them feel afraid.

PAUL COELHO, *THE DEVIL AND MS. PRYM*

FEAR AND FREEDOM—ANATOMY OF AN **Inside Job:** In chapter 9, we explored how the Market mimicked a modern-day version of bread and circuses, and in chapter 10, we saw how our collective ignorance was shredding the Enlightenment principles our country was founded upon. Here we will take a closer look at how fear has enabled the Coup and taken away our freedoms.

In the name of security, a massive and patently illegal surveillance program that would make George Orwell's *1984* look low tech, reaches into our living rooms and infects our national discourse. And consciously or not, the Oligarchy has used terrorism as both a distraction and a pretext for taking strategic aim at the culture of freedom, with the intent of changing who we are, and the society that we've collectively created over the history of this country.

Terrorism—Exhibit A in Stoking the Culture of Fear: After 9/11, we began to construct a security state. We took razor blades to the parchment and excised freedoms we had hitherto died to protect. We carried out warrantless wiretapping, systematic eavesdropping on a massive scale, even imprisonment and execution of America citizens without due process.

Why?

Because, it made us safer from the threat of terrorism, we were told. That's what Bush said; that's what Congress—especially Republicans—stated (until it gave them an excuse to bash Obama—which apparently means more to them than security); and that's what Obama, Clinton, and the Democrats claimed. And then there's Trump with his jingoistic fear-mongering, raising the fear to new levels and threatening our freedoms even more in the process.

Well, OK. Let's say all of this makes us a little safer. Does it justify jettisoning the constraints and protections that we've fought for? Does it warrant reversing the tide of history and rolling back the freedoms we've gained?

If we freely give away—out of fear—that which our attackers (and I use the term in its loosest sense) would have taken from us, don't they win? Don't we lose?

Fewer than three thousand people died on 9/11. This is about what we kill with cars and guns on a slow month, every month, month after month, year after year.

Since then, even using the most expansive definition of terrorist killings, about thirty-eight more have been killed by terrorists here in the United States.[116]

The actual risk of death from terrorism in the United States is about the same as the risk of dying from falling furniture; to put it in perspective, your risk of being struck by lightning is four times greater than your risk of dying from terrorism.[117]

How can we hold dear the grossly exaggerated freedoms in the Second Amendment, while gutting those in the Fourth Amendment, when guns result in more than one hundred thousand times the number of deaths as terrorism does over the same time period? Why do we devote more time, resources, attention, and concern than we do on almost any other problem or challenge facing us, when that threat is minimal?

Of course, terrorism demands some level of vigilance, but our national response—wars of occupation and drones—*actually increases the threat* and costs far more than methods proven to work—good policing, human intelligence, and effective screening.[118]

Writing in *Scientific American*, in an article entitled "The Five Myths of Terrorism—Including that it Works: Why Terror Doesn't Work," Michael Shermer exposes the reality behind our favorite bogeyman: the idea that terrorists are an elite cadre of competent adversaries who pose an existential threat. Citing their actual record, since 9/11, he notes they've been mostly incompetents:

Examples abound: the 2001 airplane shoe bomber Richard Reid was unable to ignite the fuse because it was wet from rain; the 2009 underwear bomber Umar Farouk Abdulmutallab succeeded only in torching his junk; the 2010 Times Square bomber Faisal Shahzad managed merely to burn the inside of his Nissan Pathfinder; and the 2012 model airplane bomber Rezwan Ferdaus purchased faux C-4 explosives from FBI agents…the 2013 Boston Marathon bombers appear to have been equipped with only one gun and had no exit strategy beyond hijacking a car low on gas that Dzhokhar Tsarnaev used to run over his brother, Tamerlan, followed by a failed suicide attempt inside a land-based boat.

Shermer goes on to summarize an in-depth empirical study of how unsuccessful terrorism and terrorists have been at accomplishing their objectives:

Finally, a fifth figment about terrorism is that it works. In an analysis of 457 terrorist campaigns since 1968, George Mason University political scientist Audrey Cronin found that not one extremist group conquered a state and that a full 94 percent failed to gain even one of their strategic goals. Her 2009 book is entitled *How Terrorism Ends* (Princeton University Press). It ends swiftly (groups survive eight years on average) and badly (the death of its leaders).[119]

How can we give away freedoms so cavalierly, when the threat we face is so small?

Are we a nation of cowards, willing to relinquish freedom at the first whiff of a threat?

Two hundred and twenty-five years ago, Ben Franklin said, "People willing to trade their freedom for temporary security deserve neither and will lose both." Franklin called us to courage; the words and actions of our leaders today call us to cowardice.

In almost all other areas of risk management and cost-benefit analysis, our society assigns a value to saving a life. In environmental regulations, which have relatively high values for a human life, it typically hovers somewhere between $2.5 and $3.5 million.

Yet in the case of terrorism, that cost is well in excess of $1 billion spent per life saved. Why the disconnect?

One can't help wonder whether the difference is because tyranny has already been visited upon our land—it came from within, in the form of corporate hegemony. Perhaps the constant drumbeat about the terrorist threat is merely cover for the fact that the social contract has been rewritten since Reagan. No longer is the compact between the governed and the government—it is between the corporations and the government.

We are now one nation, under corporations, for corporations, by corporations.

Perhaps the hoary threat of terrorism is meant to keep us from recognizing that. The fact that it also allows the government to tap your phone, observe your e-mails, and otherwise poke its nose in your business is just gravy.

And it's not just terrorism—in the United States, it's all fear all the time. Fear puts eyes on the TV news stations, it sells newspapers, and it makes books into best sellers. In the home of the brave, we are on the constant lookout for threats. We see it in immigrants; we see it in Russia and China—whose combined defense expenditures are less than one-fifth of ours. We worry about Sharia law being imposed by an infinitesimally small minority; we worry about ISIS, a group of about thirty thousand or fewer with scrounged weapons (mostly ours left over from counterproductive wars of occupation), no navy or air force, with more than seven thousand miles of open ocean separating us.

We see it in our neighbors, whom we don't know; we see it in crime from the "others" in our society—even when we are near historic lows in the rate of crimes of all kinds. Witness Trump's speech as he accepted the Republican nomination at their Convention—which was a celebration of fear, hate and prejudice.

Fear is brandished by the elite establishment to keep our eyes off the real terror—the silent Coup that is now upon us. What's different, is that we the people here in the home of the brave respond to threats—real and imagined—with such an oversized reaction that we are scared stupid. We are a nation suffering from a collective PTSD—jumping at every sound, recoiling from every threat no matter how small, hypervigilant and seeing bogeymen in our collective national closet.

And while we're jittering about, there's a new social contract being written, and we're not part of it, and that's why our rights, our freedoms, and our prosperity have all but disappeared.

CHAPTER 12

The Big Con—The Market Über Alles

● ● ●

The people that once bestowed commands, consulships,
legions, and all else, now concerns itself no more, and longs
eagerly for just two things—bread and circuses!

JUVENAL, SATIRES

WITHIN THE LAST FIFTY OR so years, there's been a fundamental change in how we perceive ourselves—a change that is so profound it challenges some two hundred thousand years of genetic heritage, and flips our cultural legacy on its head, altering everything about us as a people. Despite the revolutionary nature of this shift, it is little noted, and seldom commented upon. It goes hand-in-hand with the corporatization of America.

Let's take a quick review of where we've been, before proceeding.

In chapter 4, we examined how the MMM enabled the Oligarchy to sell policies that *screwed* the people as policies being done on *behalf* of the people. Lipstick on a pig never looked so good.

In chapter 5, we saw how the Oligarchy created the MBB to neutralize the one force capable of constraining the power of corporations and the über rich—government.

In chapter 7, we examined how politicians and corporations use rhetorical devices and marketing techniques to appeal to our inner lizard in order to favorably brand their "product," be it political philosophy, policy, legislation, or candidate. In chapters 9, 10, and 11 we saw how the Enlightenment formed the basis of our system of government; we reviewed the evidence that we are pitching these Enlightenment principles aside and literally reentering the Dark Ages; and we saw how the Oligarchy used fear to directly attack the two essential ingredients of a functioning Democracy—the notion of "a people" with common interests and beliefs and a conviction in government's obligation and ability to protect a "commonweal" composed of our commitment to assure equity, justice, and a shot at prosperity for each of us.

When we jettisoned government as a positive force, we also lost the means to make investments in bold endeavors that demanded our collective skills, talents, and brains. Projects such as the moon landing, or deciphering the human genome are increasingly difficult to fund through the government. And everyday investments in the commons, such as necessities like a functioning infrastructure, have disappeared, leaving a system that is collapsing around us, further reinforcing the idea that big government can't do anything right.

In this chapter, we will see how the MMM supported a relentless sale of an amoral worldview and changed not only our culture, but each of us individually as well, in the most fundamental of ways, and how that change contributed to the Oligarchy's successful Coup by splintering society into more and more groups—each of which looks at the other as a "them." It is the antithesis of a commonwealth and the civil society it creates. In fact, it is society as a zero-sum-game and it creates a culture that is functionally like that of *Lord of the Flies*—adolescent, violent, cliquish, competitive, and dangerous.

Bottom line: the MMM did more than simply allow plutocrats to pull off a Coup. It changed—at the deepest level—the way Americans perceived themselves as citizens, and it completely undercut our belief in government as a legitimate, let alone necessary, guarantor of the commonweal.

This particular assault on our national identity was as pernicious as it was paradoxical. Gordon Gecko championed it, Ronald Reagan enabled it, the DLC neoliberal Democrats expanded it, and the Oligarchy fed it.

The free market was not only held up to be the source of unbounded material wealth and well-being, but it also became an expression of morality. The gospel of wealth was implicit in every paean Reagan made to the free enterprise system and every knock he made on government. By the time he left office, markets were not only magic, they defined the *good*. They would help us defeat communism, eliminate poverty, and underwrite our freedoms for the generations that followed. As we've seen, that's not quite the way it worked.

The problem with setting the market up as some sort of mythical savior is that it is amoral. Not immoral, but amoral. It operates outside the context of any moral framework. What passes for "good" is what succeeds in the marketplace; what's "bad" is what doesn't maximize returns. And that in turn, means appealing to the *individual* consumer's wants, needs, and desires. As we saw, this concept, in conjunction with the fear machine, directly attacked the idea of "we the people," and as we will see in what follows, this shift also renders obsolete, all notion of a shared commons with shared responsibilities.

And here's the irony. At the same time Ronnie the Credulous was selling the MMM, he was hawking family values, and trying to sell "morning in America." To say there is a tension between the Ayn Randian über-capitalist dogma and family values or even patriotism is the grossest of understatements.

How the MMM Changed Us: For most of our history we humans were producers. As our social framework moved from hunter-gatherer, to pastoral, to agrarian to industrialist, growing, making, and creating were at the core of what we did, and even who we perceived ourselves to be. We were producers.

But within the last seventy or so years, we've been preyed upon by commercial interests on an almost relentless basis, until today we have been converted from producers to consumers. Inevitably, this shift reinforces an amoral—and intrinsically competitive and hyper-individualistic—lifestyle in which "he who dies with the most toys wins," and it directly undermines the Enlightenment principles of "we the people" and the idea of a commonweal.

Consider: By the time he or she reaches the age of sixty-five, the average American has seen two million TV commercials.[120] And the influence of media is only increasing. The average American child spends about 900 hours per year in school but spends 1,038 watching TV; researchers have determined that children can develop brand loyalty by the time they are two years old. According to another study, conducted in 2015,[121] children between the ages of five to sixteen spent an average of six and a half hours a day in front of a screen, up from three hours in 1995.

At best these assaults on reason are trying to sell an image, in place of a product. Thus, a person's status is now tied to what he or she can purchase, not what he or she can produce. We are reduced to passive consumers who are fed a steady diet of *want*, with the aim of turning it into *need*. We can become glamorous, famous, powerful, attractive, successful, fun, wise, sexy, or obtain virtually any other attribute not by the investment of effort or the roll of the genetic dice, or by the collective effort of we the people in an epochal endeavor, but by what we, *as individuals*, are capable of *purchasing*. Not making, mind you, but buying. Our national—and collective—race to put a man on the moon once riveted us as a people; now we celebrate our individual McMansion or our very own Lexus.

Want to be like Matthew McConaughey? Why hell, just purchase a Lincoln. Want to be part of a bunch of fun-loving, attractive young people? Just drink Coke. Want to be "special"—part of the cognoscenti? The ultracool? The in crowd? Don't buy a watch—"buy a precision chronometer"—buy a Rolex or a Hublot...or...or anything else that claims to confer these attributes upon you. And if the bauble or trinket in question dares to charge exorbitant fees that keeps our noses to the grindstone in order to get them...why *it just must be capable of delivering*. Bottom line: we live in a culture in which clothes (or any other piece of commercially blessed flotsam and jetsam) *do* make the man.

But the end result is the same. Vacuous entertainment with laugh tracks replaces actual discourse, and even this intellectual pabulum is interrupted every fifteen minutes or so with deceptions, distortions, and outright lies.

Our life is little more than an electronic version of that old Roman bait-and-switch con—bread and circuses—in which the masses were entertained with the purpose of distracting them from their increasingly depressing prospects.

The problem with this is not that it's wrong—although it is—rather, it is that the concept of a civil commons compromises one of the core underpinnings of democracy. The idea of a commonweal—a shared sense of responsibility that goes along with rights—is central to our democracy and our civilization.

In fact, one of the by-products of this relentless commercial assault is that we've become inured to lies, distortions, deceptions, and hyperbolic claims. It's all part of the background noise—the soundtrack to our lives. The apocryphal story about George Washington not being able to lie about chopping down the cherry tree has given way to, "Axe? What axe? I don't see no axe," even when we're holding the metaphorical axe in our hands. Because, really, what's a little lie—or even a big one—after you've heard two million whoppers over a lifetime of commercial assaults?

This contributes to the erosion of trust and the epidemic of cynicism that is the hallmark of twenty-first-century America, and this directly compromises the cohesiveness of society. As a result, we become more isolated, less social, less inclined to join organizations, sign petitions, or even meet our neighbors. Robert D. Putnam thoroughly documented the erosion of community and the rise in isolation in the twentieth century in his landmark book *Bowling Alone*.[122] It has only gotten worse since.

It is this cynicism and loss of trust in each other and in the institutions, such as the press, that enabled Trump's supporters to "know" that if he lost, it was the result of a dark conspiracy, not simply that the majority of the people didn't want an ignorant, sexist, narcissistic bore as president. Or that made Hillary supporters so sure that her loss was a result of misogyny, or Russian email hacks. Never mind that if the hacks hadn't reinforced the perception of a cynical duplicity that her record suggested, they would have had no effect. Never mind that she was a status quo candidate in the midst of a revolution. It was misogyny, dammit.

That conservatives routinely dismiss the media because they believe that it has a liberal bias is due in part to the alienation and unhealthy skepticism that a fragmented and atomized culture creates. Yet we know that the EEM has replaced truth, accuracy, facts and context with balance, giving counterfactual right-wing rants the same weight and airtime as reality.

From Producer to Consumer—the Greatest Story Never Told: For more than two hundred thousand years on this planet as *Homo sapiens*—man the double wise—we humans have defined ourselves as producers and doers. But within the last seventy or so years, under the relentless assault from advertisements, we've come to define and to value ourselves by what we consume and what we have, not by what we produce.

And it is this new vision of who we are that the MMM feeds; it is this brave new world of the Oligarchy and the elites it ushers in, fueled by a vision of ourselves as consumers. Of course, we love tax cuts—more for us—more money, more stuff, more, more, more. Of course, we worship the wealthy, consumptive lifestyle. It has been dangled before us from the day we were born.

The emergence of homo-not-so-sapiens-the-consumer changes how we relate to each other and to the natural world. Here again, the primitive wants of the lizard brain emerge triumphant over the forces of reason.

A life focused on consumption imposes enormous costs on society— such as the erosion of our communities, the exploitation of our fellow humans, the starvation of our ideals and the impoverishment of our souls, the desecration of our environment, and the theft of our children's future, and each of these costs results from a radically different perception of who we are and how we fit with each other and with the natural world.

As a society, we spend more than a quarter trillion dollars a year creating wants, then turning those wants into needs, then creating new wants. It wasn't always so. Back in the 1960s as the post-industrial society was emerging, Buckminster Fuller published a poem in *Whole Earth Catalogue*, a kind of bible of *doing* from the tune-in, turn-on, drop-out 1960s. In it, he said, "God is a verb."

We tend to think of the rebellion of the boomers in the 1960s in terms of the Vietnam War and Civil Rights, but I believe there was another component. It was a last gasp rejection of the increasingly empty world they were being sold—a world in which community was disappearing, and the pursuit of stuff was being glorified as the point of existence.

I believe Bucky's poem and the *Whole Earth Catalogue* was an anthem against this trend. Bucky had a very specific idea in mind—that we are defined by what we do, not what we have; that we are most fulfilled by what we make, not what we take; that we are most realized when we produce, not when we consume. And that when we leave that, we would lose something essential within us.

If you aren't familiar with the *Whole Earth Catalogue*, here's all you need to know: It was a compendium of tools designed to deliver us from slavery to all that was "plastic," by which we meant the sliceomatic, diceomatic, automatic everything, whose sole purpose was to make money by making life easy.

Many hoped to find within the covers of the *Whole Earth Catalogue* a life of meaning, purpose, self-reliance, and independence that was compatible with a sustainable environment and a more community-centered life. The catch phrase was "appropriate technologies"—technologies that were soft, accessible, earth-friendly, and human scaled. Some of the technologies were absurd—there was the chicken manure engine...an actual internal combustion engine that ran on methane derived from chicken poop. It worked, but it got very poor mileage—I'd venture to say less than a mile per chicken.

Some were sublime—simple solar hot-water devices made from black plastic bags, for example. They also worked. As a young man, I took hot showers in the snows of January using one I'd made for free. But absurd or sublime, the *Whole Earth Catalogue* was a kind of bible—a bible of doing. A trip ticket to a world centered around the nobility of being a producer— not a consumer.

I was reminded of how far we've traveled from that time when I attended a "60s party" a couple of years ago. Come the magic night, the music was right—Jimi Hendrix, the Beatles, the Grateful Dead (what we think of as the 1960s actually occurred between 1965 and 1975). I showed up with a T-shirt emblazoned with a peace sign. As I strolled through the crowd, a young neighbor stopped me, and after studying it a moment, she asked, "Why do you have a Mercedes sign on your T-shirt?" To paraphrase the Grateful Dead, "What a long, strange trip it's been, indeed."

I left that party a little disillusioned. It didn't help when I reached the parking lot and saw a bumper sticker on an immense Hummer that said— you guessed it—"He who dies with the most toys wins."

Something happened. Somehow, the notion that we were most divine when we were creating shifted, and we began to judge our worth not by what we could produce, but by what we were able to consume. By things and gadgets.

We got the Mercedes, but we lost some vital connections. I believe this focus on consumption is at the core of much of what ails us in the twenty-first century. And I believe we know it. There is within each of us that still small voice that tells us we've lost our way—that this isn't working. That in our quest for stuff, we haven't become happier.

We should listen to that voice. There's wisdom in it. In fact, the apogee of happiness in the United States, according to the National Opinion Research Center, was in 1957, when the average American family had one car, one TV, a house less than half as big as today's homes with one bathroom, no air conditioning, no clothes dryer, no stereo—we had less than half the stuff we have now.

Since then, as psychologist David G. Myers points out, we've gotten less happy, but astronomically richer. The moral fabric of life has been reduced to a near infantile desire for stuff. What gets more is good; what allows us to have bigger, better, faster, fatter, flashier, fluffier stuff is good. We become liquidators instead of investors; we become debtors rather than donors; we become exploiters rather than stewards.

Let's look at the hidden costs of a consumption-based life.

For Starters, It Undermines the Commonweal: Consumption is narcissistic. It's about me, not us. If more stuff is the answer, then what is good is defined by what *I get*, rather than what *we make* or what we give. A civil society becomes secondary. For example, government ceases to be the way we come together to *do* great and necessary things, and becomes instead an agent that keeps me from getting what's mine. Justice and equity, public welfare, and "the pursuit of happiness" are no longer legitimate functions of government; but "maximizing return" and protection of capital, capitalism, and capitalists is.

No wonder we hurtle toward the grim future that climate change is even now shaping, with a vacant stare and an overwhelming sense of impotence. We can hardly conceive of responding to the threat with the kind of shared collective commitment to greatness it demands. We stagger around like chickens, heads down and mindlessly mining the barnyard for goodies, while the fox digs at the fence line, and the hawk hovers above us… because…well…what else can a single person do?

Consumption Also Makes Us Exploit People: If we can get folks in China or Vietnam or Mexico to do our bidding for less, we can get more. So why not? If we can buy cheap stuff from a giant-box store, does it matter if their employees need food stamps to survive? No. Consumers want to maximize what's *theirs*, without regard for what is *ours*.

And if tens of millions of jobs are shipped overseas so that we can get more stuff at less cost, then why not? Why put requirements in trade agreements for a living wage, safe working conditions, and strong environmental protection, if it means less stuff for me? So what if those kinds of provisions would keep jobs here in the United States? It's all about the stuff, dammit. The more the better.

A Consumer-based Economy Destroys Communities: We watch giant-box stores and malls go up—temples to the getting—but we fail to see that we're cashing in the life and vitality of our local communities for a 10 percent off sale on the latest gizmo made in China. The Oligarchy prospers, while laborers are locked in a race to the bottom and local businesses wither and die.

We move across the country to chase jobs, to make more money so that we can afford more stuff, and the family and community that defined human culture for eons is weakened. In 1950, 30 percent of us lived in urban settings. In 2008, for the first time, more than half of us did. And by 2050, more than 70 percent of us will. It isn't that urban living is necessarily bad; rather, it's a sign of how much migration has occurred.

Nature, for Many of Us, Is Becoming an Alien Place—as opposed to an integral part of our community. We know the aisles of Abercrombie better than the shores of Assateague or the ancient peaks of the Appalachians or the endless prairies or the rugged Rockies or the granite peaks of the Sierras or the towering redwoods of Big Sur. And you can't love what you don't know, and you won't protect what you don't love. Once again, we get our McMansion, but the rooms are empty, our neighbors are strangers, and our connection with the world that sustains us all but severed.

A Consumer-based Society Discourages Right Relationships with Future Generations: We use the sophistry of cost-benefit calculations and discounting to justify destroying the life-giving climate we inherited, to permit the extinction of half of all living species, to leave behind seas that are oil-fouled, acidic crypts rather than bountiful sources of food, joy, and wonder.

Depending on how you count it, each newborn child in America comes into the world owing between $39,000 and $200,000. An amoral framework focused on consumption obliterates any sense of limits. Consider this: the global value of derivatives in July of 2008 was $1.44 quadrillion—not trillion, but quadrillion—with fifteen zeros. That's about twenty times the size of the entire global economy. And it's 95 percent speculative—there's nothing made, nothing tangible, nothing tying it to the earth or the air or the sea.

The upshot of all this? We are in effect conducting an open pit mining of our children's future, leaving behind the scarred remains of a once beautiful planet and a huge unpaid bill. Ah, but here's the nub, the crux, the core of the matter—we love this stuff—we know it's empty, but we love it anyway. I covet a huge monster screen TV; I want several houses, a cool car, and a home theater with a nifty popcorn maker.

Yes, it's the lizard brain at work again. The gimmee, gimmee, gimmee pleasure center that bypasses reason. We're hardwired to consume. The reward centers in our brains formed in a time of scarcity—whether it's high-calorie sweet and salty foods or plasma TVs—the same pleasure/reward pathways that make people crack cocaine addicts make us crave stuff: think of it as psychic junk food. And more and more, we purchase it with debt. If we want it, we simply put it on plastic. Plastic? Remember that 1960s phrase "That's so plastic, man"? Well here we are in 2017, and we now have islands of floating plastic junk in the North Pacific Vortex—one of them larger than the continental United States. That's so plastic, indeed.

Humanity is no longer a verb, a doer. It's becoming a noun, a thing—a miasma of stuff, a maelstrom of consumption. In the forty-eight years since the *First Whole Earth Catalogue* was released, we've traded in the idea of being producers for the hollow joys of consuming, and for a while, it looked like it worked. Like water into wine, we turned the peace sign into a Mercedes Benz symbol, and it seemed good.

The constant bombardment of advertising telling us to "please consume massive quantities" both feeds and expands our need for psychic junk food.[123] It's as if an alcoholic were asked to work as a bartender, or a dieter were forced to live in a house stocked with high-calorie junk food. No wonder we're helpless in the face of the commercial onslaught that is the handmaiden of the market über-alles mentality at the heart of the MMM.

The constant, lifelong bombardment of marketing meant to make us believe that accumulating stuff differentiates us from others and somehow elevates us above them—that it somehow can fill our lives with meaning—feeds a fundamentally narcissistic and self-centered worldview that is anathema to the notion of "we the people" and a commonweal. Is it any wonder then, that we elected a narcissist?

Splintering Our National Soul: The siren song of material wealth has prompted us to bury our collective conscience and commitment to a commonweal beneath a pile of geegaws, gadgets, and stuff…ever more stuff.

The Oligarchy is feeding the national id with a steady diet of us vs. them in which wealth and welfare is a zero-sum game with all benefits to "them" coming at the expense of an ever-narrowing set of splinter groups we define as "us." Society is becoming atomized and identity politics trumps "we the people."

Older white men—the formerly privileged, but now frightened, angry, and more and more often, impoverished—look out over the increasingly diverse landscape and see a thousand targets to blame for their diminished prospects—and Oligarchs and politicians both create and exploit this deadly combination of fear and blame. Plutocrats who write bills and instruct Congress to pass them are screwing the average American, hidden in plain sight behind the veil of blame and hate they've fostered with their politicians and their media.

Thus, the people who once were the only ones enfranchised in our system now feel left out, and they are coalescing into an angry mob. And other groups like African Americans, Hispanics, the LBGTQ community, women, immigrants—who've actually *been* left out—increasingly succumb to identity politics in the face of the backlash.

As a result, there's no one left to speak for and as "we the people." We have been divided and now we have been conquered. Of course, one of the reasons this could happen was because for decades, many whites actively worked to prevent minority groups from fully participating in our governance and from receiving an equitable and just share of the benefits of a vibrant democracy. But as whites approached a minority, their hold on the system loosened, and for a brief time, the size and extent of "we the people" grew rapidly.

Meanwhile, the Oligarchy and its media stoked an increasingly atomized and individualized version of our society, in which the commonweal was replaced with an Ayn Rand cutout figure that looked more like the Marlboro Man than any concept of a citizen that actually lives—and breathes—in the kind of civilized society a democracy demands. This disintegration of "we the people" has also been underwritten by a belief in an economy that is built around the idea that what matters is the ultrarich job creator or his Democratic equivalent, the Innovator.[124] As a result, even within identity groups, there is competition, and we are set, one against another, in an unwinnable race to transcend through greed.

Too many of us now view the world through the haze of smoke from our Marlboro Man persona, alone on the range—perhaps bestride a mythical horse and harkening back to a time and place where we were better off—and see a plethora of "thems" we declare to be guilty of robbing us of our heritage and our birthright, and preventing us from getting the stuff we crave. In reality, it is the policies and politics of the Oligarchy that are impoverishing us, and robbing us of our voice and therefore our freedoms, and snatching the future from our children.

We've replaced the power of we the people with a happy meal and a 50 percent off coupon.

And yet it has become the organizing principle of our entire global culture.

Finally, Consumption Also Discourages Right Relationships with the Natural World: When getting and taking replace giving and making, we lose something of the wisdom within us that tells us we are of nature, not above nature. If we have to liquidate a rainforest, or destroy a climate, or acidify the seas, or eliminate species and ecosystems to get more for less then we will, for the getting is what it is all about.

Producers must be stewards of the raw materials they use to produce—consumers simply want more. A family farmer nurtured the soil—a factory farm consumes it. On average, the earth is covered with about three feet of top soil. In the United States, soil is eroding ten times faster than it takes to build it up. We're not farming soils, we're liquidating them.

We don't just exploit people, we exploit species and ecosystems—giant feedlots in which cattle can't move; pigs that never see daylight; chickens with their beaks cut off, living on antibiotics and factory-farmed Frankenfood; turkeys bred to be too fat to stand, consumed by people who almost can't. All for the getting—the cheaper the better, the more the better.

The Punch Line to a Life Full of Stuff: Here's the dirty little secret. We work harder than "simple" hunter-gathers. We have less leisure time, fewer relationships, and more stress-related disease than they do. The stuff that was supposed to buy us happiness is, instead, making us sick.

Hunter-gatherers spend forty to forty-four hours a week, *total*, meeting their needs for shelter and food; we civilized folk spend more than twice that. Their time is about evenly split with twenty hours on shelter and maintenance and home-related activities such as food preparation, and twenty hours or less on gathering food and hunting. Compare that to us: we spend forty or more hours at work, ten hours commuting, and twenty to thirty more on home maintenance, food preparation, cleaning, and other home-centered activities. Hunter-gatherers exhibit almost no cardiovascular disease, diabetes is unheard of, and obesity is nonexistent in their societies.[125] They have more leisure time, they participate in more communal activities, and even their "work" is communal.

The strength of community was also evident in agrarian societies. For example, think of nineteenth-century America, where people came together from miles around to "raise barns" with a tradition of dinner and dancing afterward.

Now, think of today's equivalent, toiling away in your house or cubicle, with the curtains drawn, the doors closed—each man and woman an island, John Dunn notwithstanding. Our "barn" is likely to be a monster flat screen, smart TV, and our "barn-raising" is likely to be the two hundred hours of isolated and isolating time spent working in a cubicle needed to get it. And the smart TV will deliver more wants, less time in community, and a giant dose of must-haves, allowing the need machine to sink its talons deeper into our souls.

The triumph of the magic markets was a community shredding event, and as we will see in Part Three, this transition toward consumerism also created an existential threat to our civilization, that is orders of magnitude greater than any of the threats the Oligarchy brandishes to scare us witless.

PART THREE: Inheriting the Wind— The Sterile Seeds of Greed

● ● ●

He that troubleth his own house shall inherit the wind.

PROVERBS 11–29

Later, all this was not enough. Unhinged arrogance wished to take possession of all the harmonies of the gods.

THE WERCKMEISTER HARMONIES

CHAPTER 13

Neoliberalism and the Destruction of the Ecological Commons

● ● ●

Ruin is the destination toward which all men rush, each pursuing
his own best interest in a society that believes in the freedom of
the commons. Freedom in a commons brings ruin to all.

GARRET HARDING

IN PART ONE, WE EXAMINED how the Oligarch's Coup undermined our freedom, weakened our press, impoverished us, and took over civil institutions by means of buying elections, distracting and deceiving us through skillful use of language and appealing to our primitive lizard brain through fear.

The Coup resulted in a political monoculture in which neoliberalism—with its prescription of a society dominated by the market, with small (and weak) government, deregulation, and free trade—produced a rigged economic and political system in which government was a wholly owned subsidiary of corporate America. In the end, this is what handed Trump his victory. He was a Plutocrat who could play a populist.

In Part Two, we tracked the Oligarchy's assault on our "cultural commons"—the collection of laws, regulations, beliefs, and norms designed to assure an equitable, just, and prosperous world. We further examined how, by means of a relentless and ubiquitous media campaign featuring fear and greed, it changed our worldview, converting us from producers and stewards to consumers and liquidators. The process took us backward from the Enlightenment to the Dark Ages.

But there's another "commons" which is being undermined by the neoliberal consensus dominating our political and economic world, and it poses the greatest threat humanity has ever faced.

In his classic essay "The Tragedy of the Commons,"[126] Garret Hardin wrote about this other set of commons—the *ecological or natural* commons. These include *the natural resources accessible to all members of a society, including natural materials such as air, water, and a habitable earth.* Logic and ethics would call for these resources to be held in common, not owned privately.

The neoliberal consensus that dominates our political thought, comes with a set of earth-destroying concepts, most of which form the underpinnings of the discipline of economics. If neoliberalism is the disease, our politicians are its vectors, and economics its pathogen. Especially neoclassical economics, with its reliance on humans as perfectly rational agents and its use of excessively abstract mathematical models, and its commitment to markets as an end, not a means.

As we have seen, the stakes for us as a culture from this Coup are high, involving the continued existence of the freedoms that have been a part of our birthright and our collective culture for most of this nation's history.

But the assault on the natural commons threatens far more than the existence of our freedoms—it represents a clear and present danger to the global ecosystem we evolved in, and that in turn, threatens civilization as we know it.

There is a war going on right now between those who are working to protect these commons and the Ayn Randian capitalists, corporatists, and plutocrats who are working to privatize our economy, culture, ecology, environment, and government.

The outcome of this war will determine whether we live in a dystopian chaos, or a civil society; whether we preserve our natural life-support system, or live on life support.

At the moment, it's a rout. The Oligarchy is winning, and those very few who speak for the ecological commons are ignored, marginalized, or ridiculed. The rest of us have opted into the Oligarch's MMM and its false promise of wealth, prosperity, and equity.

In the 2016 election, the natural commons were sold out. Hillary Clinton feinted left and managed to pass herself off as a candidate of the people to enough people to beat Sanders—with the aid of a rigged system. And of course, Trump took the implicit hate, fear, xenophobia, anger, ignorance, and greed that had been the stock and trade of the Republican Party and made it explicit, and then rode it to victory in the primaries and the election.

But either way, the natural commons lost the primary races. Yes, Ms. Clinton embraced renewable energy and acknowledged the science behind climate change, but she refused to advocate the policies needed to halt it. She would not ban fracking; she would not put a price on carbon; she would not put an end to allowing exploration for new fossil fuel resources on public lands, *at a time when we have to leave 80 percent of the fossil fuels we've already found in the ground to have even a glimmer of a chance of avoiding catastrophe.*

As I noted earlier, paying lip service on the use of renewable energy without adopting policies to immediately cut carbon emissions is nothing more than a con, designed to create the appearance of taking climate change seriously, without actually taking a stand that would incur the wrath from the fossil fuel interests.

And if there's one thing the WikiLeaks revealed,[127] it's that Hillary Clinton subscribes to the neoliberal consensus that has empowered the Plutocracy, disempowered the people, and is resulting in the wholesale destruction of our planet and our climate. We will examine the politician's—indeed our entire society's—failure to tackle climate change, and the consequences separately in chapter 15, since it represents a true existential threat to our civil society. Here we will look at the danger posed to the ecological commons by the neoliberal consensus and the conservative's embrace of the Dark Ages.

The threat that Trump poses is obvious. But the danger posed by the neoliberal elite, that dominates the democratic party is, in many ways, more pernicious in that it is less overt. Indeed, if we examine the democrats' embrace of the neoliberal consensus we will see that it represents the essence of the

Oligarch's Coup. For example, their chosen candidate apologized to Wall Street for Congress's attempt to regulate the big banks, and claimed that Dodd-Frank—a bill that was too weak to make a real difference and is getting watered down even further as it is translated into regulations—was necessary only for "political reasons." As if Wall Street's central role in the worst recession since the Great Depression weren't reason enough to regulate.

The WikiLeaks reveal that Ms. Clinton believes there's a need for a public position on these kinds of issues that is different than her privately held one – a position that appears to be shared by most of the democratic establishment.

Again, what we see here is political calculation, completely devoid of any progressive values. Krystal Ball, former MSNBC journalist, captured the real problem with Clinton's attempt to hide her neoliberalism in a scathing indictment of her campaign:

> The very fact that her team is so publicly mulling these choices reveals that they have no clue that their biggest problem isn't making the proper electoral calculations, but rather that their *entire campaign* is based on electoral calculations.

The forces of ignorance and fear that fueled Trump's campaign will likely remain in the minority—remember he won with under 27 percent of the eligible vote—and the evil genie he unleashed must be stuffed back into the bottle. But notwithstanding Trump's victory, the neoliberal consensus embraced by mainstream democrats and Ms. Clinton is a majority position in politics, and it's here to stay, unless we the people recognize the threats embedded within it, and defeat it.

If we don't, the casualty will be the global ecological commons we and all life-forms depend upon to survive.

To fully understand this threat, we will need to examine key assumptions from the study of economics—the discipline which forms the underpinnings of the neoliberal consensus, and one of the chief weapons in the Oligarchy's arsenal.

CHAPTER 14

Economics and the Twin Horsemen of the New Apocalypse

● ● ●

*And I looked, and behold a pale horse: and his name that sat on
him was Death, and Hell followed with him. And power was
given unto them to…kill … with hunger, and with death.*

FROM THE RAVINGS OF JOHN OF
PATMOS—ALSO KNOWN AS REVELATION

WHAT IS THE PURPOSE OF the economy?

When you get down to it, this is one of the most important questions of our time.

How we answer it determines whether we will be able to sustain civilization as we know it beyond the mid-century.

Yet most of economics concerns itself with what an economy *does*, not what its goal *is* or *ought* to be. For example, much of economic policy can be summed up in the words of Harvard economist, Dani Rodrik, who distilled economic development down to a three-word mantra, "stabilize, privatize and liberalize."[128] You could say this is the neoliberal's national anthem.

But to what end, and for what purpose?

That question isn't even considered. The implicit assumptions, of course, are maximizing economic growth and creating more wealth.

These two unexamined assumptions are firmly embedded in the neoliberal worldview, and they represent the twin horsemen of the new apocalypse.

But what could possibly be wrong with these goals, you might ask.

Plenty, as it turns out. In the following sections, we will examine how the assumptions underlying neoclassical economics are causing us to liquidate the natural commons, and document how some of the key ecosystems we rely upon are being destroyed by these assumptions.

Steering the Ship of State with Blinders and a Broken Compass: No other discipline dominates political theory and practice as much as economics, particularly neoclassical economics. But as we will see, economics is essentially future blind and amoral, which means for the last fifty years we've been steering our national economy—as well as international economic policy—by what amounts to a broken compass and a watch with no hands. Worse, it influences policy across the board: from social welfare, to environmental protection, to educational policy, to health care, to research-and-development budgets and beyond. Only defense and security budgets escape the remorseless tyranny of cost-benefit constraints—after all, it's hard to stoke the fear machine and inflate the bad guys into an existential threat if you examine the payoff for spending close to a trillion dollars a year on threats that rank well behind those where you are relentlessly cutting budgets.

Which goes a long way toward explaining exactly why our economy is so unjust and our ecosystem is in imminent danger of collapsing.

Nobel prize–winning economist Joseph Stiglitz captured this failure when he said,

We always want to keep in mind what the function, the purpose, of the economy is […] the purpose of an economy is not producing GDP. It is increasing the welfare of citizens, and it is increasing the welfare of *most* citizens. And the American economic system has failed, and failed very badly[129].

Let's examine the neoliberal assumptions about growth and wealth to see how they undercut the commonweal while creating an existential threat to civilization.

The Folly of Infinite Growth on a Finite Planet: Ask any policy wonk, politician, or pundit—Republican, independent, or Democrat—about the sine qua non of economic policy, and the chances are pretty good their answer will boil down to one word: growth.

No matter what their stripe, a growing economy is practically synonymous with a good economy.

Yet this flies in the face of reality. It is a disconnect, a non-sequitur, an impossibility, a folly of immense proportions. Because the plain fact is, the economy can't continuously grow in a finite world, and we are already bumping up against limits.

Right now, it takes 1.5 Earth's worth of resources to maintain our current economy. By 2050, assuming only moderate growth, we'll consume nearly 3 Earth's[130] worth.

But of course, we only have one planet.

Those extra worlds we consume represent debt—assets taken from our progeny. In ecologic terms, it is called "overshoot." And living systems cannot long survive in overshoot mode.

The term overshoot comes from ecology, and a classic example of an ecological overshoot might serve to make this concept more real.

So here you go. In 1944, the US Coast Guard released twenty-nine reindeer onto St. Matthew Island to serve as a backup food source[131] for nineteen men who were stationed there to staff a long-range navigation station. In 1945, with the end of World War II, the men were recalled, and the reindeer were left behind. None had been shot, since the food supplies had been adequate.

Ecologists visited the uninhabited island periodically over the years, and by the summer of 1963, they found that the reindeer population had exploded to over six thousand animals.

Quite a success, eh?

Not really.

Visits to the island were sporadic, but sometime very shortly after they were counted in 1963, the population began to plummet, and by 1966, when scientists returned to check the population, there were only forty-two scrawny, starving animals, all females except one male who had physical deformities and probably was not capable of reproducing. By the 1980s all the reindeer had died off. Basically, they'd consumed themselves out of existence. That's a classic example of an ecological overshoot.

With our growth-a-go-go economy, we're running the risk of doing that on a planetary scale.

In fact, as the economists and politicians advocate more and more growth, we humans are getting pretty close to the reindeer's plight, and we're taking half the rest of the species with us. Fueled by increasing population and increased per capita consumption, we are perched on the edge of a global ecological abyss and calling it economic growth.

Exhibit A has to be the massive buildup of wastes in the global ecosystem, especially the buildup of greenhouse gasses (GHGs) in our atmosphere. Exhibit B has to be the diminishing reserves of life-sustaining natural resources. They are two sides to why economic growth can't be our economic polestar.

Nearly four decades ago, economist Herman Daly pointed out that our macroeconomic models were all circular, self-contained, and capable of growing infinitely; while in reality, the economy was a linear subset of a finite ecosystem. As Daley noted, the real economy required resources from the natural world to manufacture goods or provide services, and it relied on the ability of the natural world to assimilate the wastes from these processes while still sustaining us and the support systems needed for all life.

But economists and the discipline of economics have stubbornly resisted this realty and clung to the notion of their self-contained circular system operating outside of, and independent from, the natural world and capable of expanding infinitely.

Resource depletion and wastes such as carbon emissions are not priced in our growth-oriented market. Indeed, as Robert Repetto documented three decades ago, we treat resource depletion as wealth generation in national accounts such as GDP.[132]

Commodity supplies are finite, and as Chris Martenson points out in his excellent book *"The Crash Course,"* we are rapidly depleting some key nonrenewable resources. Martenson also notes that currency—the thing we use to measure growth—is simply a claim on wealth, not real wealth and that it has no intrinsic value. Thus, as we stack our pile of cash ever higher, our resource stocks—the ultimate source of real wealth—is shrinking. So essentially, we're liquidating our assets and calling it growth.

Worse, we're consuming these resources at a time when we are growing from about 7.5 billion souls to 9 or more billion. In fact, recent projections suggest the population is likely to reach 11 billion by 2100. The point is, as demand and dependence on natural resources and ecosystem services is increasing, supply is decreasing, and the economic tools we use to steer our way into the future are either blind to this trend or openly hostile to preservation strategies and policies.

In the following section, we'll take a look at what our go-go growth policies are doing to our life-support systems.

Many people, reading the tale of woe that follows will suggest these are not political issues. They will list things like immigration, terrorism, jobs, tax policy, or debt as the proper province of politics and politicians. But that's the point—the Oligarchy and their wholly owned subsidiaries, the media and politicians—want us to focus solely on those kinds of topics for three reasons. First, they are "distract, divide, and conquer" issues that can be used to weaken the commonweal and move our focus off these far more consequential concerns; second, they don't require the government to regulate corporations or limit them in any other way; and third, if we were to tackle problems like climate change, it would require a *massive collective* effort that would not only bring us together, but would also legitimize government and its role in constraining corporate power and assuring the commonwealth.

The truly astounding thing about this is that our lapdog political parties and we the people oblige them and put proximate threats to the survival of our civilization on the back burner, while we run around hysterically focusing on trumped up threats that either don't exist, or—like terrorism—barely have an effect on our well-being.

So how serious are these threats we're ignoring? How close to the tiny-brained reindeer are we? Pretty damn close. Here's a brief outline of how our neoclassical economic model is causing us to liquidate our most important life-support systems.

Water: Fresh water is becoming increasingly scarce and increasingly privatized. By 2025, some 1.8 billion people will face water scarcity, and two-thirds of the population will be living in what analysts call "water stressed" conditions[133]—which means that potable water supplies are at the edge of adequate and in imminent danger of not meeting our needs.

In keeping with the Oligarchy's drive to privatize, corporations have been moving across the globe to privatize or co-opt water systems and turn them into profit centers. Water provided by private companies costs 59 percent more than publicly supplied water systems, and in countries like Bolivia, which was forced to privatize water systems by the World Bank, privatization sparked a revolution when people could no longer afford to buy water.

Bottom line: potable water will become increasingly scarce, and the Oligarchy's response is to take advantage of the scarcity to make a profit, not to forge solutions.

Survival experts have a saying they call the rule of threes: a person can live three weeks without food, three hours without shelter, and three days without water. Because the neoliberal consensus books costs of resource depletion as if it were adding value to the economy and gives great weight to current benefits over future benefits through the practice of discounting,[134] we are not making the investments we need to assure we have enough water in the future. And because privatization increases the amount of money that can be made from water resources, our financial system supports policies and projects which favor investments in profit-making schemes over those that assure access to clean water for current and future generations.

Desertification: Fueled by global warming, increased tilling of marginal areas, over consumption of water in marginal areas, and overharvesting of vegetation—among other factors—deserts are exploding in size and popping up in previously arable areas throughout the world. Why do we do this? Growth, growth, growth.

Forests: At over twelve million square kilometers, the boreal forest, which girdles the earth at the upper latitudes covering the northern reaches of Canada, Alaska, Russia, and Scandinavia, is one of the largest biomes in the world. The entire system is under assault from an assortment of pests made stronger by climate change, and it is dying over much of its range. What isn't being eaten is under threat from an explosion in the number and severity of forest fires, again brought on by global warming.

Ironically, we're chopping down the boreals almost as fast as we're destroying them with GHG-induced diseases and forest fires. Why? Cashing in the forests helps grow the GDP. And a growing GDP is all that matters, even if it means depleting resources our lives depend upon.

But it's not just the boreals. We're threatening most of the world's forest ecosystems. For example, according to the Union of Concerned Scientists, large forest fires in the western United States are occurring nearly five times more often now than they did in the 1970s and 1980s. Today, fires are burning more than six times as much land area, and lasting almost five times longer. And the trend is global.[135]

Rainforests are a particular concern. Once, they covered 14 percent of the world's surface. Today that's down to a mere 6 percent, and some scientists believe that at current rates of destruction, they will be gone within forty years, while other forecasts suggest they won't disappear until 2100. But absent serious efforts at preservation, they will be gone.

Rainforests are home to the majority of the world's terrestrial species, but it is estimated that some fifty thousand species a year are being lost to deforestation. Again, the neoclassical model of economics so beloved by conservatives and neoliberals measures this liquidation of natural resources as economic growth, and it's backed up by macroeconomic measures such as GDP.

But this is, in fact, impoverishing us. Rainforests are the source for up to 25 percent of western pharmaceuticals, but less that 1 percent of these tropical trees and plants have been tested by scientists, so we are literally tossing out trillions in potential wealth and calling it economic growth.

Oceans: About 71 percent of the Earth's surface is covered by seas. Somewhere between 50 and 80 percent of all life on Earth lives beneath the seas. Seafood is the principal source of protein for more than a billion people,[136] oceans have a major role in regulating our climate; the top ten feet of the oceans contains as much heat as the entire atmosphere, and global currents distribute that heat across the globe.

In short, all life—including humans—depends upon a healthy marine ecosystem to survive. The seas act as the planet's thermostat, and they have been an integral part of creating the climate that has made human civilization and life as we now know it, possible. Yet the oceans and marine species are under an all-out assault from the kind of unchecked economic activity that underpins the growth mania that defines the neoliberal consensus. And conservatives? Fuggeddabout it.

Much of the carbon released from burning fossil fuels ends up in the oceans, increasing the acidity of the waters. Certain shell-forming zooplankton such as foraminifera and pteropods cannot survive even small changes in the pH levels (a measure of the acidity) of oceans. These tiny critters are at the base of the marine food chain, which means that when they are threatened, the entire food chain is threatened, including the seafood that humans depend upon.

Moreover, much of the shellfish we eat are directly affected by acidification. Mollusks—including clams, oysters, scallops, and mussels—also have a narrow tolerance for increases in acidity.

Both the zooplanktons and the mollusks cannot form shells when the water gets too acidic. We are seeing instances of thinning shells and in some areas, die-offs of these important species already, and if we continue current levels of carbon dioxide emissions, foraminifera are likely to be extinct by 2100. Removing species from the bottom of the food chain is like a poorly played game of Jenga: when the base goes, the whole edifice collapses.

Since oceanic biota generate most of the oxygen we breathe, ignoring the health of the marine ecosystem could be the equivalent of punching out the window while flying at thirty thousand feet, or pulling the plug on your own iron lung. But hey, what's a little less air here and there, as long as the economy is growing. And whoa...watch out for them terrorists...

Now, to be accurate, no one has collected enough data to positively state that climate change is depressing oxygen levels, but there is increasing support for the hypothesis that it is. Scientists have detected a sharp decline in phytoplankton in certain areas, and phytoplankton produce about two-thirds of the earth's oxygen. When scientists from the University of Leicester modeled the effects of warming on phytoplankton's ability to photosynthesize and produce oxygen, they found that the system could be compromised to the extent that it no longer provided enough oxygen to support life.[137]

Other scientists have already detected an acceleration in the ongoing decrease in atmospheric oxygen content in the past few decades.[138] This comes on top of a long, slow decline that has been going on for at least eight hundred thousand years, as measured by ice cores. But the acceleration is worrying since the margin for a viable atmosphere for humans and most other life-forms is quite narrow. Currently, oxygen makes up about 20.9 percent of the atmosphere, but concentrations lower than 17 percent are associated with impaired mental faculties.

One of the reasons you don't hear anything about the potential for oxygen depletion is that, while current trends and understanding of oxygen generation support the idea that we're flirting with a slow-motion crisis, there's very little conclusive data supporting it. It's a problem that is remote in terms of time, and it is "speculative." Scientists—rightly, in most cases—don't like speculation; they like data, working hypotheses that can be tested, and reproducible experiments that yield the same results again and again. But when it comes to spaceship Earth, the "experiment" involves the continued viability of life itself. It makes sense, when the stakes are this high, to shift the burden of proof from those who suggest a plausible concern, to those who would deny it, particularly when the consequence of the concern is irreversible or nearly so, and ubiquitous in its effect—as may be the case with chemical alterations of the atmosphere.

Now, the good news is, even if we trigger a decline, it would take thousands of years to make a significant dent in the oxygen already in the atmosphere, so we aren't talking about gasping for air in the near future. What we are talking about is the very real prospect of leaving our progeny with yet another monumental task—an extraordinarily expensive mortgage, if you will—so that we can "grow" our economy, oxygen levels be damned.

Meanwhile coral reefs—one of the most prolific nurseries for life on Earth—are struggling with acidification and warming seas, right here, right now. More than 90 percent of the corals that make up Australia's Great Barrier Reef—the largest in the world—are bleached, and a third of it has already died. Unless temperatures come down and carbon dioxide emissions are cut, the trend could become irreversible.[139]

This poses a clear and present danger to humans, who depend upon this nursery for both food and resources. But, hey, probably not worth bringing up in election campaigns…let's just focus on threats like terrorism which…well…in comparison may not pose a substantive threat, but at least addressing it doesn't require us to tackle corporate America and the Oligarchy. Besides, "there's plenty of good money to be made by supplyin' the army the tools of its trade." Gotta grow the economy, after all. Can't let a little thing like life-support systems get in the way.

Soils: But wait, the growth mania gets even more insane. Incredibly, we are using up the world's supply of topsoil, the prerequisite for all life, and we aren't even discussing it. By some estimates over 95 percent of the food we eat depends upon soil. You'd think this would warrant a mention or two. It may not be as important as whether someone wears the lapel pin or is fighting an all-out war on terrorism—which kills fewer people in the United States than falling furniture—but, hey, having no food could be a bummer.

Yet according to a UN study, the world has *just sixty years of topsoil* left at current rates of degradation. To quote the study,

> Generating three centimeters of top soil takes 1,000 years, and if current rates of degradation continue all of the world's top

soil could be gone within 60 years...Unless new approaches are adopted, the global amount of arable and productive land per person in 2050 will be only a quarter of the level in 1960.[140]

The proximate culprit is climate change and the techniques used by modern factory farms, which rely on chemical inputs and not maintenance of soil fertility. But the root cause is the neoliberal consensus which dictates that we maximize profits, not our progeny's welfare; economic growth, not natural resource preservation. In essence, we are mistaking growth in the amount of currency—a mere surrogate for wealth—for real wealth and ignoring the loss of natural resources, which is the true source of wealth. You'd think we were a bunch of stupid reindeer.

But in fact, we are very much like the reindeer on St. Matthew island in the early 1960s—growing rapidly and in imminent danger of overshoot, and our economic tools give us all the foresight of a herd of small-brained ruminants chewing up nature's bounty and farting out the waste products.

Much of the insanity in our culture and political discourse is justified by the discipline of economics—in particular, the neoclassical economic philosophy of growth, deregulation, and discounting the future. And this discipline is embraced by and supported by the Oligarchy. Remember those foundations established by the likes of the Koch brothers, Scaife, the Bradley's, Coors, Olin, and the rest of the fat cats we talked about in chapter 2? One of their main investments was to support conservative neoclassical economic advocates in academia and in think tanks. Endowed chairs at major universities assured a steady supply of ideologically correct acolytes, and a steady stream of press savvy white papers on the glories of conservative economic practices assured that the entire globe-destroying dogma of conservative economic theories achieved a level of logic-defying credibility in the media, and in our political, cultural and moral belief systems.

While Resources Deplete, Wastes Accrete: Meanwhile, on the other end of our economic growth model, wastes are accumulating at an alarming rate. Whale carcasses contain enough persistent organic pollutants (POPs) that they could be considered hazardous waste, and POPs show up in everything from mother's milk to human placental tissue, to the tissue of unborn babies. They are ubiquitous and dangerous and some last for centuries.

In the film classic *The Graduate*, Mr. MaGuire (played by Walter Brooke) turns to Benjamin (played by Dustin Hoffman) and says, "I want to say just one word to you. Just one word, Benjamin." Hoffman answers expectantly, "Yes, sir?" and then, after a few more back and forths, MaGuire reveals the magic word: "PLASTICS."

Prophetic, but not for the reason poor Mr. MaGuire believed. Nearly every bit of plastic ever manufactured is still intact today. Some plastic milk jugs take over a million years to decompose. We dump about fourteen billion pounds of trash—most of it plastic—into our oceans every year. A giant gyre of plastic debris about the size of the continental United States fills the North Pacific; and as many as one million sea creatures die each year from plastics.[141]

Here again, the economic tools we use completely leave out the devastation we are visiting upon the species we share the earth with, and on our children and their children for as many generations as we can track. It's simply not counted—or worse—it's counted as economic growth in measures like GDP, which, in particular, tells us resource depletion and waste generation and the havoc they cause, are to be measured as economic growth.

Absurd? Insane? Of course. We are wearing blinders and earplugs and navigating through time and the universe blithely unaware of the death and destruction we are causing, including, perhaps, our own, and all the while, we are calling it growth.

It's as if we were flying in a spaceship across the trackless vacuum of space and cavalierly selling off components to the highest bidder…Seats? *Sure.* Navigation system? *OK, fork over the cash.* Food and water sources? *Well, OK, if the price is right.* You say you want the oxygen system? *No problem, but it'll cost you…Wow, sure made a killing today.* Yeah, literally. Our entire approach to growing the economy actually shrinks it.

How about the Other Aim of Neoclassical Economics, Wealth Creation? Growth and wealth are used nearly interchangeably in our economic lexicon. So the first thing we need to do in this discussion is to define wealth.

Investopedia provides a definition that is fairly typical:

Wealth measures the value of all the assets of worth owned by a person, community, company or country. Wealth is determined by taking the total market value of all physical and intangible assets owned, then subtracting all debts. Essentially, wealth is the accumulation of resources.

Investopedia goes on to say that money (currency) is the means we use to measure wealth.

That's pretty typical and comparable to what any economics course might teach. It is this use of money as the measure of wealth that causes it to fail so miserably at actually creating wealth. Our entire system is designed to increase the surrogate of wealth, at the expense of actual wealth.

Note that (1) wealth is measured by money, (2) it is the total market value of all assets *minus debt*, and (3) money or currency is not real wealth, it is merely a claim on wealth.

The point is, all "wealth" is measured by currency. In conventional economic terms, then, more currency means more wealth. Simple.

Simple minded is more like it. Here's why.

As we saw in the previous section, real wealth is tied to natural resources, and natural resources are finite, while the potential supply of currency is not, and that leads to some serious disconnects.

For example, a team led by Robert Costanza found that the annual value of just seventeen ecosystem services exceeds $142.7 trillion in 2014 dollars.[142] To put that in perspective, the global world product—the total value of all goods and services—was only a little over $78 trillion that year. And remember, GDP makes no distinction between economic activity that provides benefits and economic activity which is a net negative for human welfare.

Let's take a little side trip to examine how poorly GDP performs as a measure of wealth.

Try the following thought experiment. Imagine a man who is just leaving divorce court where he's had to pay his attorney $25,000. As a result of the divorce, the family is split up, the wife and children are impoverished. Upset, the man then gets in a traffic accident and totals his car, while breaking several ribs and injuring the other driver. Chalk up another $50,000 when the other drive sues him. On the way to the hospital, he has a heart attack and is forced to stay in intensive care for a week. Chalk up another $100,000 for his medical bills. Ultimately, he dies, from an antibiotic-resistant infection he picks up in the hospital—add another $25,000 in medical costs, plus $15,000 for a funeral and burial, for a grand total of $215,000. All of this would go down as an increase in GDP and would be given the same value as if the man had sold a life-saving patent for $215,000.

In the same way, if crime goes up, and people are forced to buy expensive alarms, install bars on their windows, and hire security guards to protect their property, GDP celebrates the increase in economic activity, and it's booked as growth and a net increase in national welfare.

There are several alternatives to GDP that try to subtract out negative expenditures and resource depletion to give a true sense of how the economy is doing in terms of increasing our well-being.

The country of Bhutan has even established a measure they call "Gross Domestic Happiness." Remember Stiglitz's comment on the purpose of an economy? Isn't this the measure that counts?

The state of Maryland has been using a "Genuine Progress Indictor" for nearly a decade. It's designed to distinguish beneficial economic activity from simple aggregations of cash transactions, and it includes quality of life and environmental measures.

Economist Herman Daley and theologian Michael Cobb proposed an Index of Sustainable Economic Welfare (ISEW) in 1989, which attempted to get a truer picture of real increases in economic well-being than simply adding up all the monetary transactions. When they applied this to the period between 1950 and 1986, their analysis showed that the economic welfare for the average American stabilized after the 1970s, even though GDP continued to skyrocket upward.

It is even possible, under systems like the ISEW, or its offspring, the Genuine Progress Indicator, to have a growing GDP while experiencing a decrease in economic welfare. Just ask a reindeer.

The point is, using GDP as an indicator can make it look like we are becoming wealthier and experiencing economic growth, when we are, in fact, becoming poorer.

So now let's take another look at that $78 trillion global world product in 2014. In terms of beneficial economic activity—in terms of measuring real wealth that benefits people and society—it's considerably less.

Essentially the $142.7 trillion in ecosystem services measured by Costanza et al. are treated as an externality—that is, these services are not even priced in the market. So our definition of "wealth" leaves out value that exceeds the entire income stream from the human economy.

It gets worse. Costanza et al. also determined that some $23 trillion worth of ecosystem services had been destroyed between 1997 and 2014, and not a single penny of this vast sum was registered in conventional macroeconomic accounting. And Costanza's work was done before we had a good understanding of the extent of climate change and the enormous costs it is imposing upon us.

Finally, humans depend upon nature for far more than the seventeen ecosystem services that were measured in the study, including our very existence, so the cumulative value of natural systems are—well—priceless. As in beyond the ability to price in currency.

Now, let's look at currency. As Chris Martenson put it, money is not wealth, it is merely a *claim* on wealth. But it can grow indefinitely while the supply of natural resources is finite. So we end up with a claim on wealth that far exceeds any available wealth. Which is debt.

One of the problems with this is that there are no practical limits on currency.

For example, as noted earlier, the value of the global derivatives market is \$1.2 quadrillion. Let's write that out complete with zeroes for the full impact: \$1,200,000,000,000,000.[143]

And what is this claim made against? Well, the source of all real wealth is natural capital. Without it, all the so-called sources of wealth embraced by neoclassical economists—labor, ingenuity, and individual initiative—are basically useless. But natural capital, unlike currency is finite; it has limits.

Remember, wealth is assets minus debt, and liquidation of life-support systems—as any reindeer could tell you—is debt. So is printing paper representing claims on wealth that exceed any possible capacity to produce wealth.

So at the end of the day, our commitment to a "growing" economy is impoverishing us, and our measure of "wealth" is doing the same.

The real purpose of an economy has to be something much different than what shapes politics and what we use to formulate policy. Joseph Stiglitz's purpose—increasing the welfare of most citizens—had it half right. A billboard spotted in Johannesburg, South Africa, during the World Summit on Sustainable Development probably made as good a statement on the appropriate goal of the economy as any: *Enough for everyone, forever.*

An economy designed around this goal would look completely different than today's "Everything for a few, right now" economy does.

It would value ecosystem services and resources using taxes, subsidies, tariffs, and property rights, and it would steward them carefully. The idea of distributional equity would not be a blasphemy, but a pragmatic response to the natural tendency of capital to get concentrated in the hands of the few, and a recognition that a market economy can't function without generalized prosperity.

Co-ops and employee-owned companies would be the most common ownership model; CEOs wouldn't get eight hundred times the minimum wage. There'd be no Bill Gates making some \$218,000 an hour. Fossil fuels would have been heavily taxed long ago, and the revenue they generated would have helped fund a low cost and immediate transition to a carbon-free economy.

The daily business report would feature an index based on environmental health and resource stocks, not the Dow Jones Index of paper stocks.

But we're not likely to see such an economy. Both major parties are busy trying to maximize paper currency at the expense of natural capital—the source of real wealth.

The Natural Commons—Prerequisites to Wealth…and Survival: Costanza's work to establish a monetary value for the services the ecosystem provides us with, is in a sense, a capitulation to a worldview that is fundamentally flawed, even though it does suggest that we revise our policies to support practices that sustain our environment now and for the future.

The fact that we price the commons with currency shows a fundamental misunderstanding of what real wealth is and how it is generated.

How, for example, do you price the consequences of having no breathable air, no drinkable water, or highly acidified oceans? What monetary value do you place on the last coral reef, the last breath of fresh air, the last pollinator, or the last stretch of rainforest? To cut to the quick, how do you price the value of the climate we evolved in—the precondition for all the prerequisites of life—the one we are in the process of destroying?

The answer is, of course, you can't price these things and probably shouldn't. Denominating things that are both necessary to support life *and irreplaceable, or in limited supply* with currency is like trying to convert a stack of dollar bills into air, water, natural resources, species, habitats, or a livable climate. It doesn't matter how big the stack of cash is, it won't work.

But let's get back to that issue of currency having "no practical limits." So what? Well, capitalists are placing claims against natural capital that isn't there—in essence, they're stealing future generations blind while they gin up the biggest bubble the world has ever seen.

Capitalists get the vast majority of the spoils of this theft, we get the crumbs, and the future generations get the bill. Unless, of course, nature decides to foreclose on the debt sooner, rather than later—which, given the trends in climate change is inevitable and much closer than most capitalists believe.

Indeed, it is very likely that the bill will arrive early, payable within a decade or two, and the terms will be nonnegotiable—continuation of the ecological systems we evolved in and that shaped and defined our civilization—or not.

How and why does this insanity persist? As we've seen, the Oligarchy—essentially future-blind capitalists—have stolen the government, media, and the terms of the debate. And now, with Trump, they've not only stolen government, they *are* government.

But "we the people" have become willing accomplices to liquidating our ecosystem as if it were a garage sale designed to convert unwanted junk into cash.

Since Ronnie "government-is-the-problem" Reagan, Americans have behaved like slack-jawed yokels at a three-card Monty festival, disabling, underfunding, and discrediting government and turning the country over to a bunch of crazed capitalists, making ourselves poorer, calling it wealth, all the while destroying natural capital, our children's birthright.

CHAPTER 15

Home

● ● ●

Look again at that dot. That's here. That's home. That's us.
On it everyone you love, everyone you know, everyone you
ever heard of, every human being who ever was, lived out
their lives...on a mote of dust suspended in a sunbeam.

CARL SAGAN, *PALE BLUE DOT*

We shall not cease from exploration, and the end of all our exploring
will be to arrive where we started and know the place for the first time.

T. S. ELIOT, *LITTLE GIDDING*

EACH DAY WE AWAKE TO a miracle. A planet that, improbably, has just the right mix of chemicals, just the right physical properties, and just the right geologic history to yield a world that not only sustains us, but also immerses us in beauty.

Yet just as improbably, we seem intent on destroying this miracle. Here again, conventional neoclassical economic assumptions are the villain; in economic terms, this priceless gift is treated as an externality – that is, until recently, it was not priced or otherwise valued in most neoclassical economic models.

With the possible exception of an all-out nuclear war, climate change is the single biggest threat humanity has ever faced. In this chapter, I will lay out the full nature of that threat, the kind of response needed to tackle it, and the *actual* time have left to avoid consequences unlike any humanity has experienced in its brief time here on earth.

This is necessary because we've been misled not only by our economic conventions, but also by the media, politicians, and even some climate scientists. As a result, few people actually understand how serious the threat is and how little time we have time to act.

Ignoring the Biggest Threat Humanity Has Ever Faced for Fun and Profit: Nowhere is the Oligarchy's influence more pernicious; nowhere is the impact of the neoliberal consensus more dangerous; and nowhere is the evidence of its insanity more pronounced than in the way it has subverted attempts to deal with this existential threat.[144]

For example, during the presidential debates leading to the 2016 elections, there was not a single question asked about it for either candidate.

And after 2016 broke the record for the hottest year in recorded history, marking it the third year in a row the record was broken, the press actually reduced its coverage of climate change by 66 percent.[145]

Not too unusual, really. The media has given short shrift to the topic since James Hansen first testified before Congress about climate change in June of 1988.

On the one hand, Trump is typically Republican on the issue—which is to say a lunatic, fact-free, flat-earther full of denial—a position that would be laughable, if it wasn't for the fact that any delays he causes will likely kill hundreds of millions of people and up to half of all species, in addition to other catastrophes.

Hillary Clinton, on the other hand, was quite slick. While acknowledging the science, she steadfastly refused to back the policies needed to solve the problem, while ballyhooing her positions on renewable energy.

Here again, the neoliberals refused to take a stand against corporate America. More specifically, against fossil fuel interests. By trying to have it both ways, they got neither. Voters are fed up with politicians mumbling mealy-mouthed bromides—that's one reason why nearly half stay home.

The fact is, the policies Clinton and the rest of the neoliberals embrace on climate change pose an existential threat to civilization and the global ecosystem. And Clinton's position was about as cynical and deceptive a political stance as we're likely to see in a long time. We'll explore why this is true in the conclusion to this chapter, and why it was yet another reason she and the Democrats faired so poorly in this election. But first, let's examine how we arrived at this dangerous intersection with doom and why most of us are completely unaware that the time to avoid serious damage has already run out, and the time to avoid potentially catastrophic consequences in nearly gone.

Once again, the EEM has failed to inform people about the nature of the scientific consensus and the true extent of the threat climate change poses for going on three decades now. Gotta be balanced, you know. Even if you're weighing the opinions of the self-interested and crackpots against the findings of 99 percent of the world's leading climate scientists.

Why It's Later than You Think, and Why You Don't Know It: The use of "carbon budgets" by the International Panel on Climate Change (IPCC) has led us to believe we have time to act, and the press reports on the recent climate accord reached in Paris implied we'd gone a long way toward solving the problem.

But the Paris Agreement fell far short of solving it, and we don't have as much time as the press reported or the IPCC estimates would lead us to believe, *if we want a reasonable margin of safety for avoiding cataclysmic warming.* Meanwhile, Trump, Ryan, McConnell and the rest of the conservative deniers are trying to deny the whole thing in a desperate attempt to prop up fossil fuel interests. But at the end of the day, the practical difference between Republicans and Democrats on this issue is how fast their policies will usher in Armageddon.

Now, it must be said that the Paris Agreement was a magnificent political achievement. Getting 190 nations to agree on the *need* to cut carbon emissions, and to agree to actually *make* some reductions, was an impressive accomplishment, even if those cuts are too small, are only voluntary, and there is no enforcement mechanism for failing to make them.

And it seems churlish to criticize the men and women who worked tirelessly to hammer out such an unlikely agreement. The fact of the matter is, they were, in effect, handed the helm of a sinking ship and told to sail. But it is dangerous to confuse a political triumph with an adequate response to the physical realities we face.

The Paris Agreement is the culmination of a process that began in Rio de Janeiro more than twenty-six years ago, when countries came together and acknowledged the reality of climate change and the dire threat it posed. The Rio Accord was preceded by the establishment of the IPCC in 1988 by the UN at the request of member nations.

The IPCC—Science Meets Politics: To understand how the IPCC— which has been the gold standard for integrating science and policy—has contributed to our current state in climate change, it's useful to know a bit about its mission and methods, because the IPCC's conclusions and their five Assessment Reports have informed governments and their negotiators since it was founded in 1988.

It has not been without its critics.

The IPCC process virtually assures that all the research used in their reports will be several years old. Since it feeds peer-reviewed work into a long consensus process, it has a long lead-time and a least common denominator data set. The latest research and any research that challenges established theory is often left on the cutting room floor.

For example, in AR 4—released in 2007—the IPCC forecast sea level rise to be, at most, fifty-nine centimeters. Conventional wisdom from the data used in the report suggested that continental ice sheets took thousands of years to melt. But well before that report was issued, research had revealed that dynamic forces were causing these ice sheets to melt much faster. As a result, the AR 4 was essentially out of date on the date it was issued. Similarly, the IPCC has never included feedbacks for melting permafrost that could dramatically accelerate and worsen climate change.

These excessively conservative assumptions are baked into the IPCC process. In fact, some suggest that's the point of the IPCC—to take control of the scientific debate out of the hands of scientists and turn it over to governments.

At any rate, because we delayed so long, and bowed to "political realities," physical realities...er...trumped the political ones, including those achieved in Paris. And in a clash between physics and politics, physics always wins.

Here again, to quote climate expert Kevin Anderson of the Tyndall Center:

On the duality of climate scientists: *how integrated assessment models are hardwired to deliver politically palatable outcomes...*

The value of science is undermined when we adopt questionable assumptions and fine-tune our analysis to conform to dominant political and economic sensibilities. The pervasive inclusion of speculative negative emission technologies to deliver politically palatable 2°C mitigation is but one such example. Society needs scientists to make transparent and reasoned assumptions, however uncomfortable the subsequent conclusions may be for the politics of the day.[146]

Translation: the pervasive influence of the neoliberal consensus and the Oligarchs that rely on it has shaped the discussion of climate change even among those who should know better.

Here's the reality:

* the target long used as the upper limit of acceptable warming and the basis of the Paris Agreement—2 degrees Celsius (2°C)—is too high and risks devastating changes to our climate (something negotiators acknowledged in the Paris Agreement when nations agreed to try to limit temperature increases to 1.5°C if possible—but it's not possible, as we will see);

* but worse, the Paris Agreement will not even come close to limiting warming to 2°C;

* The methodology used to establish carbon budgets needed to meet 2°C expose us to an absurd level of risk and it is extremely deceptive;

* most of the scenarios used to estimate the amount of time we have left to get off fossil fuels assume that our children and their children and the generations that follow them will build a massive and extraordinarily expensive carbon extraction infrastructure—something

we don't know how to do, or even if it's doable in any practical sense; and

* the targets and the models supporting them ignore feedbacks that have already started which amplify the effects of emissions, which make the budgets even more risky and less achievable.

Let's examine each in turn.

2⁰ C Is Too High: The press accounts referring to the 2°C limit frequently characterize it as the "maximum safe level." In reality, there's nothing safe about it. Scientists are more careful, referring to it as a "speed limit" or "guardrail," and even this phrasing implies a level of protection that a 2°C increase simply doesn't afford. In fact, the 2°C was more or less plucked out of thin air in 1975 by economist William Nordhaus as "a first intuition."[147] Subsequent analyses more or less defaulted to this figure in what amounts to the science being molded to the political and economic paradigm, rather than to what the data tells us.[148]

In fact, we can already see some serious consequences from the increase of just 1°C above preindustrial levels humans have caused already, including much of the litany of woe covered in chapter 14. Here's a quick review of what's happening right now in case you aren't depressed enough already.

We're experiencing record-setting droughts across the earth; widespread desertification; an explosion in the number and frequency of forest fires; increases in extreme weather events; flooding; mass extinctions; irreversible melting of the polar ice cap, as well as the ice sheets on Greenland and large parts of Antarctica, and the centuries of rising seas and costal inundation this will inevitably cause; we're seeing the bow wave of a massive migration of environmental refugees, and an increase in the range of tropical diseases. Right now. Today.

The Pentagon expects this rise in refugees coupled with shortages in vital resources such as water to make climate change the major threat to global security and the major cause of conflict in this century. In fact, that's begun already—the CIA found that climate-related droughts helped spark the conflicts in the Sudan, Darfur, and the upheaval in Syria.

Those who claim terrorism is our biggest threat, but fail to take climate change seriously, are ignoring the root cause of the threat they're ballyhooing. Bottom line: these folks are either ignorant, or they are being intentionally deceptive, and using terrorism as a cudgel for the military industrial complex, and as device to distract the rest of us from the fact that the Oligarchy is screwing us, and perhaps more specifically from tackling a far more serious problem because it would hurt fossil fuel interests.

Carbon dioxide concentrations are also acidifying the oceans, turning them into giant jellyfish incubators in which many of the seafood species we currently depend upon can't compete[149]. Peanut butter and jellyfish sandwich anyone?

We are already locked into centuries of rising seas, even if we were to stop emitting all GHGs today. Right now.

If that's what 1°C has done, imagine what 2°C would do. Or, better yet, don't imagine, look to the geologic record. As James Hansen and sixteen coauthors note in their paper "Ice melt, sea level rise and superstorms: evidence from paleoclimate data, climate modeling and modern observations that 2°C global warming is highly dangerous," when temperatures were 1°C warmer than today (that's 2°C above preindustrial levels) in the geologic record, there's evidence showing that sea levels rose between six to nine meters (about twenty to thirty feet) and were accompanied by severe storms and storm surges.[150]

Bottom line: absent drastic action, most of our coastal cities will have to be abandoned ultimately, and beginning as early as 2050, we will very likely be locked into an extraordinarily expensive and massive effort to defend them against rising seas and brutal storm surges. By the twenty-second century, sea levels will have risen by more than fifteen meters (just under fifty feet) if we continue on our current path,[151] and they will continue to rise thereafter. Why don't you know this? Because the media doesn't cover climate change and most scientists end their forecasts at the year 2100, as if the consequences of everything we're doing now would suddenly stop. But they don't. Again, even if we cut GHG emissions right this minute, the seas will continue to rise for centuries.

The Paris Agreements Won't Limit Warming to 2°C: So, 1°C is already exposing us to danger, and going to 2°C above preindustrial-level risk threats that are existential in nature. But the limits countries have committed to in the Paris Agreement (called "intended nationally determined contributions" or INDCs) clearly show that the Paris Agreement falls far short of what's needed to prevent us from exceeding even a 2°C temperature increase. The best-case scenario for what the agreement can achieve is 3.5°C (6.3 F) of warming above preindustrial levels[152]—an unmitigated disaster that would essentially make Earth a different planet. But it could be worse, as Daniel Grossman reported in *Yale Climate Connections*: "a study published in *Science* in November, for instance, calculated that if all countries accomplished their INDC pledges through 2030 *and then continued cutting back at a modest rate*, there was still a 40 percent chance that the global average temperature would rise by more than 4 C (7.2 F) by 2100" (emphasis added).[153] By the way, there is nothing in the agreement that requires countries to continue to cut emissions once their goals have been met. In fact, the goals themselves are entirely voluntary, and there is no enforcement mechanism for failing to meet them.

Let's be clear: Whether the world warms by 3.5°C or 4.0°C, we can kiss good-bye the climate our civilization evolved in and say hello to a hostile, near-alien world in which virtually every bit of human ingenuity and economy will be devoted to staving off a never-ending series of self-induced catastrophes. You can think of it as Matt Damon's situation in the movie *Mars*, except there is no safe planet to retreat to.

And that's what the Paris Agreement achieved in terms of real progress on cutting emissions—too little, too late. Yes, it was a stunning political victory, and it is a framework we can—and must—build upon. But unless we understand just how great the actual threat is, we are likely to rest on our laurels, instead of insisting on more action now. Right now.

A cynic would be forgiven for believing that the Oligarchy engineered this result with backroom deals and smoke-filled corridors—but it's more likely another example of the overwhelming influence that the neoliberal consensus has on our culture, and the power exerted by many individual actors moving in the same direction. And certainly, there's evidence of

Thomas Frank's elitists carefully ignoring inconvenient truths with a collective head-bobbing affirmation of their inherent correctness and their collective disdain for the rabble-rousing masses. Even scientists and supposedly objective policy types fell prey to the elitist's conviction that all must be well when the best and brightest are in charge, as we will see when we examine how "carbon budgets" were arrived at.

But for fans of conspiracy theories, it is worth noting that the words "fossil fuels" are not even mentioned in the entire thirty-one-page Paris Agreement.

As we will examine, the method used by the IPCC to calculate how much more GHG we can emit, has been—at best—an exercise in self-delusion. At worst, considering the dangers the current allowable carbon budgets obscure, a better description might be criminally negligent.

The IPCC's Carbon Budgets—Playing Craps with the Planet: To understand just how dangerous climate change is, and how close we are to irrevocable warming, and how misleading the discussions surrounding the Paris Agreements have been, we have to understand how the IPCC has measured the time we have left to get off fossil fuels.

Most reports talk about twenty years or so to avoid "dangerous warming," by which they mean 2°C. But as we have seen, 1 C is dangerous, 2°C is folly, and we're headed toward 3.5°C or more.

But here's the dirty little secret: we don't have twenty years more emissions to avoid even 2°C—if we want a reasonable margin of safety, we have *at most* five years and probably less. And as for 1.5°C? That ship's sailed. Gone. We have no chance; there's no carbon budget left.

Here's why that's true, and why you likely didn't know it.

Hold onto your hats; carbon budgets and the sophistry behind them can get a little complicated, but there is nothing more important to the future of this planet—and therefore to you—than understanding how grossly we are understating the real risks and how quickly we have to act to avoid them. If you're under forty, you should take this whole discussion personally. If you're over forty, you should be ashamed.

Carbon budgets are established to determine the maximum amount of GHG we can emit, and for how long, to reach a given atmospheric level of GHG concentrations needed to limit warming to a given temperature increase. So, for example, if we seek to limit temperature increases to less than 2°C, then we have to limit GHG emissions to avoid atmospheric concentrations that would cause warming to exceed that limit.

In establishing carbon budgets, the IPCC used a series of probabilities for staying below the target temperature of 2 C (3.6 F). The probabilities they used were a 66 percent likelihood of meeting the target, a 50 percent likelihood of doing so, and a 30 percent likelihood. What this actually means is that 66 percent of the models result in temperatures staying below the target level, or 50 percent of them do, or 30 percent of them do.

Notice what's not included in the carbon budgets the IPCC outlined: a confidence level of 100 percent or even 90 percent. Now, think about this for a moment. We are using margins of safety for the future viability of our planet's life-support systems that we wouldn't tolerate in almost any other area of our life. Would you board a plane with a 34 percent chance of crashing? Cross a bridge that has only a 66 percent chance of holding up? NO. You wouldn't.

So why is the 100 percent probability of making our goal not included in the IPCC's scenarios—or the 90 percent probability—for that matter? Answer: because we've already blown through the carbon budgets that would achieve 100 percent probability of avoiding catastrophe, and we will exceed the 90 percent risk before the cuts are required by the agreement. So now, we're stuck with the planetary equivalent of taking risks equal to playing Russian roulette with two bullets in the chamber. You'd think this would be a big deal, something worth talking about.

But of course, you'd be wrong.

Oh, and a 90 percent chance of meeting the lofty goal of limiting warming to 1.5°C that many nations and scientists fought to include in the Paris Agreement? Forget it. Gone. No chance. Nada, zip, zero.

But by operating with a 66 percent probability of meeting the 2°C target, rather than 100 percent or 90 percent we can *appear* to buy ourselves a lot of time. The lower we set the probability of staying below 2°C, the higher the allowable carbon budget and the more time we have to get off it. Of course, that doesn't actually give us more time—but it does provide the appearance of doing so.

So, higher odds of success require lower carbon budgets, lower odds of success allow more carbon to be released over a longer time.

Now let's do some numbers.

If we wanted to have a 66 percent probability of staying below 1.5°C, our total carbon budget would be 2,250 tonnes of carbon dioxide. By the end of 2016, we burned through all but two hundred billion tonnes of that budget. Since we are emitting about forty billion tonnes per year (about forty-four billion US tons), we will blow through the budget by the end of 2020, *the year in which the Paris Agreements are to start being implemented.* If we were to choose a more rational level of risk management, such as a 90 percent or 100 percent likelihood of preventing global Armageddon, we would have had to start acting a couple of decades ago, since we exceeded those targets in 2013.[154]

Contrast this with the carbon budget based on a 66 percent probability of staying below 2°C, or 2,900 billion tonnes of carbon dioxide (GtCO2e). By the end of 2016, we would appear to have nearly 810 gigatonnes of carbon dioxide left, or twenty years' worth.

Obviously, a better margin of safety would make sense. Playing craps with the planet we live on is—to say the least—irresponsible.

Negative Emissions—or Après Moi le Deluge: There's one other way of expanding carbon budgets and giving ourselves more time: Pass the problem on to our children and their children, so we can burn more fossil fuels now and still *appear* to stay within our carbon budget.

You can think of this as the Neville Chamberlain approach to climate change: it allows our carbon budgets to exceed the limits "in our time" while requiring our children and their children to mount the most ambitious and costly effort ever undertaken by humanity—one we don't even know how to do, or even whether it *can* be done—to wit: extracting massive amounts of carbon dioxide from the atmosphere and safely sequestering it. The idea here is, it would somehow be OK to exceed the limits on emissions as long as "we" got carbon down to an acceptable level by 2100.

This runs the risk of crossing tipping points and triggering self-reinforcing amplifying feedbacks, which would guarantee hell on Earth.

But hey, anything that would make it appear OK to keep doing what we're doing. As for the kids? Well, perhaps they could undertake this monumental effort to extract carbon in their spare time when they are not engaged in the life or death struggle with sea level rise, famine, droughts, diseases, and a billion or so refugees they will already be dealing with, using whatever left over budget they might—or might not have.

And that's precisely what the IPCC carbon budgets do. Most of them require our offspring to create extraordinarily expensive new technologies that will take massive quantities of carbon dioxide out of the air and *safely* sequester it. What we are saying is that it's OK *for us* to exceed concentrations that would put us above the 2°C limit, as long as by the end of the century, we are sufficiently below the level, even if it risks triggering irreversible feedbacks. Basically, this is a giant fuck you to future generations.

The Carbon Budgets Ignore Positive Feedbacks that Have Already Started and These Will Make Warming Happen Faster and Be Worse than the Models Suggest: In 2016, there were two influential reports on climate change that help demonstrate why feedbacks are important, and how we are conning ourselves about having more time. Both were issued in March.

The first report, issued by NOAA[155] on March 9, said that 2015 saw the biggest rise in atmospheric concentrations of carbon dioxide on record. Like most climate-related stories, it was lightly reported by the EEM.

The second report issued by the International Energy Agency exactly one week later, received slightly more coverage in the EEM, and it noted that, for the second year running, in 2015 carbon dioxide emissions were flat, even though the economy grew.[156] The reports hailed this as real progress in our attempt to slow the steady march of climate change.

This begs a couple of questions, one scientific, one cultural—if not psychological. Let's start with the science.

If emissions are static, why did the increase in atmospheric concentration of GHGs actually accelerate to record breaking levels, rather than slow down?

The answer is simple, but not well understood by policy makers or the media—and the IPCC has been in denial about the reason.

Basically, the amount of carbon dioxide being absorbed by the planetary sinks went down.

A word of explanation is in order here.

The atmosphere can be thought of as a bathtub, with GHGs flowing in, and GHGs draining out. Although the flows and "drains"—or sinks—vary slightly over the epochs, they are typically in equilibrium, which lends the system some stability. In fact, for the entire span of human civilization, the climate has been remarkably stable. Beginning with the industrial revolution, humans began to add more carbon (as well as methane and other greenhouse gasses) at a faster rate, and the "bathtub" began filling.

And even though 2015 saw a leveling in the amount of human-caused GHG emissions, we are still adding more than the sinks drain, so levels will continue to go up, but all things being equal, they should go up at a *slower rate*.

So once again, the question is—and it's one of the most important questions of our time—if we're not *increasing* the amount of *emissions* we're adding, why did 2015 set a record for the biggest increase in *atmospheric concentrations* ever observed?

The answer lies in the sinks, and it doesn't bode well for the Paris Agreement having the kind of impact we need.

Sinks include things that absorb or sequester carbon. Some of the major ones include forests, peatlands, the oceans (both the water itself and the biota in the ocean), and soils. Basically, because of warming, the sinks aren't functioning as well as they used to. For example, as we saw in chapter 14, one of the largest terrestrial sinks—the boreal forests—have been devastated by disease and pests caused by warming, and they have been burning down at record rates. As a result, now they are not taking in as much carbon as they used to. In fact, in some areas, they have become a *source* of carbon emissions, not a *sink*. And this appears to be happening with rainforests and other important sinks.

So even if we manage to turn the emissions down a bit, the bathtub will continue to fill faster and faster because the drain is becoming increasingly clogged. In short, atmospheric concentrations of carbon dioxide could continue to rise and even rise at a faster rate despite the fact that we are reducing emissions. Nothing in the IPCC models or the carbon budgets underlying them, factors this in.

Moreover, the calculations of how much time we have left assume that temperatures stop rising the moment we stop emitting GHGs, and this is simply not true. At best, they continue to go up for about a decade.

Bottom line: the IPCC budgets are wildly optimistic—and given what's at stake, insanely so. Speaking of insanity, we now have to factor in Donald Trump and his EPA chief, Scott Pruitt, both of whom deny the existence of climate change and advocate backing out of the Paris Agreement.

But it gets worse. The sinks have already stored trillions of tons of carbon over the eons. In fact, fossil fuels are basically hundreds of millions of years of stored photosynthetic energy. One of the more sensitive sinks, permafrost, contains an estimated 1,672 gigatonnes of carbon (more than double the amount currently in the atmosphere), and due to rapid warming, it is releasing some of this carbon—much of it in the form of methane, a GHG that is seventy-three times as strong as carbon dioxide in the short term.

Just three of these feedbacks could, by themselves, increase the global temperature by nearly 2.5°C. The first is a result of decreases in sulfur aerosols from phytoplankton, as the seas become more acidic and these critters begin to die off. Sulfur aerosols are known to moderate solar gain and mitigate global warming. This could increase warming by close to 1°F by 2100.[157]

Extreme weather events could add another 1.5°F, since they effect the earth's ability to sequester human-caused emissions and in some cases increase those emissions directly.[158] Add these to the 2 F expected from methane releases—a conservative number if one compares the results of similar events in the geologic record—and these three feedbacks alone could add just under 4.5°F, or 2.5°C, to our worst-case projections of 3.5°C to 4°C for 2100, resulting in a net increase of 6°C to 6.5°C, or nearly 11–12 F. Again, humans have never existed in a world this warm—it is essentially equivalent to an alien world to our species and many others we share the planet with. And of course, Trump is threatening to scuttle the Paris Agreement, so the actual increase in global temperatures could be considerably higher.

There are other feedbacks at work, each serving to release more GHGs.

This compromising of the sinks, and the triggering of feedbacks, may be among the reasons that most of our models—including those that the IPCC uses—haven't matched the observable geologic record in terms of damage, and that means we've grossly understated the difficulty of mitigating climate change.

But even if these feedbacks don't occur as forecast, the amount of GHGs that can be sucked out of the atmosphere by natural sinks is going down, and that means atmospheric concentrations will go up—in fact will accelerate—even if we succeed in flatlining emissions. It also means that the time we have left to cut emissions is less than the IPCC budgets forecast, as are the volumes of emissions that are allowable.

The bottom line is that, keeping emissions static or decoupling GHG emissions from economic growth are good things, but they are woefully inadequate to address the existential threat of climate change in a world with compromised sinks.

In reality, the true nature of the threat from climate change demands far more that the Paris Agreement provides—indeed, far more than the press, politicians or even many scientists acknowledge. And against this urgent need for greater effort in a shorter time frame, we have Trump and his cabinet pushing fossil fuel-friendly policies and scuttling climate protection programs.

And now for the cultural question these two reports suggest—why did a report that says we've flatlined emissions in 2015 get more coverage than one which tells us we've just set a record for the biggest increase in atmospheric concentration of GHGs in our history in that same year? After all, warming is directly affected by the atmospheric concentrations of GHG emissions, not the volume we emit.

The answer may lie in the fact that humans appear to be hardwired for optimism,[159] particularly with regard to future events. This bias makes it difficult for us to make a realistic assessment of data, by tipping the scales to the most positive outcome when competing information is presented. We give greater weight to the information that paints a rosier picture.

And as many have noted, we tend to focus on threats that are proximate in time and space, and tend to ignore threats that are distant in time or space. There's even evidence that this bias is genetically hardwired as part of our evolutionary baggage.

But the role of the Oligarchy can't be ignored. For example, the press maintained the illusion of a "controversy" about whether climate change was happening for decades after the science was conclusive by giving weight and airtime to unqualified blowhards and insisting on "balance" (as we saw in chapter 3). And when that was no longer credible, they carried denier talking points about whether humans were responsible for it. And it wasn't just corporate-owned media. For example, PBS has provided scant coverage of climate change, and their flagship science program NOVA has done only three programs on climate change in the last five years, and those programs essentially reported the IPCC orthodoxy, without noting that many leading climatologists believe it grossly understates the depth of the problem.

Three programs on the most significant problem facing humanity in five years by the nation's flagship science program would seem to be inexplicable.

Unless you consider that David Koch of the Koch brothers, co-owner of one of the largest privately held oil and petrochemical companies in the world, and as we saw in chapter 2, cofounder of several of the conservative foundations used by the Oligarchy in their Coup, is on the boards of WGBH, WNET, and NOVA and is one of the principal financial contributors to PBS for science coverage. Knowing this, the fact that PBS's treatment of climate change ranges from ignoring it, to barely scratching the surface of the science in those few instances where it is covered, makes sense. WGBH and WNET by the way, are responsible for most of PBS's programing, so Koch's position on their boards allows his influence to reach wide and deep.

Ignoring Risk Management—or Risky Business: The frightening thing is, with climate change, we are doing exactly the opposite of what we do with other risks.

A core precept of risk analysis and risk management is that dangers which are irreversible, consequential, and ubiquitous demand very high safety margins. People intuitively understand this with near-term threats, and that's why the airplane example is so obvious. We're genetically hard-wired to recognize risks that are proximate in time and place. We understand that when the alarms start sounding at thirty-five thousand feet, we can't simply exit the plane and grab another that's flying by, and so we insist on reducing risks associated with flying to as close to zero as is feasible.

Yet, the same is true of our planet, and we're cavalierly accepting a 34 percent chance of failure. If we screw it up, we can't hop off and wait for another planet to pass by. But the scale of this danger is so large and the time frame sufficiently long (exceeding a single life span) that we don't experience this threat in the same way. Responding to this danger will require us to exercise wisdom, not simply rely on the genes we've been given by natural selection.

But when it comes to climate change, wisdom is obviously in short supply.

It's the Physics, Stupid: If we want a reasonable margin of safety for the world, we have to get off fossil fuels as soon as possible, preferably within the next decade.

Impractical? No more impractical than pretending it makes sense to adopt a carbon budget that risks global catastrophe simply because we failed take the action we needed to take in the past.

The amount of GHG we can emit without ushering in Armageddon is determined by physics, not politics.

The thing is, we have everything we need to switch to carbon-free energy within the next five to six years, except the wisdom and the political will to do it. The cost of renewable energy alternatives and low-carbon technologies has literally plummeted in the last few decades. For example, between 2008 and 2015

* utility scale photo-voltaics (PVs) dropped by 64 percent;
* distributed solar dropped by 54 percent (distributed is typically rooftop or on-site energy for houses or commercial buildings);
* land-based wind power has dropped by 41 percent;
* Modeled battery costs have come down an astounding (73 percent); and
* LED light bulbs have dropped by 94 percent.[160]

Wind and solar are currently among the cheapest source of new power in many areas. And battery storage—once a pipe dream—has been improving in both performance and cost. In 2010, the price per kilowatt-hour for energy storage approached $1,000; in 2016, the price broke the $350–$300 per kilowatt-hour barrier, and analysts anticipate that with scale, manufacturing improvements will drive the price lower. In fact, some analysts believe Tesla's ability to build at scale, together with some key manufacturing improvements, has already reduced their costs to between $150 and $200 per kilowatt-hour.[161] And they've achieved a range of over three hundred miles on a charge. At these prices and performances, electric vehicles (EVs) outcompete comparable internal combustion cars in terms of net cost on a life-cycle basis.

What this means is that we can completely decarbonize our transportation system within the decade, if policies providing incentives to turn in internal combustion cars in exchange for EVs were put in place. Over a ten-year period, such a program could provide half the price of a new EV and replace all the registered cars currently on the road, at a cost of less than half the defense budget. That buys a lot of security—a hell of a lot more than wars of occupation costing twice as much.

Similarly, cheap storage opens up the opportunity to completely decarbonize our national grid. In fact, EVs and used EV batteries could take the issue of intermittency (the sun doesn't always shine and the wind doesn't always blow) and make it irrelevant at a very low cost. Here's how: EV cars can feed the grid when they are not in use, shaving peak demand. And used EV batteries—which have 85 percent of their useful life left when they can no longer meet the stringent requirements for powering a vehicle—are an ideal and low-cost way to provide grid storage. There's already a company purchasing used EV batteries for storage at costs of $100 per kilowatt-hour, and they are offering a ten-year guarantee on their repurposed batteries.[162]

The one bright spot in the area of climate change comes from a suit brought against the federal government by Our Children's Trust[163] which has a proceeding against the United States based on the "public trust doctrine." Writing in the *Huffington Post*, Peter Niall described the doctrine succinctly, in language that readers of this book will readily understand.[164] The public trust doctrine is:

> a long-standing legal concept designed to protect the common wealth, our natural resources, precedent and outside statutory law, for the benefit of future generations. In effect, government acts as a "trustee" for this trust, with the management responsibility and accountability similar to that of oversight of an estate or investment account, not just to preserve value but also to enhance and sustain value over time for the benefit of heirs and beneficiaries, in this case the public.

Neoliberals – Trying to Have It Both Ways: Which brings us to Hillary Clinton—who tried to use her commitment to protecting and helping kids as one of her claims to being a progressive—and why her neoliberal position on climate change not only poses a clear and present danger to them, but also goes a long way toward explaining why she lost.

But wait, you say: Ms. Clinton embraced renewable energy and acknowledged the science behind climate change, and she backed Obama's Clean Energy Plan.

Well, yes, she did. But it's one thing to back efficiency and renewables, quite another to do what needs to be done to avoid catastrophic climate change.

For example, as we noted, Ms. Clinton backed fracking and new exploration on federal lands, but the science dictates we leave more than 80 percent of the oil *we've already found* in the ground. How does permitting fracking and allowing exploration for new reserves square with leaving 80 percent of the already known reserves in the ground?

Answer: it doesn't.

The fact is, she vehemently fought inclusion of the kind of policies and positions needed to actually avoid cataclysmic climate change in the Democratic Party platform.[165]

As we said earlier, paying lip service to the use of renewable energy without adopting policies to immediately cut carbon emissions is tantamount to putting a spot of duct tape on a broken airplane wing, while you're flying at thirty thousand feet. It's like trying to jump the Grand Canyon in a series of ten-foot leaps. It's like jumping off a cliff and trying to knit a parachute on the way down. It's like...well, you get the idea. It's just plain stupid, and it's bad politics too. It's this kind of value-free, ethically challenged equivocating that makes the Democrats lose elections.

Climate change is an existential threat to civilization and to the ecological life-support systems we evolved in; it is far too dangerous to allow pay-to-play politicians to push half measures as solutions; and if we want better than a 66 percent chance of avoiding truly catastrophic climate change, then the clock starts NOW for starting immediate and comprehensive efforts to get off fossil fuels, as soon as is technologically feasible, not twenty or more years from now as the IPCC scenarios suggest, and as Clinton's policies would have done. It's this kind of split-the-difference politics that has caused the democrats to lose ground for going on fifty years now, and with climate change it goes well beyond politics—it is literally an existential threat.

As climate expert Kevin Anderson said, the reason we don't take the kind of actions actually needed to address climate change is because it would "upset the dominant paradigm" of economic growth at all costs. The irony here is that countries and states—such as Germany and Demark or California and the Regional Greenhouse Gas Initiative (RGGI) member states in the Northeast—which have implemented measures to mitigate climate change have actually exhibited faster economic growth than those countries and states which haven't.

Which begs a question: Just why would anyone except a crazed Republican denier oppose policies that get us off carbon?

The answer should be obvious—pay-to-play politicians cannot afford to anger potential corporate benefactors, and neoliberals put the market before reality. And so, the citizens are handed planet-wrecking platitudes and sophistry instead of solutions.

And Trump and many of his new cabinet members are motivated not only by campaign contributions—in fact they've been the ones making the contributions on behalf of the Oligarchy—but also by ideology. As plutocrats in their own right, they've managed to cut out the middleman by getting appointed to key government positions, and now they *directly* benefit from climate denial. They've gone from buying government to being government.

Now, some readers may question whether a long and somewhat detailed harangue on climate change has any relevance to a book that purports to explain what's wrong with American politics and how we can get back on track.

The answer is quite simple—the MMM, the MBB, and the EEM have all conspired to make it impossible for us to take the kind of actions we need to survive and prosper in the twenty-first century. And these became dominant forces in our political culture because both parties were taken over by the Coup. Whether we maintain a civil society and inhabit a sustainable world past the middle of this century is a political issue—indeed, they are the political and moral issues of our time. We have both the technology and the resources to get off carbon, now, and it would cost very little—far less than inaction would cost. And the science is settled. In fact, with each passing year it becomes more obvious that our models have understated both the magnitude of damages from climate change and the speed with which they occur.

With the science settled and the technology available and affordable, that leaves only politics as an impediment. Indeed, meeting the challenge of climate change is a *completely* political issue. The only reason we don't acknowledge that, the only reason we aren't grappling with this grim reality, is that the Oligarchy doesn't want us to.

There's a reason the Oligarchy has us chasing our tail on marginal threats while they invent fake threats and ignore the existential threat that is climate change. There's a reason most people don't understand—even today—the magnitude of the threat climate change poses and how little time we have to tackle it. And, finally, there's a reason neoliberal sophists like Clinton and the rest of the neoliberal Democrats are losing to the new know-nothing party. By trying to be all things to all people, they've ended up being nothing to everyone. By being Republican-lite, they lost to the real thing.

The Democrat's problem—and therefore the country's—is not simply a failure to address the needs of poor uneducated whites; it's not simply that Hispanics, blacks, and women didn't turn out—or support them when they did—in sufficient numbers; it's not even that Trump lied his way into office. Rather, it's that they abandoned the values that made them successful and made this country prosperous; it's that they refused to defend the role of government as an arbiter of justice, equity, and a needed constraint on corporate power—in fact, it's that they embraced the corporate Oligarchy and abandoned the people.

That's been the point of the book up to now—and climate change is exhibit A on what the stakes are for continuing the politics of the Plutocracy, and why it dooms Democrats to lose. Whereas once we won world wars, went to the moon, and proudly proclaimed government to be the champion of the people and the defender of freedom, now the government is a punch line or an all-purpose bogeyman, and the Magic Market is our savior.

But to paraphrase the immortal words from *Ghostbusters*, when the life-sustaining climate we depend upon to survive is haunted by fossil-fueled corporatists (or when the Republic is threatened by income inequality, or loss of freedom, etc., etc., etc.), "Who ya gonna call?"

The Republicans have an answer, even if it's wrong. Democrats? Not so much. A pocket full of mumbles, at best.

And that, ladies and gentlemen, is why we have a President Trump.

PART FOUR: Putting America Back on Track

● ● ●

Stand for something or you will fall for anything. Today's mighty oak is yesterday's nut that held its ground.

ROSA PARKS

We stand now where two roads diverge. But unlike the roads in Robert Frost's familiar poem, they are not equally fair. The road we have long been traveling is deceptively easy, a smooth superhighway on which we progress with great speed, but at its end lies disaster. The other fork of the road—the one less traveled by—offers our last, our only chance to reach a destination that assures the preservation of the earth.

RACHEL CARSON

Switchman's sleeping, train hundred and two is on the wrong track and headed for you.

JERRY GARCIA; GRATEFUL DEAD

CHAPTER 16

A Revolution Is Coming

● ● ●

A revolution is coming—a revolution which will be peaceful if we are wise enough; compassionate if we care enough; successful if we are fortunate enough—but a revolution...is coming whether we will it or not. We can affect its character; we cannot alter its inevitability.

ROBERT KENNEDY

ON APRIL 30, 2015, A relatively unknown democratic socialist from Vermont announced in an e-mail to potential supporters that he was running for president. His name was Bernie Sanders. At seventy-three years old, with disheveled hair, a wrinkled suit, and a Brooklyn accent, without the support of corporations, the rich, or the party, he had only three things going for him: the truth, the courage to tell it; and the fact that a majority of voters who were hungry to hear it.

The political establishment's reaction ranged from bemusement to outright hostility, but they all agreed on one thing: he had no chance of winning.[166] A democratic *socialist*, for God's sake? A *Jew?* From the rural state of *Vermont?* What could he be thinking?

By the time the nomination was gifted to the Democratic establishment's preordained candidate, Sanders had won twenty-three primaries, garnered more than thirteen million votes, and raised more than $207 million, nearly all of it from small donors. And as we saw in chapter 8, absent the Democratic Party's establishment apparatchik and the EEM, Sanders could well have won the nomination, and if he'd won the nomination, polls consistently show he would have walked away with the election. And no, he was not vulnerable to charges of socialism etc. He'd weathered that storm already, and polls also show most voters don't respond to the old commie bating tactics of the right.

In many ways, Sanders's success built on the Occupy Movement, which had raised the issue of income inequality five years before. But the revolution he called for was rooted in a struggle that is older than our nation. To quote Thomas Jefferson,

> I hope we shall crush…in its birth the aristocracy of our moneyed corporations, which dare already to challenge our government to a trial of strength and bid defiance to the laws of our country.

Sanders was the first politician to talk openly about the Oligarchy and the "rigged" system, and it resonated across a broad spectrum of society. It took the combined forces of the Democrat's arcane nominating system (which often excluded independents and new registrants, both of whom overwhelmingly supported Sanders), the EEM, and the so-called civil institutions to defeat him.

One of the most remarkable things about the Sanders's campaign was how it electrified the young, reinvigorated progressives, and forced Hillary Clinton to feint to the left, abandoning her cynically slick strategy of winning the nomination solely on the basis of being "the inevitable candidate," saying nothing substantive about anything so she could pretend to be everything to everyone, without offending her corporate benefactors so she could continue to collect and cache obscene amounts of corporate cash for her campaign.[167]

But if history has a tide, then Sanders caught an epic and—epochal—wave and nearly rode it to victory. In fact, over the next few years the movement he mobilized might just persist and win—but only if we have the wit and wisdom to build upon it—a reality that strikes fear into the stony hearts of the few establishment types who understand this.

Because, make no mistake, Sanders launched a missile at the soul of the Oligarch's Coup that has taken over the United States.

His campaign was centered on a revolutionary concept—he sought nothing less than to wrest the political power from the Oligarchy and return it to the people.

What he called for was a political revolution. Critics have ridiculed the notion of a "revolution," calling it naive, impractical, unrealistic, or—in Paul Krugman's terms—"happy dreams." Yet despite the press's blackout on all things Sanders and the establishment's attempt to marginalize both him and the movement he inspired, he was gaining momentum until the confederacy of dunces representing the elitists and corporatists conspired to defeat him.

Meanwhile, another outsider, Donald Trump, crashed the Republican Party's attempt to coronate JEB!, their presumptive nominee. Whereas Sanders's revolution was rooted in progressive values, such as getting money out of politics; restoring economic equity and social justice to our society; taking climate change seriously; preserving Social Security, and establishing Medicare for all...Trump's bid was regressive and depended upon appealing to our baser instincts.

Trump—Hypocrisy Unbound: Although Trump got elected by posing as a populist and an outsider, at the end of the day, he's a corporatist through and through, and his playbook comes straight out of the Oligarch's Coup as outlined by Powell. Trump differs from the mainstream Republican Party only in his position on trade policy, but given his political team, and the short shelf life of his various promises, it would be no surprise to see that change.

Meanwhile, his transition team is a collection of hard right ideologues, fat cats, plutocrats, and privatizers that look more like something a Republican on steroids might support than what a populist reformer would assemble. Of the seventy-five people named to his transition team, 70 percent were in the pockets of corporations and hard right foundations.[168] And though he excoriated Goldman Sachs throughout his campaign, once again, they have an outsized role in government, with seven current or former Goldman Sachs senior officers serving in his cabinet or in senior positions, including his proposed treasury secretary and his chief economic advisor.

Beyond that, his cabinet appointments are a collection of rich corporate foxes assigned to guard the chicken coop, together with ultraconservative government-hating ideologues tapped with governing. Just seven of his appointments are worth more than $11 billion.[169] And remember the DeVos foundation from chapter 2, "Funding the Coup"? Well, Betsy DeVos, one of the Coup's big funders, is in charge of the Department of Education. She's on record as wanting to make our educational system more "Christian," and she wants to privatize the whole shebang. Oh, and by the way, her family is worth $5 billion.

With Exxon CEO Rex Tillerson taking the reins of the State Department, the plutocrats are getting a lock on governance.

But nowhere are Trump's antipopulist, pro-Oligarchy policies more evident than in his treatment of EPA. And as we saw in chapters 15 and 16, nowhere are the stakes higher. Once again, the thumbprint of the Coup is all over Trump's hypocrisy. Remember the Competitive Enterprise Institute— one of the Coup's think tanks charged with eliminating real thinking? Well, their chief climate denier, Myron Ebell, head of their "Center for Energy and the Environment" (an entity whose track record would suggest it would be more accurately called the "Center for Fossil Fuel Energy and against the Environment) was selected to lead Trump's EPA transition team.

Talk about antipopulist—The Competitive Enterprise Institute gets its funding from the Olin Foundation, the Koch Family Foundations, several foundations funded by the Scaife family, and the Lynde and Harry Bradley Foundation, as well as funding from corporations including tobacco and oil companies. If that list sounds familiar, it's because we met them in chapter 2, and they are charter funders of the Oligarch's Coup.

Not surprisingly, Myron Ebell recommended another climate denier and staunch supporter of the fossil fuel industry—Scott Pruitt—to head EPA, and, of course, Trump promptly selected him as his nominee. Pruitt has sued EPA over regulations designed to mitigate water and air pollution, and he's on record as wanting to roll back the United States' involvement in the Paris Agreement. Pruitt was confirmed on February 17, 2017 despite the fact that a judge had ordered the release of twenty-five hundred e-mails that had been withheld from the Senate the day before. They contained communications between Pruitt and fossil fuel interests that were at best inappropriate, at worst illegal. But hey, why wait and see before confirming him? Just our Earth we're dealing with here. No biggie.

Trump's promise to "drain the swamp" in Washington is risible— in fact, his cabinet is composed of men and women who could personally profit from gutting government authorities and budgets. Talk about arsonists posing as firemen – these guys are crazed pyromanias wearing a fire hat and sporting a badge while they carry flamethrowers.

His promise to get lobbyists off the team was in the same vein as his politically clever confrontation with Carrier over outsourcing jobs: a highly visible, but completely symbolic stand designed to give the appearance of populism, without the costs of actually being a populist. It's noteworthy that when Pence kicked three former lobbyists off the transition team, they were replaced by three *former* lobbyists who had represented the same interests as the displaced lobbyists had. But people were desperate for a populist, so they suspended disbelief and voted for him. The Democrats made it easy by running a neoliberal.

Trump, it turns out, uses the same distract, deceive, and blame tactics the Republican Party has been using for decades and—with the exception of his rhetoric on trade—he is essentially mirroring their trickle-down, deregulatory chicanery in terms of fiscal and social welfare policies. When it comes to national security, his policies are like a caricature of the Republican's conventional playbook—a macho, power-obsessed, knee-jerk militarism that looks more like WrestleMania than a coherent strategy for seeking a peaceful world. Except, of course, for his strange attachment to fellow macho man Putin. But even that dissolved in the vapors of political expediency. And speaking of WrestleMania, Linda McMahon, the former CEO of World Wrestling Entertainment, was his pick to head the Small Business Administration. Figures.

The reason this plutocrats' plutocrat was able to pass himself off as a populist is that the neoliberal Democrats and mainstream Republicans alike ceded the populist ground to him. With Sanders out and Hillary Clinton unwilling to confront the Oligarchy—even on a symbolic level— Trump could walk away with the rust belt and the electoral votes that enabled him to win.

Interestingly, Sanders, the only candidate who actually took on special interests and the Oligarchy, would have trounced Trump in the election by historic margins.[170]

If progressives are smart, Trump's victory can be a wake-up call—no more false prophets, no more neoliberal posers, no more identity politics. We need to vote on values and mobilize an electorate hungry to do so. But sadly, it looks like the DNC is doing its best to continue with the DLC/neoliberal catastrophe.[171] Perez, in his tour with Sanders, has resolutely tried to preserve the neoliberal, corporatist wing of the Democratic Party.

The sound bite from the punditocracy is that this election was about the angry white males, not a cry for progressive politics, and that they only lost because Comey and Putin intervened, but they are wrong. Whites and white males were a factor, but as we've seen, the sickness infecting our body politic goes much deeper, and the cure must strike at the heart of the two great myths that have animated political debate for decades, undermining our democracy in the process.

The 2016 elections were the bow wave of change, the harbinger of a revolution to come. This time, voters were given a choice between a faux progressive elitist and a man who at least pretended to represent the people, while simultaneously appealing to hate, fear, greed, and ignorance. If the United States is to avoid the siren song of fascism, we will have to give people a real choice—one that explicitly seeks to overturn the Oligarch's Coup and restore power to the people.

The bottom line is this: the genie is out of the bottle. The revolution may not be televised, but it will not be denied. Indeed, we are in its midst now. The only question is, how it will end.

Martin Luther King said, "The arc of history bends toward justice."

But Fredrick Douglass said,

Those who profess to favor freedom and yet deprecate agitation are men who want crops without plowing up the ground; they want rain without thunder and lightning. They want the ocean without the awful roar of its many waters. This struggle may be a moral one, or it may be a physical one, and it may be both moral and physical, but it must be a struggle. Power concedes nothing without a demand. It never did and it never will.

It is the thesis of this book that sometimes history's arc needs a little help if it is to continue its journey toward justice, and that now is such a time. In the coming years, we the people must generate some thunder and lightning, and we must take history's arc in hand and bend it ourselves, because the alternative is continuing the march toward injustice, inequity, and fascism we are on now.

CHAPTER 17

Mounting the Resistance—
Administering Political First Aid

● ● ●

It is easier to resist at the beginning than at the end.

Leonardo Da Vinci

It's important to remember that the election of Donald Trump is a symptom of a deeper disease. But it is just as important to recognize the grave threat this symptom poses to our freedom and our future survival.

While we must ultimately attack the root causes of the Coup that made Trump's victory possible, we must also mobilize in the short term to stop the grave damage he is—even now—doing to our country and the world.

As we noted in chapter 3, the first thing the Oligarchy did was to take over the press. We see in the early days of the Trump Administration, the tactics of the despot—discrediting the news, creating "alternative truths," and bypassing the conventional media. To accomplish the latter, despots in times gone by created official news sources such as Pravda, which carried propaganda and engaged in distraction, deception, and distortion. In keeping with his small-bore ideas, Trump uses Twitter.

The fact that much of the media is currently attempting to hold Trump accountable for his lies is a sign of how far from the mainstream he is. Even the Oligopolies fear a reaction from the people from his obvious overreach, not to mention the real-world consequences. Their preferred candidates—JEB! or Hillary—could fly under the radar, while carrying corporate water. Trump cannot.

Yet we've watched Republicans—who were nearly united in their opposition to him—fall meekly into line and kiss his imperial ring. And we must be mindful of the press's tendency to function as mute stenographers, charged with generating revenue and devoid of any commitment to truth, accuracy, context, or ethics.

Remember, the public editor of the nation's flagship newspaper the *New York Times*, actually asked readers if it was a reporter's responsibility to tell the truth.[172] It's this kind of crap that has discredited conventional news sources to people across the political spectrum, and it means we can't trust the EEM to function as watchdogs.

And in just his first 100 days, the press repeatedly reported on the moments that Trump became "presidential."[173] All it takes, apparently is to read a speech without lunatic ad libs, and to launch a few Tomahawk missiles. The only reason the press isn't giving him the same he-said/she-said treatment they gave Bush is that he continues to send out a steady stream of self-indulgent, self-destructive, and self-incriminating tweets with all the self-restraint of a caffeinated six-year old. But you can almost feel the sickening slide towards Trump as the new "normal."

So, before we attempt major surgery on our nation's diseased body politic, we must administer first aid to head off the life-threatening symptom that is Donald Trump.

Short-term Actions Needed to Save the World: In the short term, we will have to take a page from the Tea Party and swarm our representatives at every possible opportunity, pressing for progressive positions on everything from health care to climate. At every town hall meeting, before every legislative vote, and, in between, there must be a steady drumbeat of activists demanding social justice and a responsible and responsive government. Trump did, after all, lose the popular vote—even with a neoliberal sophist running, so we're in a better position to pull this off than the Tea Party was.

This book won't attempt to outline all the short-term *political actions* required to stop the Trump regime from laying waste our social and ecological commons. There are any number of books and websites devoted to this. One of the most valuable recent additions to this body of work, Indivisible,[174] can be found on line. Written by former congressional staffers, it succinctly lays out some of the best techniques for getting your member of Congress to listen to you and, more importantly, to respond on issues. The same tactics can and should be applied to your state representative, your local mayor, and your local assembly representative.

Sanders himself lays out a good set of strategies in his latest book, <u>*Our Revolution*</u>.

One area that most guides for political action do not address is getting the press to report Trump's policies accurately. We must move the media from reporting on politics as a food fight and to drop "balance" as the journalistic polestar and adopt a policy of using facts to pursue truth, accuracy, and accountability. To do this, we will also have to aggressively work the press.

And while the press is doing a credible job covering Trump as of this writing, we can't count on that to continue as Trump becomes the new normal. Moreover, it's one thing to report on Trump's cavalcade of lies and ineptitude, quite another to cover progressive policies, politicians, and candidates. Remember the Bernie Blackout and the complete failure of the press to cover the Congressional Progressive Caucus's (CPC) popular budget proposals? As Vox put it, "Every year the Congressional Progressive Caucus releases a budget, and every year it gets roundly ignored."

It will be up to us—we the people—to ensure that progressive policies and politicians get covered and covered fairly, and to do that, we will have to actively "work the refs" as Eric Alterman put it.

Too often in the past, the press has ignored reasonable and popular progressive proposals while providing wall-to-wall coverage to counterfactual right-wing rants disguised as legislation.

Indeed, when you contrast the Republican budget proposals with the CPC's budgets, it becomes obvious just how badly the press is doing. This complete failure by the press has become an annual event. Each year,

Paul Ryan presents a budget that guts social programs benefiting poor and middle-class Americans, gives the ultrarich exorbitant tax cuts, all while exploding the deficit, and it is hailed as "serious" by the cognoscenti. Meanwhile, the CPC puts together a budget that preserves social programs and balances the budget far sooner than Ryan's, all while using strategies that are popular with the majority of Americans.

Guess which one gets widespread coverage and praise from the media? Hint: not the one developed by the CPC.

This little tableau of hypocrisy and censorship goes on year after year.

You can go back to 2011, when Ryan's proposed 2012 budget—issued as a fiscally responsible way to cut the deficit—actually failed to balance the budget until the 2063 and ran up an incredible $62 trillion in additional debt in the meantime. It was widely covered—and covered favorably—by the press, despite the fact that it was an exercise in self-contradiction.[175] Where did all Ryan's debt come from? Tax cuts for the rich, of course. The EEM felt no need to mention this, of course.

At the same time, the People's Budget—issued by the CPC—eliminated the deficit by 2021, while protecting Medicare, Medicaid, Social Security, and a variety of other social programs, using policies that the majority of Americans favored. Yet it was virtually ignored by the press and both parties.

And this kind of selective reporting by the EEM is not restricted to budgets. Obamacare—admittedly a less-than-ideal solution to the healthcare crisis than, say, a single-payer approach built on Medicare might have been—was vilified by the Tea Partiers with lies, distortions, and innuendos, and the press merely reported on the food fight, rarely attempting to set the record straight. Remember death panels?

But, hey, it's not the press's job to be "truth vigilantes" right?

How bad was their coverage of the health-care debate? Well, as the Bill was being considered, in many cases, the EEM would note that it was unpopular in polls, without also noting that there were more people saying it didn't go far enough than there were saying it went too far, leaving the impression that the Tea Partiers' nihilistic viewpoints were in the majority. In fact, when people were asked if they favored a universal-health-care plan, 58 percent of Americans favored it, and only 37 percent opposed it. The point is, the press largely reported a bipolar perspective in which all those who opposed Obamacare (or do so now) were in the camp of the Tea Partiers.

In fact, their position comprised a small minority of the public's position, then and now.[176] The largest faction of those opposing Obamacare wanted *greater* government control of our health-care system, not less. If you were to rank the positions of citizens at the time Obamacare was initially being debated, the single biggest block would have been those wanting more government involvement in health care, followed by those who felt Obamacare struck the right balance, followed by those who objected to it. But you'd never have figured that out from the press coverage. And because their distorted reporting gave conservatives such an expanded voice, the shape of public opinion shifted as the radical right got to brand Obamacare. In truth, the silence of the Obama administration and the cowardice and complicity of the neoliberal Democrats made it easier than it should have been to hijack the press.

And now that Republicans have been charged with governing instead of taking gratuitous potshots at government, they've had to unveil their health care alternative, and Obamacare has suddenly become popular with a majority of Americans. If progressives were able to penetrate the media blackout on single payer, you'd see much the same result. The thing pundits call too left-wing would be revealed as exactly what the people want.

This kind of misinformation—aided and abetted by the EEM—is a big reason why the conservative/neoliberal perspective frequently drowns out progressive views. And why Trump won. As Paul Krugman pointed out in his January 23, 2017, column many Trump voters went to the polls accepting all manner of counterfactual lies:

Two-thirds of them believe, falsely, that the unemployment rate rose under Obama. (Three-quarters believe George Soros is paying people to protest Mr. Trump.) Only 17 percent of self-identified Republicans are aware that the number of uninsured is at a historic low.

This list could go on and on. Few know that the rate of increase in medical costs has slowed under Obamacare. Most Americans believe crime is on the rise, even though there's been a two-decade drop in all crimes, according to government statistics (with a very slight blip in violent crime within the last year).

By February, social media and the press were aflame with stories about "fake news." But in fact, as this book has documented, fake news has been an issue for decades now.

If this kind of "he-said, she-said" coverage continues under Trump, we're in deep trouble. The only thing standing between fascism and freedom at the moment is the truth and the media's willingness to tell it. But don't hold your breath.

There is no hope for a democracy when the media doesn't inform. But as we've seen, when the media is a wholly owned subsidiary of the Oligarchy, the news is shaped to fit the Coup's purposes. Whether it happens from corporations censoring the news, or from fear that actually taking a stand will alienate some part of their audiences and reduce their revenues, or because politics as a food fight attracts a wider audience and feeds their coffers, or because the media is composed of the liberal elites it's supposed to cover, or simply because of a deep ideological bias, when the EEM ignores its First Amendment responsibilities, we the people, need to storm their headquarters, flood them with complaints, cut off our subscriptions, and boycott their advertisers.

In the age of the Internet and social media, social activism can have two important new components. It can perform the more traditional actions of connecting the 99 percent who've been left out and left without a voice far more efficiently than we've been able to do in the past. This aspect of the so-called Fifth Estate can make the kind of political activism advocated in *Indivisible* more effective, and it can help address the EEM's failures. We saw that happen in Occupy Wall Street, in the Sanders's campaign, and in the phenomenal response to the Million Woman March—the largest protest event in the history of the world. And yes, Trump used the Fifth Estate to ride to victory.

Beyond Political Action—Harnessing the Market to Effect Change: The Internet and social media can also allow us to collectively exercise our market power. Each purchase—and each decision not to purchase—is in effect a vote. If we seek to make the media more responsible and responsive to…well…reality, we now have recourse, when they fail to do so. By organizing on the web, we can stop buying their stuff, collectively stop watching their propaganda, cancel subscriptions to those who propagate myths or repeat Trump's lies without holding him accountable; we can collectively turn the dial and let them know we're doing it. If that doesn't work we can arrange boycotts of their major advertisers. If Exxon wants to fund global warming denial, we can stop buying Exxon goods and services; If NPR wants to let the Koch Brothers determine climate coverage, we can stop contributing. (In all fairness, on February 1, 2017, NOVA had a program on batteries that emphasized the need to stop global warming. Nice to see, but too little, too late).

Remember, Trump only got less than 27 percent of the voting age people to back him. These were the passionately ignorant and the desperately disaffected. If there was ever any doubt that they were duped, Trump should be dispelling it now with his corporate cabinet. That leaves 73 percent of the eligible voters as potential participants in boycotts, and it has the potential to give voice to those too young to vote—and the overwhelming majority of them oppose Trump and his policies.

We are the marketplace, and we decide who wins and who loses in the market by where we park our money, what we invest in, what we choose to buy and who we choose to buy it from.

Think about it. We purchase about $100 billion worth of stuff a day[177], not including what we spend on our homes, cars, and normal household bills. We hold about $25 trillion[178] in retirement funds—the single biggest source of money the big banks, Wall Street, fat cats, and assorted other speculators use to play their very own version of hi-risk Texas Hold'em.

This, in a market economy, is power. Raw, naked power. All we need to do is to organize so that we can exercise it.

Here again, conservatives understand this. For example, if you Google "Boycott conservative advertisers" what you'll get is a list of sites telling you how to boycott *liberal* advertisers.

Yes, there have been numerous attempts to organize progressives into a coherent political and economic power in the past, but they have not met with much success. Yet if you stood on the streets with the more than four million others who marched on January 21, you know the time is nigh; you know the shape of the political landscape and the range of the politically possible can be changed—the sleeping giant of "we the people" has been awakened. Trump's election has, ironically, created new opportunities for the progressive majority to take back the country.

But this window can close, just as quickly as it opened. The siren song of consumerism can highjack our good intentions, the bread and circus Kardashian nonevents, lapel pin bullshit, and serial lying by Trump can still distract and derail us. Occupy may have planted a seed, but it is up to us to nurture it and bring it to maturity.

There are a number of organizations that can serve to help us to consolidate and exercise both our political and economic power and bring accountability to our political debate and our media coverage of it Our Revolution, women's march, Sleeping Giants, Moveon, or any number of other sites can offer the frame work for accomplishing this, although it is critical that the sites we invest in be independent from the neoliberal/ DLC branch of the Democratic Party and frankly the elites who represent it, including Secretary Clinton, Chuck Shumer, or any of the other status quo–chosen ones who have been contributing to the four-decade slide of the Democratic Party.

Building the electronic framework is easy. The message and mission discipline needed for it to transform the Democratic Party—or to create a third one if it refuses to be reformed—is the hard part. It is also critical that the organization(s) focus on common and shared values, not identity politics.

For this reason, my own preference is to build on the Our Revolution site, although it, too, would need some adjustments if it were to be effective and achieve buy-in. Chief among them would be to build in greater transparency, with more accountability, and a greater sense of agency on the part of those who participated. The details of how to accomplish this are laid out in an article I wrote on the topic.[179]

And of course, it's likely that more than one group can and should emerge as leaders and focal points for the revolution. But if we are to be successful, we will have to have the same unity of purpose as the Oligarch's Coup did.

Once we've mobilized and organized to address the acute problems posed by a Trump presidency, we must turn our attention to tackling the MMM and the MBB and restoring the Enlightenment culture that underpins our democratic republic. If we don't also address these, the future will belong to Trump-like fascists and neoliberal tools of the Oligarchy.

CHAPTER 18

Catch-22—Can't Change the Laws without Changing the Culture; Can't Change the Culture without Changing the Laws

● ● ●

"That's some catch, that Catch 22," [Yossarian] said.
"It's the best there is," Doc Daneeka agreed.

JOSEPH HELLER, *CATCH-22*

ON THE FACE OF IT, overturning the Oligarchs' Coup should be easy. All it involves is passing a few pieces of legislation that enjoys popular support and returning to the Enlightenment principles that had been the basis for prosperity, freedom, and a civil society. Seems hard to argue with that.

But the current crop of legislators and appointees is dominated by antiscience, anti-Enlightenment ignoramuses who are actually members in good standing of the Oligarchy and most of the rest are slaves to it, so they are about as likely to pass such legislation as Trump is to read a book.

Hopefully, the short-term actions and tactics outlined in chapter 17 will force enough of the legislators from their servitude to the Oligarchy not only to head off the worst of what Trump can do, but also to begin to lay the legislative groundwork for the changes we need to recapture our country.

But while the changes needed are relatively straightforward and simple, they will not be easy. The reason for this is stated in the title to this chapter—we have a version of a catch-22 going on here. We need to change the culture to change the laws, and we need to change the laws to change the culture.

Here again, we the people can lead the process. As a starting point, we should start by broadly sharing draft legislation and constitutional amendments addressing

* restoring FCC rules governing the media;
* limiting corporate personhood; and
* completely revamping our election process, to eliminate gerrymandering, get money out of the process and limit campaign contributions in size and source, and, ideally, shorten the length of campaigns.

There are already drafts of legislation addressing Citizens United and restoration of FCC powers over the media.[180] The point of providing specific language accomplishing this is to have something we can circulate widely for the purposes of getting petitions of support for them—something that should be relatively easy, since each of these has broad support from the people.

For example, a Rasmussen poll found that 47 percent of Americans favored rules requiring broadcasters to provide equal time for conservative and liberal perspectives, while only 39 percent opposed it. That's consistent with other polling on the topic. And this level of backing comes without any concerted effort designed to mobilize support for restoring fairness and accuracy in the media. One can think of this as fertile ground awaiting the seeds of sanity.

One of the few areas that conservatives and liberals agree upon is that we need stop giving corporations the rights of citizens. In poll after poll, large majorities—typically between 70 percent and 80 percent of Americans—favor overturning Citizens United and stopping corporate involvement in elections. Period. And the overwhelming majority of people would also like to limit corporate lobbying in Congress.

In a *New York Times*/CBS News poll on the role of money in politics,[181] 84 percent of Americans thought money had too much influence on campaigns, while only 10 percent thought it was about right.

With regard to revamping our campaign system, the same *Times*/CBS poll found that 85 percent of Americans thought the way we fund elections needed fundamental changes (39 percent) or that it needed to be completely rebuilt (46 percent).

With this kind of support from the people, a democracy should have no problem making the changes the people want—but of course, we don't live in a democracy any longer.

Bottom line: the conservatives and their enablers—the DLC, neoliberal Democrats--who dominate Congress, the EEM, and the civil institutions that should hold corporations accountable have simply not raised any of these issues in a public way. Indeed, when it comes to the FCC, the Democrats were responsible for eviscerating it and turning media over to the Oligarchy.

But with specific legislative language, and the aroused populace, it will now be possible to seize the debate. Too much of what we plan is focused on discrediting Trump—but you can't beat something with nothing. And these would give us something. Using social media and specific legislative proposals allows us to pursue the political and the cultural debate simultaneously.

We will have to push these initiatives in a way that makes them fit into more broadly articulated values frame—specifically, taking power from the moneyed interests and restoring it to the people.

But to succeed, we will have to pursue cultural change simultaneously. As we've seen, within the last four decades, our culture has moved *from* one rooted in the Enlightenment principles that formed the basis of our government, that have been the source of our prosperity, and the wellspring of the advancements that have made civilization possible, *to* one rooted in myth, religiosity, and magical thinking or, in the case of Trump, no sign of any thinking whatsoever. Just a bubbling cauldron of emotion that periodically erupts in spontaneous twitters with little context and less thought, infecting the national discourse with a shallow, vapid stream of intellectual sludge, which the press promptly reports as if it were serious policy making.

As we saw in chapters 7 and 10, absent a real choice, and given scapegoats and bogeymen to blame, people vote on broad—frequently fabricated—frames rather than on issues that directly affect them. And with the success of the Oligarch's Coup, only one frame is being presented. As long as conservatives and neoliberals can rely on distraction, division, and the broadly shared perspectives that the market is our savior and the government our enemy—or at least inept and hapless—people will be prone to voting for candidates who favor small (as in weak) government, few regulations, austerity budgets, and market über-alles policies, rather than for the candidates who want to regulate corporate excesses, rebuild a functioning government, and restore competition that harnesses the market's ability to stimulate innovation.

And with more and more people opting out of participating in the two-party plutocracy, an ever-increasing proportion of the remaining voters are made up of those who operate on misinformation and who reject the Enlightenment principles that used to frame our culture. These people will continue to embrace empty rhetorical frames and, as a result, vote against their interests. Particularly if they are not offered real choices on the issues that matter most to them, while being offered scapegoats for the blame that should fall on the Oligarchy.

And they aren't being offered real choices in most cases.

The bottom line is, we have a de facto political monoculture in which any real agents of change are weeded out, and people's choices are between Tweedledee and Tweedledum. In the end, the thing the press and the assorted wise men and women have been missing is that neoliberalism and modern conservatism are more alike than they are different. Both celebrate relatively unconstrained free markets, deregulation, small government, a measure of austerity, free trade, and capital enhancing policies in general—at the expense of labor and working-class people.

As long as people aren't offered real choices, they won't have power. We see this in the low turnouts among voters and in the flight from party affiliation. This bodes ill for progressives. It's long been known that conservatives do best when turnout is low.

As Cornell West put it in a recent op-ed in *The Guardian,*

> In short, the abysmal failure of the Democratic party to speak to the arrested mobility and escalating poverty of working people unleashed a hate-filled populism and protectionism that threaten to tear apart the fragile fiber of what is left of US democracy[182].

Or, in the words of W. B. Yeats, from his poem *The Second Coming*, "The best lack all conviction, while the worst are filled with a passionate intensity." As long as this is the case, enacting even simple, common-sense laws will be difficult.

So the attempt to change the culture currently underpinning our political worldview will require a sustained and simultaneous commitment to both a long-term effort to create and nurture a progressive infrastructure with the scale and discipline that the Oligarchy practiced for its Coup and a parallel effort to pass legislative fixes that undo the takeover of our press and the electoral system and a short-term effort to stop the excesses of Trump and his cronies.

The medium-term effort of passing legislation restoring democracy can be a part of the short-term activism. By presenting popular bills that roll back corporate money, influence, and intervention in governance, progressive Democrats can create a debate that has been absent from our body politic since Reagan.

At the moment, progressive groups are receiving record contributions, but the progressive landscape is fragmented and focused on single issues or identity politics. Until they coalesce around long-term objectives designed to rebut the myths and restore a culture of trust, tolerance, and inclusion, the money will not make the difference we need to make.

So yes, the elements of the Countercoup are easy, but the implementation is not simple.

CHAPTER 19

A Blueprint for a Cultural Revolution

●　●　●

*Strength lies in organization, in careful long-range planning
and implementation, in consistency of action over an
indefinite period of years, in the scale of financing available
only through joint effort, and in the political power available
only through united action and national organizations.*

FROM THE POWELL MEMO

THE PEOPLE'S COUNTERCOUP MUST TAKE a page from the Oligarchy and invest in creating passionate advocates in foundations, academia, and think tanks on the importance of an effective government and the perils of a market über-alles society, and they need to develop the same skills at linking the findings of these institutions to the media.

In fact, step one for the progressives should be to make sure that Trump voters understand he didn't drain the swamp; he filled it higher and deeper with a rogue's gallery of Oligarchs, ideologues, and corporatists, many of whom have been opposing policies designed to help the average American for decades. If the middle-class and working-class folks understood just how much Trump has double crossed them, they would be marching on the White House with torches, pitch forks, and sharpened sticks demanding Trump's scalp—or his hair piece.

But there's no one to mount the Countercoup, at the moment. Yes, the press is full of daily outrage over the insult du jour, and Democrats are all but busting their jugulars over Trump's initial actions. As we noted in chapter 17, even the press is taking Trump on. But the larger story of how his appointments and policies fall into the playbook of the Oligarch's Coup is being left untold. And unless we engage people in this broader debate, we run the risk of more Trumps in the future or, at best, more neoliberal Democrats, and both are beholden to the Oligarchy.

Most of the so-called liberal foundations and think tanks in existence at the moment represent the neoliberal consensus—that is, they buy into the idea that the private sector should have the primary role in managing and structuring the economy, and they generally favor privatization, deregulation, small government for its own sake, and free trade. This is not only electoral suicide, its presumptions about outcomes are counterfactual, as we saw in chapters 4 and 5. The prescription not only doesn't cure, it makes us sick.

Hell, even the conservatives' favorite bête noire, George Soros, backed neoliberal Hillary Clinton, rather than a real progressive populist like Sanders.

As we saw in chapter 6, the watchdogs who used to keep civil society civil, have also been taken over by the elites, Oligarchs, and the neoliberals.

Even the few organizations that actually advocate progressive policies tend to invest in one-off projects and crisis response, rather than in sustained, strategic initiatives. As Reclaim Democracy put it:

> One of our great frustrations is that foundations and funders who prefer a democratic republic to corporate domination have failed to learn from the success of these corporate institutions. They decline to invest in long-term education and culture-shifting that we and a small number of allied organizations work to achieve. Instead, they overwhelmingly focus on damage control and short-term goals. This approach stands no chance of yielding the

systemic change needed to reverse the trend of growing corporate dominance.

The few truly progressive organizations operating today are frequently single issue or single constituency, and that diminishes their impact on society at large and on the culture the Oligarchy has bequeathed us. One of the great challenges for progressives will be figuring out how to address specific and valid grievances of minorities and issue-oriented groups without devolving into identity or single-issue politics, which the Oligarchy has skillfully used to divide and conquer.

Predictably, the Democratic Party is focusing on tactics designed to slow down Trump's assault on government and his consolidation of power. And to be sure, they need to organize into an effective opposition party. Trump's collection of Oligarchs, defense hawks, climate deniers, and oilmen are a clear and present danger to the world, the nation, and—ironically—particularly the people who voted for him.

But progressives need a long game. And we can't be merely against Trump. If we don't stand *for* something more than identity politics, tactics, and power, the Democratic Party will become a footnote in history's dustbin. Progressives need the equivalent of their own Powell memo—a long-term, strategic blueprint for taking back our country that allows us to either take over the Democratic Party or lay the groundwork for creating a new one.

"Taking Back Our Country": Consider that phrase for a moment. It was the battle cry for the Tea Party, for Trump supporters, and it is the phrase rolling off the tongues of elitist neoliberal Democrats and true progressives now. The reason it resonates across the ideological spectrum is that there is an inherent truth in it. As we saw in Part One, this country no longer belongs to the people.

The election in 2016 was between politicians with a fascist bent and those from the neoliberal elitist establishment, but both represented the Oligarchy. The more authoritarian group won because they were more effective at passing themselves off as populists.

Either one would lose to real progressive populists in a fair fight, as polling just before the election clearly showed.[183] But as we've seen, there's nothing fair about the political system as it stands now, and the deck is stacked against anyone who calls out the rigged system.

The desire—and need—for a people's champion, without the presence of a progressive populist alternative, explains the rise of right-wing faux populists across the world.

As Oxfam pointed out, globally, just eight people have as much wealth as the least wealthy half of the world's population.[184] The economic disenfranchisement of the masses is a global phenomenon, as is the concentration of political power that inevitably flows from such inequality. And the embrace of neoliberalism across the world means there has been no effective progressive alternatives to counter the hard right's attempt to capitalize on people's justifiable anger. When people are hungry, economically threatened, and feeling insecure, they are not likely to be tolerant, welcoming of strangers, or accepting of those who are different. They become tribal, and they hunker down with their tribe.

Thus, we see the rise of right-wing faux populists not only here in the United States, but in Britain with Brexit, in Italy with the Five Star Party, as well as in Austria, Australia, France, Sweden, and the other Scandinavian countries.

But as we saw in the previous chapter, we need to operate in the strategic and tactical theatre simultaneously, to put it in military terms. We need to change culture and law at the same time.

There are two impediments to accomplishing this. First, there is the notion that corporations have the rights of citizens. We address this in chapter 20. The next is that government, at the moment, has been rendered ineffective by Republican sabotage, so we must have a plan to restore its effectiveness before we take on the MBB. A method for accomplishing this is outlined in chapter 21.

CHAPTER 20

If It's Called Free Speech, Why Does It Cost So Much?

● ● ●

I believe there are more instances of the abridgment of the
freedom of the people by gradual and silent encroachments of
those in power than by violent and sudden usurpations.

JAMES MADISON

GILDED MEGAPHONES DROWNING OUT THE **Citizen's Voice:** Any attempt to change our culture or to enact legislation limiting the role of money in elections will have to deal with a shibboleth that the Oligarchy uses to justify their theft of the public forum: to wit, "freedom of speech."

As we saw in Part One, the Oligarchy has used money and power to take over the media, influence academia, purchase elections outright, and to actively discredit government as a force for public good, while creating a broadly shared illusion that markets will accomplish all good things by pure serendipity. They've used the power derived from this process to rip off workers, the middle class, and anyone not part of the über rich or corporate collective.

They've fought off objections to this epochal theft by brandishing the term "free speech" like a garlic encrusted cross before a vampire. In what has to be an irony of historic proportions, they've excluded "we the people" from the political process by claiming to be champions of First Amendment rights. This has been the justification for granting rich people and corporations the "right" to drown out the average citizen's voice with gilded megaphones.

It seems obvious that the First Amendment was never intended to allow a very small minority to drown out the voices of the vast majority. Indeed, it could be convincingly argued that by using money and power to hijack the political debate, the ultra-rich and corporations were not so much exercising their rights to free speech as infringing upon others' right to be heard.

And then, of course, there is the questionable assumption that corporations should have rights that were obviously meant to be afforded to citizens. In fact, this bizarre notion could be marked as the opening salvo in the Oligarch's Coup. Regardless, the power of corporations and the rich can be rolled back with legislation.

It's worth remembering Thomas Jefferson's hope of crushing "in its birth the aristocracy of our moneyed corporations, which dare already to challenge our government to a trial of strength and bid defiance to the laws of our country," particularly since he is so often quoted by the hard right.

What Jefferson understood was that while the Constitution the founders developed made sure government power was subject to the people (albeit, a fairly exclusive subset at the time it was written), power vested in an aristocracy of the wealthy or the corporations was subject to no such constraint. The entire Constitution is based upon the notion of establishing competing branches that served to check the abuse of power. It is certain that had corporate power approached anything like what we see today, the founders would have established specific checks on it, as well. If freedom is to be preserved, hegemony and tyranny must be opposed, regardless of whether they come from the private sector or government.

Defenders of corporate personhood have a long record of court decisions supporting their perspective. But a close analysis of the origins of the Supreme Court's treatment of corporations as "people" reveals that this, too, was an inside job that had more to do with undue corporate influence than it did with good jurisprudence.

A Brief History of Corporations as Citizens: Until the late 1880s, in the heart of the Gilded Age, the Supreme Court's decisions regarding corporations' rights to personhood were strictly jurisdictional. That is, they were accorded that status merely to allow legal challenges involving corporations to be heard in federal courts. Since corporations were chartered in states, only by treating them as "citizens" could federal courts claim jurisdiction over them.

In fact, in 1853, in Marshall v. the Baltimore and Ohio Railroad, the Supreme Court went out of its way to limit the interpretation of corporations as citizens to jurisdictional matters only.

But in an act of legal jujitsu, corporations used this mere jurisdictional convenience of citizenship, to gain the substantive rights of citizenship and establish the notion of corporations as persons. One of the pivotal cases setting a precedent for corporate personhood, County of Santa Clara v. Southern Railroad, was heard in 1886, the heart of the Gilded Age.[185] The court recorder, a former president of a railroad company, appended language onto the decision that implied that granting corporations the rights afforded by the Fourteenth Amendment was a matter of "settled law," and this assertion was used in subsequent decisions to uphold and even expand the notion of corporate personhood.

The court's actual decision in the case did not make this precedential claim. Indeed, before the case was argued, Chief Justice Waite specifically excluded consideration of the question of whether the Fourteenth Amendment, which forbids a state to deny to any person within its jurisdiction the equal protection of the laws, applied to corporations. So this question was not part of the case, or the court's decision in the case. And while the chief justice had suggested in an offhand comment that the court was of the opinion that protections under the Fourteenth Amendment did apply to corporations, this was his personal observation, offered outside the context of any argument presenting a legal counterargument to this presumption, nor was it endorsed specifically or officially by any of the other justices.

Thus, a former railroad president, with no legal authority, unilaterally altered the course of jurisprudence on corporate citizenship, to the detriment of democracy, by inserting extrajudicial language in a mere summary of the case that was not, in fact, considered in the case.

But in the corporate-friendly era of the Gilded Age, the ex-railroad president's nonjudicial take on the proceedings was used in subsequent decisions to justify a more broadly construed application of the Fourteenth Amendment to corporate personhood *as if it were a court decision with the power of precedent*, when it was no such thing. It is a measure of how much power the Oligarchy has that this bizarre history of corporations as citizens is still cited by so-called strict-constructionist justices and legal scholars to justify an activist interpretation of the Bill of Rights that was clearly not the intention of the founders.

How Chief Justice Roberts Perverted the Process in Citizens United: As strange as County of Santa Clara v. Southern Railroad was, Chief Roberts' role in Citizens United may top it, in terms of judicial overreach.[186]

In fact, in Citizens United, Chief Justice Roberts framed the case in the broadest and most expansive context possible, so that it would have the greatest effect on the rights of corporations. The case, as presented by Citizens United attorney Theodore Olson, merely sought to determine whether a documentary shown by an on-demand format was something that Congress sought to prohibit under the McCain-Feingold Act. Thus, there was no need to consider the constitutionality of McCain-Feingold— it was essentially a technological question of whether that particular electronic format was subject to the McCain-Feingold law.

Roberts assigned the case to himself, which meant he would write the court's opinion. He issued a ruling that was narrowly applied along the lines that Olson argued. Justice Kennedy wrote a concurring opinion that agreed with Roberts's decision, but suggested that the court should take a much broader view of the case, and declare McCain-Feingold to be unconstitutional. Roberts's then withdrew his opinion and tasked Kennedy with writing the majority opinion, which did, in fact, substantially expand the notion of corporate personhood and citizenship, while declaring McCain-Feingold to be illegal.

When Justice Souter—who'd announced his retirement—wrote the brief for the dissenting minority, he basically accused Roberts of maneuvering the narrow case to reach the much broader conclusion Roberts wanted all along. Roberts was boxed in, and the court's decision was vulnerable to charges of overreach. Roberts responded by withdrawing the brief and seeking to rehear the case in the following session.

The scope of a case is defined in part by the "Questions Presented" and Roberts rewrote these for the rehearing of Citizens United so that the case called into question the constitutionality of the law—as well as creating the possibility of overturning two previous Supreme Court decisions on campaign finance law. The announcement that the case would be reheard in the fall, and that its scope had been so broadly expanded shocked even the attorney representing Citizens United.

Conservatives like to talk about liberal judges as "activist," but the Citizens United case is one of the most activist decisions in recent history, and, as we have seen, the basis for the whole concept of corporations having the rights of citizens, rests on the writings of a former president of a railroad company, appended to the decision in what amounts to an extrajudicial musing by a former industry CEO.

Thus, the legal agenda of empowering the FCC, limiting corporate personhood, and retooling our elective process does not limit free speech—it limits corporate tyranny. Politicians hate complexity, and this is complex terrain; in an age of Twitter communiques, bumper sticker slogans, and bread and circuses, trying to explain that monopolies can monopolize politics as easily as they can markets can be daunting for a politician. But it is absolutely necessary, and it is eminently doable in the context of a foundation-funded think tank with a little media savvy.

CHAPTER 21

Making Government Work Again

● ● ●

I know of no safe repository of the ultimate power of society but people.
And if we think them not enlightened enough, the remedy is not
to take the power from them, but to inform them by education.

THOMAS JEFFERSON

AS WE SAW IN CHAPTER 5, the charge by conservatives that government can't do anything right started as a baseless assertion lobbed at a highly functional government and a credulous public. It only evolved into a reality when Republicans used a combination of starve-the-beast tax cuts, obscene defense budgets, cynical-arsonist-posing-as-Firemen strategies, and complete intransience to make the charge true. Neoliberal DLC Democrats joined in the weaken-the-government feeding frenzy under Clinton. And the corporate-owned press fed it as well.

But there is an important difference between neoliberal Democrats and Conservatives. The neoliberals at least want a functional government. They may be fine with serving the needs of the Oligarchy, but they want to pass a budget, keep the debt in check, make the trains run on time, and fill empty vacancies in important positions. They also constrain themselves—for the most part—to the empirical tests of reality that Francis Bacon outlined in the *New Organon*. You know, science, as opposed to tossing chicken bones or making shit up.

Republicans, on the other hand, have such a naked contempt for governance that they run insane deficits, openly blockade budgets and appointments, and routinely threaten to shut the place down whenever things don't go their way.

Under Obama, Republicans set a record for the number of filibusters when Democrats held the Senate. They refused to set a hearing date to replace a Supreme Court Justice. They openly stated that their most important goal was not making the country run, but assuring that Obama failed in all that he tried to do. Failure, in the end, was their chief product, and actual governing was a casualty.

Political analysts, Norman J. Orenstein and Thomas E, Mann, writing in the *New Republic* back in 2012, had this to say about the Republican Party:

> The GOP has become an insurgent outlier in American politics. It is ideologically extreme; scornful of compromise; unmoved by conventional understanding of facts, evidence and science; and dismissive of the legitimacy of its political opposition.
>
> When one party moves this far from the mainstream, it makes it nearly impossible for the political system to deal constructively with the country's challenges.[187]

Since they wrote that, it's only gotten worse. Orenstein is a resident scholar at the Conservative American Enterprise Institute, so this observation cannot be dismissed as the rantings of a liberal ideologue. Other Republicans have made similar observations. For example, Orenstein and Mann note that Mike Lofgren, a Republican staffer who had worked on the Hill for three decades, wrote what they describe as an "anguished diatribe" after quitting in disgust. Here's a quote they include from Lofgren's article in Truthout:

> The Republican Party is becoming less and less like a traditional political party in a representative democracy and becoming more like an apocalyptic cult, or one of the intensely ideological authoritarian parties of 20th century Europe.

As we noted in Part One, the Republicans engineered dysfunction as part of the Coup, while the hapless Democrats watched in near silence, and then joined in the Coup.

The point here is to assess blame for the dysfunctional government we now have. Democrats may have wanted to make government a wholly owned subsidiary of corporate America, but at least they wanted to make it a functioning subsidiary. Republicans wanted to vilify it, starve it, sabotage it, disable it, and drown it.

And thanks to Democratic perfidy they just about succeeded.

The reason it's important to assign responsibility is because it's a prerequisite to fixing the problem.

We know two things. First, government can work. As we saw in Part One, the most prosperous periods in our history are when government regulated the market's natural tendency toward excess and monopoly and when it created a level playing field by using tax policy, supporting unions, guaranteeing minimum wages, assuring a relatively transparent financial system, building infrastructure, and conducting world-class research and development. Government also won two world wars, sent a man to the moon, and managed a green revolution that is the only reason we aren't experiencing widespread starvation today.

Second, we know it's not working now.

Government Generally Grows under Republicans and Shrinks under Democrats. Before we outline some general principles for making government more effective and less costly, let's dispense with one of the great fabrications of the last seventy years—the notion that Republicans favor small government. Fact is, they don't give a damn about small government; what they're interested in is weak government.

Doubtful? Well, here's the data. We'll start with how much spending increased in each president's term.[188]

* Nixon increased spending by about 8 percent
* Ford by just under 10 percent
* Carter by about 6 percent

- Reagan by nearly 20 percent
- Bush I by about 2 percent
- Clinton by about 6 percent
- Bush II by more than 45 percent
- Obama by about 4 percent

I chose this measure because basically, each president inherits a spending level from his predecessor, and what he (or she, hopefully one day soon) controls is what he does with that level. In the case of Obama, for example, he inherited the greatest recession since the 1930s and two wars that were essentially being funded off budget. The apparent dramatic increase in Obama's term was thus hardwired into the spending levels determined by Bush's policies and by Bush's attempt to hide spending off-line.

But basically, any measure of government growth would reveal the hollowness of the Republicans' claim of favoring small government. For example, consider the increase in the number of federal employees under each president:

- Reagan *increased* the number of federal employees by 237,000;
- Bush I decreased it by 30,000;
- Clinton decreased it by 381,000;
- Bush II *increased* it by 56,000; and
- Obama decreased it by 30,000 as of 2015.

Since Reagan, Republican administrations *increased* federal employment by 263,000, while Democrats *decreased* it by 411,000.

Republicans' claim of being against big government is about the emptiest rhetoric in a town built on empty rhetoric. Here again, the fact that this isn't common knowledge is directly a result of the EEM's failure to inform citizens about the basic truths of government.

What Republicans favor is weak government—a government that can't constrain the corporations and the excesses of the market; a government that can't keep the plutocrats from getting all the money; a government that can't and won't protect the environment, ensure public health, ensure the safety of the workplace and the safety of our food—in short, anything that might get in the way of corporate excess and the interests of the über rich.

Building a Government That Works: So let's face two facts. First, at the moment, government doesn't work particularly well. Second, Republicans have no interest in making it work; in fact, they want to disable it.

But the solution to bad government is good government, not no government.

One of the more systematic approaches to improving the efficiency and effectiveness of government was the Reinventing Government effort under Clinton and Gore.

After consulting with agencies, they developed a comprehensive blueprint for streamlining everything from procurement policies and rules to funding R&D, to hiring, firing, promoting, and paying the federal workforce. The plan also introduced competition into the system across a broad range of activities including policies on pay increases and promotions. Finally, the effort focused on ways of making government more accessible and understandable to people who used its products or who had to comply with its regulations.

As someone who was responsible for managing the development of several major environmental regulatory efforts, I can attest to the impact it had. Allow me to give a personal anecdote illustrating this. I joined the federal government's EPA after working at a small environmental engineering firm. At EPA, I served as a technical representative on several litigation efforts and assisted in rewriting rules that the litigation required. I was also tasked with the effort of managing the developing regulations governing the disposal of hazardous liquid wastes through underground injection, when Congress passed new legislation governing it. As it happens, the vast majority of the nation's waste gets handled in this way.

The new rules required a fair amount of technical knowledge, and so together with my technical staff, I ended up drafting most of the proposed regulatory language and the justifications for the requirements (the pre-amble, in administrative law jargon). EPA's Office of General Council and their Office of Enforcement—among others—reviewed the various drafts, and their concurrence was necessary before publishing proposed or final rules. My experience at the small engineering firm had instilled in me two important lessons: 1) the notion that time was money and 2) the realization that wading through regulations that were incredibly complex and nearly impervious to reason didn't contribute to increased compli-ance. I was determined to write simple rules, and to do so quickly.

I'm happy to report that in a career that spans more than thirty years, with stints in academia, the private sector, and two of the nation's premier think tanks, I have never encountered employees who exhibited a level of dedication, skill, and expertise greater than what I found in the federal workforce. Is there deadwood? Yes. Is it hard to get rid of it? Yes. But on balance, it's not appreciatively different than what I found in the other sec-tors in which I worked, and most federal employees are attracted to public service precisely because they want to make a difference. We were rou-tinely able to attract and hire the best from leading universities in every field, from law, to finance, to science and engineering.

Back to the regs…The Office of Enforcement favored complex, arcane, and multilayered administrative requirements because more complex regs made it easier to bring cases against folks. Sort of like the Al Capone-went-to jail-on-tax fraud school of law. So, our initially clear and relatively simple proposed regulations based on technically verifiable performance standards became far too complex, arcane, and administratively burden-some than they needed to be.

Similarly, the Office of General Council wanted to cover every possible contingency in the rules, which also contributed to increased complexity.

Under the Reinventing Government initiative, the Office of Enforcement began to perceive its mission more in terms of encourag-ing compliance than prosecuting noncompliance and the final rules were simpler and clearer as a result. After all, if you want people to comply, clarity is your friend; if you merely want to punish, then complexity is the order of the day. With regard to the Office of General Council's desire to cover every contingency, we began to see that specifying means got us into the weeds, while specifying ends—the desired performance standard as opposed to the technologies used to achieve the performance—allowed us to stay out of what could be pages of arcane technical requirements. By sticking to performance standards rather than design standards, we also freed the regulated companies to get innovative, and experience showed that they could frequently figure out ways to achieve better performance at lower costs than anything we'd envisioned.

We even began to think of those we regulated as our "customers."

Sadly, many of the ideas from the blueprint developed by the Reinventing Government process ended up on the cutting room floor. Ironically, Congress—including Republicans who routinely criticize government for being inefficient—failed to act on most of the rule changes the Reinvention Task Force proposed to make it more efficient. And when Bush II came in, the desire to make government more effective simply vanished.

The twin goals of the Reinventing Government effort offer an important clue as to why the Republicans—who have spent the last century telling anyone who would listen, how inefficient government is—had zero interest in backing an effort designed to make it more efficient. The process was designed to make the government more effective at accomplishing its objectives, as well as more efficient—as in less costly. As we've seen, Republicans don't want an effective government, and they exhibit no interest in an efficient one either.

But for anyone who actually wants a government that performs at a high level, and does so at the lowest cost possible, the process used by Gore and Clinton in the Reinventing Government effort would yield a good guide for making it happen.

Problem is, there doesn't seem to be a constituency for that at the moment, and until we explode the MBB, that's unlikely to change.

CHAPTER 22

Making the Media Serve the People, Not the Plutocrats

● ● ●

With a fascist the problem is never how best to present the truth
to the public but how best to use the news to deceive the public into
giving the fascist and his group more money or more power.

HENRY A. WALLACE

AS WE SAW IN CHAPTER 3, until the 1980s, the FCC was charged with assuring there was a diversity of views covered by the media, that there were a diversity of stations and owners in both local and national markets, and that the airwaves were first and foremost treated as a public trust, not a private profit center.

A central part of any attempt to restore power to the people has to involve restoring the Fairness Doctrine, re-empowering the FCC, and reclaiming the policy of treating the media as a public trust.

Any attempt to reclaim a measure of restraint over the media will prompt the Oligarchy to accuse progressives of impinging on freedom in general and free speech in particular, but as we saw in chapter 20, putting the Oligarchy and corporations on the same level as people does more to limit the freedoms of the majority of the people than it does to protect the rights of the rich. Moreover, it rests on an interpretation of the First and Fourteenth Amendments that is based on shaky legal ground, and that represents an aggressive reinterpretation of law that serves the corporate interest.

The fact is, regulation of the media serves to increase freedom of speech rather than impinge upon it, by preventing the Oligarchy from simply buying up the media and completely controlling the terms of our national debate. Until Reagan, the policy of preventing those with a gilded megaphone from drowning out the voice of the people had been the rule in the United States from the dawn of the media age.

Federal regulation of the airwaves began before the first news program even existed, with the Radio Act being passed in 1910 and the first news program going on air in 1920 in Detroit, Michigan. In 1912, the Act was expanded, and it was expanded again in the Radio Act of 1927, then again in 1934, when the FCC was established. Finally, in 1949, the FCC put the Fairness Doctrine in place.

The broadcast media, unlike newspapers or the Internet, has a finite number of outlets, and this introduces the need to regulate on both a practical and theoretical level. Practically, some entity needed to assure that stations and transmitters didn't broadcast over each other on the same frequencies and to guarantee that emergency frequencies were available to serve vessels in distress as well as other appeals for emergency assistance, all dictated by the reality of a finite bandwidth.

On a more theoretical level, the fact that there is a limited bandwidth increases the likelihood that monopolies could emerge, and that introduces the prospect of someone controlling the flow of information, particularly since, as the first FCC chairman put it, reliance on advertising threatened "a further commercialized, conservative-biased and corporate-dominated medium." Exactly what we see today, now that regulation of the media is essentially nonexistent.

The point is, from the moment mass communication was born, it has been regulated, and the airwaves have been viewed as public property owned by "we the people," with the government acting on our behalf. And it worked reasonably well. Balance wasn't a slogan; it was a requirement that was guaranteed not only by restrictions on content, but by controls that assured that leases were issued to a variety of owners, and held for limited terms. People could "vote" with their dials or channels, and there was real competition—the basis of market effectiveness— because of it.

In general, the history of media regulation represented a steady march toward greater diversity and was designed to prevent monopolies and oligopolies from forming. For example:

* In 1941, rules for prohibiting a broadcaster from owning more than 35 percent of the nation's market were established.
* In 1946, rules prohibiting a major network from buying another major network were put in place.
* In 1964, rules prohibiting a company from owning more than one station in the same market were put in place—in markets with more than eight stations the rule didn't apply.
* In 1970, broadcasters were prohibited from owning both a radio and television station in the same market.
* In 1975, a rule was instituted barring ownership of both a television station and a newspaper in the same market.

All this came to a screeching halt under Reagan, and the reversal accelerated under Bill Clinton. Since 1980, the airwaves and the media have been increasingly turned over to the forces of a free market, and the inevitable concentration and monopolization that results, until today—just six Fortune 200 corporations own 90 percent of the media. Today, "balance" is a slogan that allows an imbalance in the forces of the market, uttered by those who use "free speech" as a shield against honesty, accuracy, context, and competing perspectives in the news.

Attempts to restore some semblance of diversity and responsibility within the media will not only be met with accusations of government censorship; they will also mount a spirited defense of the free-market by advocates and claims that big government will only screw things up. And this will come from the folks who own the media and the message.

Progressives will have to lead the charge to end media monopolies and restore market forces to the media, and they will have to be prepared to accept the assault on them it will trigger. It won't be popular at first, but without a media that is free from the corporate control, there can be no functioning democracy. It may seem counterintuitive to assume that more regulation creates greater freedom, but the facts are clear: if we don't accept government intervention in the media markets, we will have to accept corporate hegemony over them. The media is no less free simply because its censors come from the private sector; indeed, the private sector is not directly answerable to the people, and it is free to run the kind of "bread and circus" appeals that are anathema to a democratic republic, but that dominate our media today. Government, however, can be held accountable for its actions by we the people.

Returning the press to the people simply requires that we reinstate the constraints on media monopolies that the Oligarchy removed, including.[189]

* limiting the number of outlets any one company can control in a given market—ideally to the pre-Reagan limit when no entity could own more than seven stations; licenses were limited to five years and they had to be purchased at auction;
* requiring stations to carry a diversity of views and to carry at least the specified minimum number of non-entertainment programs; and
* requiring stations to carry opposing views.

And media monopolies are not the only threat to our freedom—propaganda, false news, "balance" for its own sake, and misinformation are the true source of any despot's power.

Progressive Need to Work the Press: One of the most pernicious effects of emphasizing balance in reporting is that it frequently ends up introducing false equivalencies. For example, the press frequently treated Hillary Clinton's troubles with the truth as if it were in the same league as Trump's. Now, Ms. Clinton did lie, and she frequently was deceptive, or distorted the facts. That's why the e-mails caused her such trouble. But she was within the range of many politicians when it came to truth telling. Her main problem was that she simply wasn't very good at it.

But Trump? His lying was—and is—pathological, random, self-contradictory, and continuous. There is no precedent in modern politics for it. But after an initial shock, much of the press began to treat him as if he were no different—or only slightly different—than Clinton. Balance demanded false equivalency.

This is yet another reason why Trump is in the White House.

Anyone who has read or heard a climate story is all too familiar with the degree to which false equivalency can distort public opinion. For decades, reporters for both paper and broadcast media would present a climate scientist recounting carefully researched conclusions, but feel obligated in the name of balance to present an opposing view—usually from a crackpot, or someone on the payroll of the fossil fuel interests. In short, a climate denier. As Bill Nye recently put it to CNN, if you want to present a "balanced view" on climate, they you should have 97 scientists who endorse human-caused climate change for every denier you include in the broadcast.

The recent campaign was littered with false equivalencies, as are the so-called fact-checking sites. For example, when Bernie Sanders said that climate change is directly linked to the growth in terrorism, Politifact rated it "mostly false," despite the fact that the US intelligence community, the Pentagon, and the CIA largely agree, although some might quibble with the word "directly." But the real offense here is that, based mostly on semantics, Politifact assigned Sanders's statement the same "mostly false" rating that they gave to the various climate deniers, many of whom were candidates. Here's a list of denier statements from Media Matters that Politifact rated as "mostly false" [190]

* Austin, Texas, city council member Don Zimmerman declared: "You don't have to be as smart as a fifth-grader to know what causes the climate is the sun...I have people tell me, 'carbon dioxide warms the Earth.' No, it doesn't. The sun warms the Earth."

- Texas senator Ted Cruz claimed "Many of the alarmists on global warming, they've got a problem because the science doesn't back them up. In particular, satellite data demonstrate for the last 17 years, there's been zero warming."
- Florida senator Marco Rubio asserted: "[T]he left loves to go around saying there is a consensus, there is a consensus. There is a majority of scientists that say that global carbon emissions by humans cause some changes in the climate. What there is no consensus on and (what) they conveniently ignore is there is no consensus on the sensitivity of the climate. How much is it changing and how much of it is directly attributable to human carbon emission? There is no consensus on that, which is why the models vary so greatly, which is why, despite 17 years of dramatic increases in carbon production by humans, surface temperatures (on) the earth have stabilized."
- Fossil-fuel industry advocate Patrick Moore alleged: "It has not warmed for the last 17 years. We know that for sure. And that brings into question the whole hypothesis."

Talk about false equivalence. Putting these head-in-the-sand blatant attempts at misinformation in the same category as Sanders's statement is tantamount to equating an all-out nuclear war with a kid's squirt gun battle. Literally. Each of these statements is flat-out false, and they repeat conservative memes that have been disproved more often than it's a sunny day in San Diego. To rate them the same as Sander's basically true statement is to grossly misinform the public.

A close relative of false equivalence is the practice of always using a pro-and-con format and never intervening to question the validity of each "side's" statement.

Even supposedly liberal outlets like NPR are notoriously bad at this, with nearly every report featuring someone from each "side."

Thus, recently on a story about repealing Obamacare, NPR presented the usual "for and against" duo. After the supporter wrapped up the problems that would occur from repealing Obamacare, he noted that the rate of increase in medical costs has gone down since Obamacare was passed (a fact), that twenty million previously uninsured people now had medical coverage (a fact), that premiums have actually gone down in some states, but even where they've gone up, subsidies have kept premiums flat for the vast majority of those covered (both are facts). The reporter then turned it over to the critic, saying, in effect, "but some say Obamacare has been a costly disaster," by way of introduction.

The critic then launched into the favorite memes about the system collapsing of its own weight (it's not) and declared that Republicans would replace it with something much better at a lower cost (their efforts will reduce the number of folks covered by between 22 and 23 million people, and it will dramatically increase costs for anyone who actually needs health care) and he completely ignored the enormous tax windfall the Republican versions give to the superrich.

When the critic was done, the NPR reporter made no attempt to critique either speaker. Since both "sides" had presented their perspective, his job was done…Back to you, Joe…As a result, empty assertions, bald-faced lies and slogans were accorded the same weight as factual statements, and context was completely absent. No wonder a sizable number of Americans hate Obamacare, despite strongly supporting virtually all of its individual provisions. No wonder Trump won.

How bad is it? Here's a statement from an NPR fact-check on the Obamacare debate:

Both sides are trying to position themselves as the protectors of Americans' health care, while branding the other party as a dangerous threat.

As usual, the truth may be somewhere in between. Here we take a closer look at some of the claims being floated by both parties.[191]

But when you read the "closer look," there's no contest. Conservatives are hurling counterfactual nukes and mouthing idle conjectures, while defenders of Obamacare are essentially hewing to facts. Look, Obamacare is a product of the neoliberal consensus—in fact, it was developed in the conservative think tanks the Oligarch's funded. The only reason conservatives hate it so is because Obama sponsored it. It's not an ideal program, and it has its flaws. Real progressives should work to replace it as soon as possible. But it's a hell of a lot better than what we used to have, and it beats the pig-in-poke program the Republicans are trying desperately to conjure up out of their antigovernment, anti-tax cauldron.

Thus, truth, context, and accuracy are victims to the cult of balance.

Consider the allegedly liberal *New York Times*. In 2012, the *New York Times* "reader's representative" Andy Brisbane actually asked readers whether reporters should be concerned with the truth.[192] Honestly. He did. And in so doing, he acknowledged that it was not part of a *Times* reporter's normal portfolio. At the *Times*, apparently, a pound of bullshit is equivalent to a pound of truth. Just get the money quotes right.

If this is how NPR and the "liberal" *New York Times* treat the news, imagine how the rest of the EEM performs.

As noted earlier, over the next two years, progressive organizations—and individuals—must mount an aggressive campaign to hold the media accountable, while simultaneously pursuing legislation to empower the FCC. Every time some reporter emphasizes "balance" over accuracy, truth, or context, every time an empty, counterfactual statement is allowed to stand, without challenge, no matter how "super-terrific" the assertion is, we the people need to let loose with millions of letters, cards, and phone calls. We must be willing to drop subscriptions, picket outside the headquarters of the media giants, and boycott their products. If the news organization won't respond, then we need to go to their masters—Time Warner, Disney, Murdoch's News Corporation, Bertelsmann of Germany, and Viacom—and threaten them with boycotts and divestments.

The media is ground zero in the war to take back America. Changing the laws will take time. In the meantime, we the people have it in our power to hit them in their wallets and purses.

This is why the fight to reclaim the Enlightenment culture that underlies our government must proceed in tandem with the campaign to reinstall legislative constraints on the power of the plutocrats. We can't get people to back legal constraints if they don't believe in government or if they believe markets will deliver what people want and need without any constraints. In the meantime, we can vote with our values in the market. In the end, it may be the most powerful tool we have.

Fortunately, people are beginning to understand that unconstrained media markets—like unconstrained capitalism in general—serve only a handful of rich folks and the corporations. Indeed, one could explain this whole election—including Trump's victory—as a desperate search on the part of the people for a candidate who acknowledged it. Clinton certainly didn't—but Trump at least pretended to.

But while they are becoming suspicious of the MMM, they still buy into the MBB, and they don't believe that government can—or will, or in some cases, should—effectively represent their interests.

In the next chapter, I outline how to reform out electoral process.

CHAPTER 23

Reforming Our Electoral Process

● ● ●

The death of democracy is not likely to be an assassination
from ambush. It will be a slow extinction from
apathy, indifference, and undernourishment.

ROBERT M. HUTCHINS

NO OTHER COUNTRY IN THE world makes electing its leaders such a pro-tracted spectacle, nor such an expensive one. But when government is for sale, we the people get outbid, and the tyranny of the rich is no less odious than government tyranny.

Here again, the fixes are simple and popular, but not easy.

The progressive revolution should aim to

* reverse corporate personhood;
* limit spending to a set amount of publicly provided funds;
* make it easier for third-party candidates to run in local, state, and national elections;
* eliminate gerrymandering; and
* get rid of the electoral college.

Corporate Personhood: A majority of senators have already voted for a constitutional amendment overturning Citizens United v. the Federal

Election Commission and its evil mini-me's, Buckley v. Valeo, and McCutchen v. the Federal Election Commission. That was in 2014, when Democrats had control of the Senate, but they were blocked by forty-two Republicans.[193] And so, money still talks and the people walk.

Clearly, this needs to be addressed, and just as clearly, we need a countercoup to address it. But the mechanics of addressing it—a constitutional amendment that limits corporate participation in elections—are quite simple and popular among voters, with 78 percent favoring it.[194]

Limiting Campaign Spending: Limiting campaigns to using only publically provided federal funds to run a campaign would also eliminate the influence of money on politics.

The role of money in politics has two root sources:—first, there is currently the need for billions of dollars to run a campaign, and second there is a "revolving door" which rewards politicians who have faithfully served the plutocracy and provides a steady stream of self-interested corporatists and insiders to serve as cabinet members, subcabinet members, judges, advisers, and other high-level appointees.

There are two impediments to implementing a limit on money in the election process. First, there are claims about violating First Amendment rights. But as we've seen, both the logic and the effect of corporate personhood and money as speech do more to violate the rights of the majority, and they actually work to increase the power of the powerful. And the people understand this. Only the absence of a voice calling for a change has enabled the Oligarchy to retain their lock on funding elections. When the Democrats decided to compete for the Oligarchy's money rather than to speak up to eliminate it from the system, the Oligarchy's victory was assured. To overturn this lock, the people will have to take over the Democratic Party or start a new one.

The second impediment is more subtle but still significant. The media and press make enormous sums of money on the current mode of campaigns in two ways.

First, they raked in nearly $6 billion of the $11.7 billion spent on elections in 2016 directly in the form of advertising dollars.[195] A system that didn't go on forever assuring unlimited amounts of cash going into media coffers can hardly be expected to garner support from a media that makes so much money off it. But the media and the press benefit in yet another way—by turning our campaigns into a food fight, they get viewers in front of screens, radio audiences on dial, and newspapers in more hands, all of which increases circulation and ad revenue.

This means the EEM will not be allies in attempts to get money out of elections. But with half of Americans polled favoring a law that requires all federal campaigns to be funded by the federal government and that bans private contributions, and some 79 percent favoring at least limits on Senate and House races, it should be possible to mobilize enough support to overcome the vested interests.[196]

Make it Easier for Third-Party Candidates to Run: At the moment, it is difficult for third-party candidates to get on the ballot in local, state, or federal elections, or to participate in debates. As a result, they are just about ignored by the media. This means we live in a political duopoly that is a de facto monopoly, now that neoliberals and conservatives subscribe to many of the same positions—and certainly answer to the same constituency.

Nearly everybody accepts that monopolies are bad for the economy—reducing choice, stifling innovation, and allowing wholesale theft of our national wealth—so it seems odd that the same recognition seems to escape folks when it comes to our political system.

Actually, it doesn't. Once again, the majority of voting age Americans—57 percent woup like to see a viable third party in the United States.[197]

With popular support for third parties, a long-term strategic approach to electoral reform should make it possible to remove barriers that are now in place at local and state election processes and allow them to participate in public funding. Indeed, any fix to the campaign-funding laws should incorporate rules that make it difficult for third parties.

Eliminate Gerrymandering: Gerrymandering is anathema to democracy. It intentionally undermines the notion of "one person, one vote," which is the basis of any democratic system, and its effects are real, not theoretical. For example, Republican donors funded a massive—and strategic—campaign to influence the state races for governor and legislatures with an eye toward shaping the scheduled redistricting efforts after the 2010 census. In the first election after the redistricting took place, Democrats won 1.37 million more votes for the House than Republicans did, but won only 201 seats to the Republicans' 234.[198] In one of their targeted states, Pennsylvania, Democrats received 44 percent of the vote, yet they won only 27 percent, or 5 out of the state's allocation of 18 House seats. Yeah, that's democracy at work, all right.

If you want to see the full depth of the advantage that a strategic approach gives the Republican Party, Google project Redmap, or read *Ratf**cked*, by David Daley, which details the Republican's sophisticated strategy, generous funding, and the impressive results. Daley talks about districts whose boundaries are so tortuously drawn that one Pennsylvanian district was described as resembling "a horned antelope barreling down a hill on a sled," while another looked like a cartoon of "Donald Duck kicking Goofy in the groin." Except in this case, we're Goofy, and it's our groin that's getting kicked. Some of the gerrymandered districts are so strangely drawn they've earned nicknames—there's Michigan's "eight-mile mess," North Carolina's "Hanging claw," and Maryland's "Pinwheel of Death" (one of the few examples of Democratic gerrymandering—not because Democrats are too noble, but because they are too busy steering by their hood ornament to do something as strategic as Redmap).

The origin of the term explains what it is. Gerrymandering was first used in the *Boston Gazette* on March 26, 1812, to describe a bizarrely drawn district done under Governor Elbridge Gerry in order to ensure his Democratic-Republican Party (a single party with no relationship to today's two parties) retained power against the Federalists. One of the districts was shaped like a salamander, and the *Gazette* created a portmanteau from Governor Gerry's name and a salamander. The practice has been in place even before this; in fact, in Virginia in 1788, former governor Patrick Henry persuaded the state's legislature to use redistricting to force

James Monroe—his political enemy—to run against the popular James Madison. Monroe won anyway, and as history shows, both James ended up doing OK.

But democracy has not fared as well. As *New Yorker*'s invaluable Elizabeth Kolburt points out, project Redmap was extraordinarily successful at changing a political map that was dominated by blue states and blue districts to one that was red. As Ms. Kolburt notes,

> All told, in 2010 Republicans gained nearly seven hundred state legislative seats, which, as a report from redmap crowed, was a larger increase "than either party has seen in modern history." The wins were sufficient to push twenty chambers from a Democratic to a Republican majority. Most significantly, they gave the G.O.P. control over both houses of the legislature in twenty-five states. (One was Pennsylvania.) The blue map was now red.[199]

There is no reason, given the popularity of progressive positions, that progressives can't reverse engineer this process to our advantage. Republicans were able to raise $30 million to support the effort with relatively little effort, but we should be able to get the money required "$27 dollahs" at a time.

There has not been a lot of polling on gerrymandering, but what there has been suggests that the overwhelming majority of the public would like to get the politics out of districting. Virginians favored a nonpolitical approach by a wide margin. A national poll—not from a statistically valid sample, but from volunteer respondents—reported by ISideWith.com found that 85 percent of Americans wanted to use a nonpolitical method of establishing districts.

One of the most equitable and easy ways to assure that redistricting hews as closely as possible to one person, one vote is to use an algorithm to set up districts, as one computer programmer did.[200] Brian Olson of Massachusetts drew up a computer program that defines "optimally compact" geographical districts of equal populations. Writing in the

Washington Post's *Wonkblog*, reporter Christopher Ingraham compares maps of districts defined by Olson's program with those developed by politicians—the contrast is stark. In Olson's system, there are no salamanders, while the current districts drawn by politicians looks like the terrarium from hell.

The Supreme Court has been loath to get involved in the issue of gerrymandering, and Roberts is downright hostile to the idea. But as the inequities becoming so grossly obvious, suits are being ginned up as I write this, and in the next few years, the Supreme Court is likely to be entertaining many such suits, based on the Fourteenth Amendment and the Voting Rights Act.

While the Constitution gives states the responsibility for drawing districts, it also guarantees individuals competing rights under the citizen's rights to equal protection under the Fourteenth Amendment. It seems that a reasonable balance between a state's right to draw districts and the rights of individuals under the Fourteenth Amendment could be struck by using algorithms like Olson's to define what is the rebuttable presumption of what is neutral and equitable, and require states to have a legally defensible justification for deviating from it. Alternatively, the use of an independent, nonpartisan commission could be used as the presumed and rebuttable standard, with deviations subjected to high standards of proof.

In any case, this issue should be a focus of the network of think tanks, media efforts, and citizens' political action needed to effect the culture change we seek.

Eliminating the Electoral College: The electoral college gives smaller states proportionally more power, and since there are more smaller states than larger, the hurtle for getting the needed constitutional amendment is high. Nevertheless, we should pursue it.

If we are to bend history's arc toward justice, then we must make each individual's vote count the same as any other's. The idea of equal voice in a democracy should be an easy sell, and studies that expose the relative inequality of voters in our current system could help sway public opinion. For example, a voter in Vermont or Wyoming has about four times the impact on the electoral college outcome as does a voter in California or New York.[201] If conservatives could overturn the incredibly popular New Deal and discredit government after it helped usher in the most prosperous, long-lived, and equitably shared economic boom in our nation's history, then surely progressives have a shot at making our system more democratic.

It Will Take Massive Amounts of Money to Get Money out of Politics: Yes, it's ironic that we will have to spend money to get money out of politics. But as we noted earlier, it will have to come "27 dollahs at a time" from individuals. We'll have to do a reverse Powell—establish foundations, think tanks, academic chairs, and media-savvy operatives to attack the twin myths and the dysfunctional media that fosters them. We are already seeing an influx of money for progressive causes.

The institutions we fund will have to focus on creating a progressive infrastructure that provides sustained, enduring, and continuing support designed to insert the progressive message into every facet of society including academia and the media. And we will have to show the same kind of strategic sense that Republicans did in executing project Redmap—arguably one of the most antidemocratic efforts ever undertaken by a political party. And no, if progressives invest in trying to move toward one-person, one-vote policies, we're not "just as bad." That would be false equivalency.

We Will Have to Address All Levels of Government: Remember, Republicans managed to win more House seats than Democrats did while getting fewer votes after electing state legislators in key states prior to the redistricting after the 2010 census. Call it gerrymandering for fun and profit. Texas led the way with a highly unusual—and legally questionable—mid-decade redistricting in 2003, which was politically motivated and which enabled Republicans to win the state for the first time since Reconstruction, although their plan was eventually struck down by the courts.

Progressives should take aim at gerrymandering early with analyses, articles, and public education about how antidemocratic it is. There is broad public support for the concept of hewing as closely as possible to the principle of "one person, one vote," but any attempts to pass actual legislation constraining the state's ability to disenfranchise its voters might have to await a more favorable Supreme Court.

Another reason progressives will have to develop and support down-ballot candidates is to create a bench or "farm team" to replace the neoliberals who now dominate what passes for the Left in today's political word.

Finally, the conservative Republican domination of state politics is causing pain to middle-class and working-class people[202] and[203] even as it eviscerates the institutions that brought prosperity to this country. Public education from kindergarten through the university level is threatened in states with Republican control as is infrastructure, the social safety net, health care, job growth, and economic growth in general. Getting Republicans and conservatives out of governance is therefore necessary to reduce the misery index of American citizens.

The good news is, this could be a one-time only effort, even if it does take a decade or more. Once the laws have returned the media to the people and silenced the gilded megaphone, once we've established a level playing field in the electoral process, and once the cultural effort is restoring some notion of "we the people," the fact that reality has a progressive bias should keep things on track with relatively less money needed.

CHAPTER 24

Funding the New Coup with "Viewers Like You"

● ● ●

If you want to build a ship, don't herd people together to
collect wood and don't assign them tasks and work, but rather
teach them to long for the endless immensity of the sea.

ANTOINE DE SAINT-EXUPERY

THE CENTRAL CHALLENGE TO CHANGING the existing system is that those who created it have set up a political framework that depends upon money and monetary rewards, and they have the money, while those who have been cheated by it have relatively little.

Sanders showed that cumulatively, when the people believe in a goal, their combined assets can rival—or even exceed—the assets of the Oligarchy. His famous refrain, "Just 27 dollars apiece" led to a total of $230 million for the primary race alone. However, individual contributors suffer from what I call the "PBS effect."

You know those noncommercials right before NOVA, or All Things Considered or the NewsHour where they thank funders from foundations and corporations and finish with "and brought to you by viewers like you?" Even when viewers like us are, cumulatively, the major contributor, we lack the voice that a single contributor like...say...David Koch might have. Doubt that? Try calling up the president of PBS and say, "Good morning, this is viewers like us. Can we talk?" You wouldn't make it past the operator or the secretary. David Koch or the president of a corporation or foundation, on the other hand, would promptly get ushered into the inner sanctum, or have a lunch meeting immediately scheduled. That's what I call the PBS effect.

Politics works the same way. The people may, cumulatively, contribute more than large donors, but we won't get the access they have. And mass mailings or e-mail campaigns are dismissed as just that—campaigns revved up by some political group like Move-On—rather than the genuine interests of voters which will get reflected in elections. The bottom line is that money talks, but our money can only talk if it comes only from us. Hillary Clinton and Barack Obama showed that when corporations and plutocrats pay, only they get to play—the rest of us get neutered by the PBS effect.

One of the things that made Sanders successful was his commitment to eschew corporate contributions and people's faith that he wasn't beholden to moneyed interests.

Progressives need organizations that will raise money to fund the Countercoup. And these organizations have to operate in the same focused way the Oligarchs' Coup did. This means a commitment to broad values, not simply tactics. It requires us to defend government as the means of assuring freedom, not accept the meme that it is an impediment to it; it demands that we embrace a politics defined by justice, equity, fairness, tolerance, and empathy to all, not the politics of identity. It demands, in short, that we forge a coalition representing the rights and aspirations of the 99 percent. This does not mean we cannot recognize the unique challenges that individual groups face, nor that we should ignore historical attacks that they have experienced, nor that we shouldn't accept that some of these groups require unique remedies. What it does mean is that we cannot allow these differences to divide us, to weaken us, or cause us to abandon the solidarity we need to make the political changes we must make together.

As Maya Angelou said:

I note the obvious differences
Between each sort and type,

But we are more alike my friends,
Than we are unalike.

As with the Oligarch's Coup, the focus has to be continuous and not tied to a specific party or election, but rather to the nation's political worldview, its cultural identity, and on influencing the existing media and harnessing the Internet to create a level playing field in which facts, truth, and reality are dispositive once again. This requires the same kind of network of foundations, think tanks, and academic resources as the Oligarch's Coup.

After the primaries, Sanders launched Our Revolution (OR)—an entity that was meant to serve exactly the need outlined above—an entity that could be core of the progressive's Powell Movement.

The level of support Sanders got from those under forty-five was unprecedented. If that support can be consolidated and mobilized, the future belongs to progressives, and more importantly, the ideals of progressivism.

Which makes getting OR or an equivalent organization right, all the more important. Unfortunately, the launch of OR failed to ignite the same passion and commitment that Sanders's campaign did.

Many of the concerns progressives have about OR were outlined in a petition[204] released by the Bernie Delegates Network entitled, "Support and Improve 'Our Revolution.'" One particularly important one was the omission by OR of anything about the essentially neocon foreign and defense policy that dominates establishment politics. Another is whether OR will support only Democrats or whether it will also support third-party candidates.

The pathway to the status quo is composed of revolutions that devolved into chaos, and the revolution Bernie ignited is in danger of becoming yet another footprint on that trail.

If we want the same level of engagement and commitment toward OR that made the Sanders campaign so effective—if we want to inherit the future—then we must understand what Sanders got right, and why his campaign resonated with progressives and united them, then replicate that in OR or an equivalent organization or group of organizations.

What Sanders offered progressives, for the first time, was agency and transparency, and they go hand in hand. There can be no sense of agency without transparency, and no transparency without agency.

Let's explore why these ideas are linked, why they appear to be missing in OR, and how they can be better integrated into it.

Agency and Transparency: Most politicians try to run on as vague a platform as possible, under the assumption that it's better to avoid alienating anyone with specifics, than it is to inform them about where they stand.

Clinton is a classic example. Back in July of 2015, I referred to her as the cypher candidate "who won't answer questions; who equivocates on the issues; and who speaks in vague generalities and stunningly calculated language that is designed to say nothing.[205]"

When it became apparent that Sanders's progressive stands were a serious threat to her coronation, she became "the progressive who got things done." What things? Well, that was a subject she avoided.

I made the same point in 2008 about Obama's "Hope and Change." Hope *for* what? Change *to* what? We never found out. Still hard to tell.

What resonated with people about Bernie was that he staked out very specific positions that fell into a coherent framework, and he insulated himself from influence by appealing directly and nearly exclusively to the people for funds.

He was not only for a more equitable economic system; he was against a "rigged system." He favored reinstating a modern Glass-Steagall; he wanted to overturn Citizens United; he wanted to defeat the TPP; end overseas tax shelters…the list is long, specific, and intellectually consistent. Or take climate change. He not only wanted to back renewables—a political no-brainer that Clinton also endorsed—he also wanted to ban fracking, end fossil fuel exploration on federal lands, and tax carbon. Again, specific policies that were integrated into, and flowed from, a coherent framework.

In short, when you gave Bernie money, or a vote, the transparency enabled you to know what you were backing, and it also gave you a sense of control. There was no intermediary, no "trust me, I'll do the right thing," no feel-good abstractions that didn't pin him down. No mega-donor who's interests would trump yours. This kind of empowerment—or agency—was and is central to what made Sanders successful.

After decades of poll-tested spinmeisters whose main attribute was to say nothing without appearing to, this kind of specific, honest, and transparent candidate was the perfect antidote to people grown justifiably cynical about a process fueled by the rich that left them out. If the Russians had hacked Sanders campaign, they would have gone away empty handed and disappointed.

Building Transparency and Agency into OR: Under its current framework, OR denies people that direct sense of agency, and is less transparent than it could be. There is an explicit "trust me, we'll do the right thing" that is exercised by an intermediary. The appeal is based on the promise to support "progressives"—an abstraction—rather than the specific list of policies Bernie offered.

Without a specific definition of what progressive means, it may be a level of abstraction that's a little too close to "hope and change" or "a progressive who gets things done" or an "I feel your pain" approach to work when the people have been lied to and intentionally deceived for most of their lives about everything from their deodorant to their president. There is also the issue of accepting money from the ultra-rich and corporations.

The fix is for OR or its equivalent to address these two issues directly, starting with the notion that accepting anonymous contributions from the über rich in the context of a 501(c)(4) is somehow consistent with a people's movement. This simply won't work in a world in which lies are aired 24-7 in the name of commerce.

First, to achieve transparency, progressive organizations should establish a set of core values that any candidate they back must subscribe to and do so in cooperation with the community they are seeking support from.

These don't have to be exhaustive, but they should articulate more than a commitment to a candidate who self-identifies as progressive. Or one who is identified as a progressive by a self-ordained leader. The list of issues might include requirements, such as

- refusing to accept corporate money and limiting the size of contributions from private citizens;
- supporting aggressive campaign finance reform (we could even limit the length of campaigns to mirror that in other—still functioning—democracies);
- supporting universal health care;
- supporting fiscal and other policies that restore the middle class and protect the poor;
- reining in big banks and Wall Street, breaking up too big to fail banks, restoring a modern Glass-Steagall;
- supporting a transfer tax on Wall Street and other security exchanges;
- supporting a carbon tax—perhaps a fee and dividend structure which would return the tax to consumers while banning fracking and establishing a path to getting off fossil fuels completely;
- supporting a fifteen-dollar-an-hour minimum wage;
- Assuring that any trade agreements have real, enforceable protections for American workers and for the environment;
- Supporting a rational and humane immigration policy that includes a pathway to citizenship;
- Revamping the criminal justice system so that the United States is not the world leader in incarceration and making sure that it is free from bias due to race, ethnicity, nationality, religion, or sexual orientation;
- committing to end the endless wars, making war our last resort, and demanding a rational and relevant defense budget; and
- restoring needed authorities to the FCC, including the Fairness Doctrine, and rules which require a greater diversity in ownership at both the local and national level.

This is probably too extensive, but the key is to have specific criteria and to allow the people who contribute to OR to define what a progressive is by allowing them to vote and select which elements are required. This would provide both transparency and agency. But note that this is more than a laundry list—it is an internally consistent set of actions that can be summarized in the context of a broader moral framework of making the system more equitable, protecting our environment, and being sure that *all* people's interests are represented.

Second, in order to sustain a sense of agency, we must give the community that contributes a say in who OR backs. In the age of the Internet, it should be easy to solicit participation in this process.

None of this is easy; and it's not convenient. It would be far less burdensome to simply trust Jeff Weaver or whoever to do the right thing and back the right people. And to be sure, OR will likely be a positive force in politics regardless of whether they institute something like this or not.

But if OR wants to replicate the kind of success Bernie had, if they want to occupy the future, this is what it will take. If OR doesn't adopt strategies that confer both agency and transparency to the people, then we will have to develop organizations that do.

CHAPTER 25

Why the Establishment Will Tell You to Ignore this Book And Why You Shouldn't Listen to Them

● ● ●

Start by doing what's necessary; then do what's possible,
and suddenly you are doing the impossible.

Francis of Assisi

Those who make peaceful revolution impossible
will make violent revolution inevitable.

John F. Kennedy

The political pundits, politicians, self-proclaimed pragmatists, journalists, the cognoscenti, academicians, and assorted other wonks will reject this book, its premises, and its solutions out of hand. It will stimulate eye rolls, knowing smirks, even sad, empathetic nods.

They will write it off as beyond the province of politics, pie-eyed, paranoid, or even…gasp…unrealistic.

Before you accept their judgment on the ideas presented here, consider these four facts:

First, nearly all these critics are the same people who told us Hillary Clinton had this election in the bag; whereas a very small number of us correctly forecasted Clinton's defeat. My first article warning of this prospect was published as far back as 2014, and I explained why it could—and probably would—occur several times thereafter.[206]

Second, they universally predicted an immediate crash in the stock market if Trump were elected, whereas we got the "Trump Bump." But the Oligarchy knows one of its own, even if the politicos and the pundits were fooled. The stock market will, in all likelihood, ultimately go down, but it won't be because of Trump's policies, it will be because of his incompetence.

Third, as we have seen, most of these commenters are wholly owned subsidiaries of the Oligarchy, or committed members of the elitist club that dominates the press and our civil institutions and as such are more interested in obscuring the Coup and the people's revolt against it, than in shedding light upon it.

And finally, what they are dismissing as "unrealistic" is merely what's necessary to save the planet; what they are dismissing as paranoid, is backed by fact; what they are dismissing as pie-eyed is simply deciding to reembrace the Enlightenment principles this country was founded upon.

A final reason the cognoscenti will see the ideas posed in this book as beyond the province of politics or possibility is because they are all viewing the world through the same narrow lens of politics as a horse race between two parties, with one representing the Left, the other the Right. In reality, that world was under assault in the late 1960s, and it died completely in the 1980s. Today, the EEM sees politics as all about the quest for power and the exercise of it—rather than the search for effective policies and solutions that assure equity, justice, and a sustainable future for the majority of Americans—so it is blinded to all that really matters.

It is likely that the residents of conservative and mainstream think tanks, assorted pundits, and most of the politicians themselves will drop out somewhere shortly after chapter 5, sputtering with rage that any would say that the United States is not a democracy, that the press is not free, that the market will not deliver all good things by pure serendipity, and that "big government" is not the source of our problems. In fact, as we have seen, government is the only possible guarantor of freedom and prosperity—that it has been in the recent past and must become so again.

The self-proclaimed pragmatists, the practitioners of realpolitik, tri-angulators, corporate lackeys, other useful idiots, and their ilk probably began rolling their eyes sometime around chapter 8, by which time they were told that society's watch dogs have been neutered, that they themselves have been sold a bill of goods which they've resold, and that their favorite illusion—America as politically right of center—is dead wrong. Once the eye-rollers are dispatched, the rest will reach Part Two.

The few economists who would remain after hearing that markets aren't perfect will have fled by the end of Part Two, unable to accept that the neoliberal consensus they and their Davos buddies have been using to steer the ship of state is a giant con game, little better than a Ponzi scheme, which destroys the Enlightenment principles that are the basis of modern democracies. Many, if not most of the elected Democrats and Democratic Leadership Council acolytes, and the few remaining members of the EEM still reading will have joined them.

Most of the rest of the academics and denizens of "liberal" think tanks and the "liberal" online media will have dropped out somewhere early in Part Three when the litany of environmental and resource woes begins. Impractical, they will mutter; can't be giving people bad news; can't sell people doom and gloom.

But the premise of this book is that the agenda for our future has to be shaped by what *must* be done, not by what *can* be done. As we saw in chapters 15 and 16, we have not left ourselves the time to pursue only what is *possible*; we must do what is *necessary* and we must begin—literally—today.

That will leave philosophers, scientists, and hopefully, the people—who generally have more wisdom and courage than they are given credit for when they are dealt with honestly. If the general population of the United States is doing its best to turn *Idiocracy* from a cult movie into a documentary, it's not because they are stupid; it is because they have been kept in a state of ignorance using distraction, fear, and a modern-day version of bread and circuses.

At any rate, the reviews and the judgment coming from the commentariat will say the problems and solutions in this book are beyond the province of politics. Unrealistic they will say. Attacking the fundamental assumptions underlying our economy, culture, and political system is a fool's errand. Not worth the paper, ink, or electrons it's carried out with.

Here's the thing. In ordinary times, they'd be right. I'd be in full agreement with them.

But to paraphrase Neil de Grasse Tyson, the bad thing about reality is that it is true, whether or not you believe in it.

The bottom line is this: If we don't address the challenges we face, we are on our way to the New Dark Ages and all that it implies. Not simply because we are abandoning the Enlightenment principles that form the basis of our government, but also because we will need the power of Enlightenment thinking to solve the problems we have been and still are creating. Relying on necromancy, myth, religiosity, and medieval thinking to solve our problems will doom us to catastrophe.

We are on the cusp of the most devastating environmental and economic crisis humanity has ever witnessed, brought on by climate change, ocean acidification, and overconsumption. If we fail to address these problems they will not only compromise our life support systems, they will also create global social upheaval the likes of which we've never seen. Indeed, the crises in Syria, Darfur, and Libya are the bow wave of the secular apocalypse to come if we fail to act, and they were caused in whole or in part by disruptions triggered by climate change.[207]

Indeed, trying to raise the specter of the global threat of terrorism while denying climate change is like dining on a fast-food diet of fatty fries, burgers, bacon, and cheese and wondering why you've just had a heart attack.

The window of opportunity to prevent *some* measure of ecological catastrophe has closed, but the opportunity to *mitigate it to tolerable levels* still exists, although it is rapidly closing.

The proximate cause of these problems is the widespread use of fossil fuels, the liquidation of natural resources, and the release of massive quantities of wastes, particularly greenhouse gasses, into the biosphere.

Their ultimate cause lies in the belief systems that enable us to cavalierly dismiss these dangers, while we compound them. These are cultural, political, and epistemological, and no matter how ingrained they may be in our society or culture, they must be dealt with if we are to avoid a secular Armageddon. Much of what is destructive in our culture comes from the worldview shaped by modern conservatism, neoclassical economics, and neoliberal politics.

The people have an innate understanding of how completely the system has failed them, and how completely it's been taken over by the Oligarchy. Republicans have long been allies with—and in the pocket of—corporations and fat cats; since Bill Clinton, Democrats have joined them.

We need a new consensus if we are to avoid a second Dark Ages. It is my hope that this book contributes to forging it. But that will depend upon you, the people. If we continue to follow the "prudent" path; if we continue to put conventional wisdom over real wisdom; if we fail to understand that we are at a singular moment in the history of our country and our people, and our planet, then we will continue to rocket into oblivion while we set trim tabs on our course, thinking as we do, that it will suffice.

But look at what we've done; look where we are. We have elected a buffoon to lead us, and he has done nothing more than accelerate our toboggan ride to hell. These times demand the "unrealistic," they demand unconventional wisdom, and most of all, they call for the passion and the courage of ordinary people to take control and change course.

It is time, at last, to actively define our future by what is necessary, not what is possible, sensible, pragmatic or reasonable.

CONCLUSION

● ● ●

The world is indeed full of peril, and in it there are many dark
places; but still there is much that is fair, and though in all lands
love is now mingled with grief, it grows perhaps the greater.

J. R. R. TOLKIEN, *THE FELLOWSHIP OF THE RING*

THESE ARE PERILOUS TIMES.

At a time when the window of opportunity to avoid the worst—and increasingly, the irrevocable—consequences of climate change is closing, we have an anti-science president and Congress that is already doing its best to usher us into the new Dark Ages.

At a time when the social fabric of our nation is in danger of being ripped to shreds, we've elected a leader who feeds divisiveness.

At a time when the world is in danger of slipping into fascism, we've elected a fascist.

At a time when the bases of our freedoms are threatened, we've elected a president and a majority in Congress who have contempt for democracy and the principles which sustain it.

At a time when bread and circuses, beads and baubles, and Kardashian nonsense threatens to rip values, morals, and the meaning they confer from our lives, we've elected a man devoid of values who encases himself in gold—a modern day Midas, who understands the price of everything and the value of nothing.

At a time when we need a government that is strong, capable, responsive, and responsible, we've turned it into a punch line.

At a time when the unconstrained power of the free market is consuming our souls even as it consumes our planet and funnels the wealth from the many to the few, we've elected a man and a Congress intent on serving the plutocrats, not the people.

At a time when we need a political system that represents the people and advocates for them, we have only the Republicans who worship at the altar of wealth and represent the interests of the 1 percent and the neoliberal Democrats who have been reduced to pale doppelgängers of them.

Finally, when we need an aroused citizenry willing and able to mount a sustained revolution that will counter the Oligarch's Coup, we have only the complacent, the fat, the spoiled, the entitled, the willfully ignorant, the overfed and distracted children of a lesser god...a god defined by the trappings and toys dangled before us...familiar with a Coke, but not a Koch; more intent on getting a Lincoln than we are on electing one; more interested in consuming than producing.

But wait. I see, everywhere, evidence that this last thing—this soporific excuse for a citizen—is waking up. I see it in the tens of millions who supported a rumple-suited Vermonter with wild hair and an unvarnished commitment to the truth. I see it in the nascent wisdom that, after lying dormant for decades—attenuated by Reagan's false promise of morning in America if we would just get government out of the way—is even now sprouting. I see it in the growing awareness that government isn't the enemy—that in fact, government is us, we the people. And if it is to be good, then so must we be good. If it is to work, then so must we work. If we are to be great, then it must be the vehicle we ride to greatness.

And I see it in the millions who marched together on January 21 and April 22, and in the protests and continued resistance being mounted by we the people since then.

The next two years will be critical. If we've hit bottom with Trump, then we must start our climb. And we must climb together. The middle-aged white man, huddling in his basement, facing diminished prospects, shooting heroin, and clutching his gun must be given hope and the opportunity that makes hope real.

The angry young black man who's never had prospects, who's been denied a shot at an education, at a job—who has been a victim of frightened or prejudiced police, who sees people cross the street to avoid him—needs to be welcomed.

The women who've been cheated out of wages, opportunities for advancement, and recognition—who've had to face misogyny, unwanted advances, and inflexible roles for their life choices need to be granted equality at last.

Immigrants, the LGBQT community, native Americans—each must be allowed to live in a land that values us for who we are and what we give, not for how we fit someone else's template of what it means to be American.

And all of us—black and white, women and men, native born and immigrant, straight or other, young and old—must be willing to reach out a tentative hand each to the other because only by standing together can we win as individuals or as groups.

We must know that tyranny comes more often from within than without. Our freedoms and our opportunities have not been taken by foreigners, but by the rich and the powerful here at home.

Corporate tyranny is no less vile than any other. Living in a land that is fast becoming a company store will enslave us more quickly and more surely than terrorism or Russians or any of the bogeymen of the moment conjured up to keep us afraid and distracted.

We must know that the very people who have eroded our opportunities or prevented us from having any are posing as populists and champions of the people while they steal us blind, grab our pussies, and divide us one from another.

We must know that if our country is no longer the land where hard work and steadfast commitment turn dreams into reality, it can be again.

We must know that if we stand shoulder to shoulder the way we did by the millions on January 21, we are the most powerful force on Earth.

It will take work, it will take commitment, it will demand sacrifice. But we can take our country back again. We can end the four-decade-long con job that has robbed us of our freedoms, our wealth, and our honor.

Ironically, the Oligarchy has showed us how. We need only emulate what they did in the name of greed and power, to restore a measure of dignity, decency, morality and wealth to each of us.

Yes, these are perilous times. But from peril can come promise. The reality we find ourselves in now—the daily outrages, the gross incompetence, the shear folly that has taken over our politics—is the culmination of four decades of our own neglect.

Perhaps we needed to hit bottom. If so, we certainly have. We must start today to climb out of this dark cave and together start our march to the summit—united, as one.

An informed citizenry is a check on tyrants and tyranny, an aroused one is an antidote to them. Let us continue to move forward together with passion, purpose, and promise. Let the Revolution begin. It's high time it did.

Preface

1. I first wrote about the Silent Coup in 2005, here: http://www. informationclearinghouse.info/article10407.htm Since that article appeared, the situation has only gotten worse, and yet it remains the greatest story never told.

2. As we will see in later chapters, the corporations' attempt to take over our country goes back to its prerevolutionary days, but the modern-day success of its efforts can be dated to the publication of Lewis Powell's Memo to the Chamber of Commerce on August 23, 1971. See: http://reclaimdemocracy.org/powell_memo_lewis/.

3. Michael Moore, Nathan Robinson, and Thomas Frank warned that the Democrats were in trouble, and I warned that Clinton's candidacy was likely to doom Democrats as far back as November of 2014. See: John Atcheson, "Backing Hillary in 2016: Bad for Progressives and Bad Politics, Too," *CommonDreams*, November 29, 2014; or see here or here or here.

4. Patrick Cadell, Scott Miller, and Bob Perkins, "It's Candidate Smith by a Landslide," *Huffington Post*, July 2, 2014, http://www.huffingtonpost. com/patrick-caddell/its-candidate-smith-by-a-_b_5552229.html.

5. Julianna Goldman, "Donald Trump's Cabinet Richest in U. S. History, Historians Say," *CBS News*, December 20, 2016, http://www. cbsnews.com/news/donald-trump-cabinet-richest-in-us-history-historians-say/.

Chapter I

6. "Put Away the Fireworks: You Don't Live in a Democracy Anymore," John Atcheson; *Common Dreams*,; July 4th, 2016,. See: http://www.

commondreams.org/views/2016/07/04/put-away-fireworks-you-dont-live-democracy-anymore.

7.   Emily Atkin, "Voters Want Pretty Much the Opposite of What Congress is Doing," Think Progress, June 16, 2015. See: https://thinkprogress.org/poll-voters-want-pretty-much-the-opposite-of-what-congress-is-doing-5bc936a668c6

8.   ibid.

9.   Brad Johnson, "Poll: 74 Percent of Americans Support Ending Big Oil Subsidies," Think Progress, May 3, 2011. See: https://think-progress.org/poll-74-percent-of-americans-support-ending-big-oil-subsidies-8ef5d6ac4a50

10. Paul Steinhauser, "Do Americans want to extend tax cuts for the wealthy?", CNN Political Ticker, September 16, 2010. See: http://politicalticker.blogs.cnn.com/2010/09/16/do-americans-want-to-extend-tax-cuts-for-wealthy-3/

11. Robinson Meyer, "Most Americans Favor Staying in the Paris Agreement," *The Atlantic*, May 31, 2017. See: https://www.theatlantic.com/science/archive/2017/05/most-americans-support-staying-in-the-paris-agreement/528663/

12. Alison Linn, "Americans Will Pay to Shore Up Social Security: Poll," *Today*, CNN, February 1, 2013, 8:50 AM. See: http://www.cnbc.com/id/100426765

13. "Polls Show Vast Majority for More Wall Street Regulation," *New York Times*, March 12. 2010, 2:46 AM. See: https://deal-book.nytimes.com/2010/03/12/poll-shows-vast-majority-for-more-wall-st-regulation/

14. Gabriel Levy, "Senate Votes Down 4 Gun Bills After Orlando Shootings," *US News*, June 20, 2016, 7:29 PM. See: https://www. usnews.com/news/articles/2016-06-20/senate-votes-down-4-gun-bills-after-orlando-nightclub-shootings

15. Martin Gilens and Benjamin I. Page, "Testing Theories of American Politics: Elites, Interest Groups and Average Citizens," *Perspectives on Politics* 12 (2014): 564–81.

16. Jay Costa, "What's the Cost of a Seat in Congress?" *MapLight*, March 10, 2013. See: https://maplight.org/story/whats-the-cost-of-a-seat-in-congress/

17. Mark Abadi, "One metric puts into perspective just how unpopular Donald Trump and Hillary Clinton were with voters," *Business Insider*, November 9, 2016, 4:41 PM. See: http://www.businessinsider.com/more-votes-for-down-ballot-than-president-2016-11.

Chapter 2

18. One of the more popular short hand terms used to describe chaos theory is the "butterfly effect," which suggests that when a butterfly flaps its wings, it can change the weather in a far- off place. In scientific jargon: a small change in one state of a nonlinear system can create large changes or even completely new equilibria states in relatively short time frames. For a more sophisticated understanding of this concept start here: http://tuvalu.santafe.edu/~wbarthur/Books/Preface.html.

19. See: The Powell Memo [also known as the Powell Manifesto], Reclaim Democracy, http://reclaimdemocracy.org/powell_memo_lewis/.

20. For a thorough and fascinating look at how these foundations have been used to shape everything from academia to the media, at the

state and federal level, see: https://www.pfaw.org/sites/default/files/
buyingamovement.pdf.

CHAPTER 3

21. Conservatives Bashing the Liberal Media Aided by Think Tanks,"
    BuzzFlash, November, 12 2015, http://truth-out.org/buzzflash/
    commentary/conservatives-bashing-the-liberal-media-aided-by-
    think-tanks

22. Sally Covington, "How Conservative Philanthropies and Think
    Tanks Transform US Policy," http://mediafilter.org/CAQ/caq63/
    caq63thinktank.html.

23. Economists proudly proclaim that the market is amoral— not
    immoral—but non-normative. That is, it stands outside the frame-
    work of good or evil, right or wrong, ethical or unethical.

24. See: Ashley Lutz, "These Six Companies Control 90% of the
    Media in America," *Business Insider*, June 14, 2012, http://www.
    businessinsider.com/these-6-corporations-control-90-of-the-
    media-in-america-2012-6.

25. Eric Alterman, *What Liberal Media? The Truth about Bias in the
    News*, New York, Basic Books) 2003. https://www.amazon.com/
    What-Liberal-Media-Truth-About/dp/0465001769

26. Eric Alterman, "What Liberal Media? The Right Is Working the
    Refs and Its Working," *The Nation*, February 24, 2003.

27. Glen Kessler, "Recalling Hillary Clinton's claim of 'landing under
    sniper fire' in Bosnia," *Washington Post*, May 23, 2016. See: https://

www.washingtonpost.com/news/fact-checker/wp/2016/05/23/recalling-hillary-clintons-claim-of-landing-under-sniper-fire-in-bosnia/?utm_term=.dfa623e351ff

28. See: http://www.cc.com/video-clips/yv88qv/the-daily-show-with-jon-stewart-the-gop-whisperer

29. Ron Susskind, "Faith, Certainty, and the Presidency of George W. Bush," *New York Times Magazine*, October 17, 2004, http://www.nytimes.com/2004/10/17/magazine/faith-certainty-and-the-presidency-of-george-w-bush.html.

CHAPTER 4

30. Smith's famous invisible hand quote: "He intends only his own gain, and he is in this, as in many other cases, led by an invisible hand to promote an end which was no part of his intention. Nor is it always the worse for society that it was no part of his intention. By pursuing his own interest he frequently promotes that of the society more effectually than when he really intends to promote it."

31. Decision 2012, "Bachman's husband got $137 thousand in Medicaid funds," NBC News.com, http://www.nbcnews.com/id/45570552/ns/politics-decision_2012/t/bachmanns-husband-got-medicaid-funds/#.WPF5uVPyuu5

32. Remington Shepard, "Reagan, Ryan and Exploding Deficits," *Media Matters*, August 13, 2112, http://mediamatters.org/blog/2012/08/13/reagan-ryan-and-exploding-deficits/189313.

33. David Corn, Alan Shrugged, *Mother Jones*, October 24, 2008, 3:00 AM, http://www.motherjones.com/politics/2008/10/alan-shrugged

34. George Brown Tindall and David E. Shi, *America: A Narrative History (Brief Ninth Edition) (Vol. 2)*. (New York: W. W. Norton & Company, 2012), 589, and Steve Fraser, *The Age of Acquiescence: The Life and Death of American Resistance to Organized Wealth and Power* (New York: Little, Brown and Company, 2015), 66.

35. Hyperhistory.com, See: http://www.hyperhistory.com/online_n2/ connections_n2/bust1.html

36. Wealth Inequality in the United States since 1913: Emmanuel Saez and Gabriel Zucman, Evidence from Capitalized Income Tax Data, Working Paper 20625, National Bureau of Economic Research, www.nber.org/papers/2065.

37. Bryce Covert, "Thomas Piketty Ran the Numbers on Wealth Inequality. Here's What He Found," *Think Progress*, January 6, 2016. See: https://thinkprogress.org/thomas-piketty-ran-the-numbers-on-income-inequality-heres-what-he-found-77475863e421

38. Raquel Meyer Alexander, Steven W. Maza, and Susan Schultz, "Measuring Rates of Return for Lobbying Expenditures: And Empirical Case Study of Tax Breaks for Multinational Corporations," Journal of Law and Politics 25, no. 401 (2009): 401–57.

39. See: http://sunlightfoundation.com/blog/2014/11/17/fixed-fortunes-biggest-corporate-political-interests-spend-billions-get-trillions/.

40. Kevin Drumm, "Are Corporations Hoarding Cash?" *Mother Earth News*, March 18, 2014, 2:31 AM. See: http://www.mother-jones.com/kevin-drum/2014/03/are-corporations-hoarding-cash-its-complicated/

41. David Cay Johnston, "How to Repeal the Tax Loophole that Allows Companies to Hide their Profits in Offshore Accounts," *The Nation*,

August 4, 2015, https://www.thenation.com/article/how-to-repeal-the-tax-loophole-that-allows-companies-to-hide-their-profits-in-offshore-accounts/

42. "Fact Sheet; Taxing Wealthy Americans," Americans for Tax Fairness, http://americansfortaxfairness.org/tax-fairness-briefing-booklet/fact-sheet-taxing-wealthy-americans/.

43. Matt Taibbi, "Secrets and Lies of the Bailout," *Rolling Stone*, January 4, 2013, http://www.rollingstone.com/politics/news/secret-and-lies-of-the-bailout-20130104.

44. Chris Isadore, "Fed Made 9 Trillion in Emergency Overnight Loans," *CNN*, December 1, 2010, 6:05 PM. See: http://money.cnn.com/2010/12/01/news/economy/fed_reserve_data_release/index.htm.

45. Derrick Thompson, "America's Monopoly Problem," *Atlantic*, October, 2016, http://www.theatlantic.com/magazine/archive/2016/10/americas-monopoly-problem/497549/.

46. Joseph Stiglitz, "The New Era of Monopoly Is Here," *The Guardian*, May 13, 2016, https://www.theguardian.com/business/2016/may/13/-new-era-monopoly-joseph-stiglitz.

47. Oxfam Media Briefing, "Broken at the Top," Oxfam America, April 14, 2016. See: https://www.oxfamamerica.org/static/media/files/Broken_at_the_Top_4.14.2016.pdf

Chapter 5

48. With the passage of the Clean Air Act, the Clean Water Act, the Resource Conservation and Recovery Act, and the Toxic Substances Control Act—all promulgated and amended between 1970 and the 1990s—most of the *acute* environmental insults were addressed. But

it was becoming obvious by the 90's that significant and even more serious environmental insults resulted from the *chronic* and ubiquitous release of wastes—toxic and nontoxic alike, with climate change representing an existential threat. But with the Coup, it became impossible to take action even to save ourselves.

49. Steve Idemoto, *Social Security Privatization in Chile: A Case for Caution* (Seattle, WA: Economic Opportunity Institute), last modified September 29, 2000, http://www.eoionline.org/wp/wp-content/uploads/social-security/SSPrivatizationChileCaseCaution-Sep00.pdf.

50. Institute for Public Accuracy, Press Release, July 28, 2015, See: http://www.accuracy.org/release/medicares-50-years-of-low-overhead-vs-acas-increasing-bureaucratic-bloat-merger-mania/.

51. Dana Liebelson, "POGO Study: Contractors Costing Government Twice as Much as In-House Workforce," The Project on Government Oversight, Sept, 13, 2011. See: http://pogoblog.typepad.com/pogo/2011/09/by-dana-liebelson-the-us-governments-increasing-reliance-on-contractors-to-do-work-traditionally-done-by-federal-empl.html.

52. See http://inthesetimes.com/article/17533/how_to_sell_off_a_city.

53. Ben Herschler, "Exclusive—Transatlantic Divide: How US Pays Three Times More for Drugs," *Reuters*, October 12, 2015, http://www.reuters.com/article/us-pharmaceuticals-usa-comparison-idUSKCN0S61KU20151012.

54. See: http://useconomy.about.com/od/usdebtanddeficit/p/US-Debt-by-President.htm.

55. I express the debt in terms of percentage rather than absolute dollars, since a comparison on a dollars basis is essentially comparing apples to oranges.

56. Wikapedia, "List of Countries by Military Expenditures." See: https://en.wikipedia.org/wiki/List_of_countries_by_military_expenditures

57. Michael Shermer, "The Five Myths of Terrorism—Including That It Works: Why Terrorism Doesn't Work," *Scientific American*, August 1, 2016, https://www.scientificamerican.com/article/five-myths-of-terrorism-including-that-it-works/.

58. Sally Kohn, "Hell from Above: Drone Strikes Are Creating Hatred for America that Will Last for Generations," *Quartz*, December 9, 2015, http://qz.com/569779/drone-strikes-are-creating-hatred-towards-america-that-will-last-for-generations/.

59. National Priorities, "Federal Spending: Where Does the Money Go." See: https://www.nationalpriorities.org/budget-basics/federal-budget-101/spending/

60. Tobin Harshaw, "It's the Lapel Pin, Stupid," The Opinionator, *The New York Times*, April 17, 2008, 9:12 AM. See: https://opinionator.blogs.nytimes.com/2008/04/17/its-the-lapel-pins-stupid/

61. Sarah Ferris, "Showdown Scars: How the $4 Trillion 'Grand Bargain' Collapsed," *The Hill*, http://thehill.com/policy/finance/268857-showdown-scars-how-the-4-trillion-grand-bargain-collapsed.

62. See: Michael Shermer, "The Five Myths of Terrorism—Including That It Works: Why Terror Doesn't Work," *Scientific American*, August 1, 2013.

63. Steve Eder and Dave Philips, "Faith in Agency Clouded Sanders's [sic] V. A. Response," *New York Times*, February 6, 2016, http://www.nytimes.com/2016/02/07/us/politics/faith-in-agency-clouded-bernie-sanderss-va-response.html

64. Richard Eskow, "A Secret Plan to Close Social Security's Offices and Outsource its Work," *OurFuture.org*, June 24, 2014, https://ourfuture.org/20140624/a-secret-plan-to-close-social-securitys-offices-and-outsource-its-work.

65. "Thomas Frank: Bill Clinton's Five Major Achievements Were Longstanding GOP Objectives," Interview with Thomas Frank by Mark Karlin, Truthout, May 15, 2016, http://www.truth-out.org/news/item/36035-thomas-frank-bill-clinton-s-five-major-achievements-were-longstanding-gop-objectives.

66. See: http://inthesetimes.com/article/18889/bernie-sanders-president-bill-clinton-1995.

67. Eric Levitz, "The Republican Party Must Answer for What It Did to Kansas and Louisiana," *New York*, March 18, 2016, 11:48 AM. http://nymag.com/daily/intelligencer/2016/03/gop-must-answer-for-what-it-did-to-kansas.html

68. Michael Lindon, "Kansas' experiment with tax cutting failed spectacularly — on its own terms," *Business Insider*, June 14, 2017, 1:39 PM. See: http://www.businessinsider.com/kansas-experiment-with-tax-cutting-failed-on-its-own-terms-2017-6

69. California requires a two-thirds supermajority to pass most tax bills.

70. "Tracking Trends in Party Affiliation, 1939–2014," *Pew Research Center*, http://www.people-press.org/interactives/party-id-trend/.

71.   Josh Sagler, "Is the USA Center-Right? An Issue-by-Issue Breakdown," May 2, 2014, *The Progressive Cynic*, https://thepro-gressivecynic.com/2014/05/02/is-the-usa-center-right-an-issue-by-issue-breakdown/.

CHAPTER 6

72.   Facebook has introduced tools to identify fake news and reduce its influence, as has Google. Recently Slate issued a tool that can be used to neuter fake news. See: http://www.slate.com/articles/technology/technology/2016/12/introducing_this_is_fake_slate_s_tool_for_stopping_fake_news_on_facebook.html.

73.   John Atcheson, "The Oligarchy vs. the People: Why We Need a Political Revolution," *CommonDreams*, November 18. 2015. In this article, I summarized key endorsements and link to references outlining the disconnect between the members of these civil institutions and their leaders. https://www.commondreams.org/views/2015/11/18/oligarchy-vs-people-why-we-need-political-revolution

74.   See League of Conservation Voters National Environmental Scorecard at: http://scorecard.lcv.org/moc/hillary-rodham-clinton

75.   See League of Conservation Voters National Environmental Scorecard at: http://scorecard.lcv.org/moc/bernie-sanders

76.   A poll from about this time can be found at Real Clear Politics. See: https://www.realclearpolitics.com/epolls/latest_polls/president/

77.   Mario Vasquez, "Machinists Union Members Outraged Over Hillary Clinton Endorsement, Say They Want Bernie Sanders," *In These Times*, Monday, August 17, 2016, 1:34 PM. See: http://inthese-times.com/working/entry/18321/bernie_sanders_machinists1

78. Ibid.

79. Emily Atkin, "Big Green Groups Line Up behind Clinton, While Smaller Ones Stick to Sanders," *Think Progress,* June 10, 2016, https://thinkprogress.org/big-green-groups-line-up-behind-clinton-while-smaller-ones-stick-to-sanders-9ff97dd6ebd#.haglorag9.

CHAPTER 7

80. Poll after poll supports the fact that Americans are overwhelmingly progressive when viewed on an issue-by-issue basis—see: https://our-future.org/report/american-majority-project-polling, for example.

81. Hedrick Smith, "How GOP Gerrymandering Is Disrupting the House," *Reclaim,* October 1, 2015 http://reclaimtheamericandream.org/2015/10/how-gop-gerrymandering-helped-topple-boehner/

82. See: Ballotopedia at: https://ballotpedia.org/State_government_trifectas.

83. See: https://en.wikipedia.org/wiki/List_of_United_States_state_legislatures.

84. Lydia Saad, "Conservatives Hang onto Ideology Lead by a Thread," *Gallup Poll,* January 11, 2016, http://www.gallup.com/poll/188129/conservatives-hang-ideology-lead-thread.aspx

85. Joseph Romm, *Language Intelligence: Lessons in persuasion from Jesus, Shakespeare, Lincoln and Lady Gaga,* July 11th 2012. See: https://www.amazon.com/Language-Intelligence-Lessons-persuasion-Shakespeare/dp/1477452222

86.   Kevin Drum, "Liberal Branding," *Mother Jones*, October 11, 2010, http://www.motherjones.com/kevin-drum/2010/10/liberal-branding.

87.   "Differences in Conservative and Liberal Brains: 16 Peer-reviewed Studies Show Liberals and Conservatives Physiologically Different," *ProCon.org*, February 3, 2015, http://2012election.procon.org/view.resource.php?resourceID=004818.

Chapter 8

88.   Harry Enton, "Americans' Distaste for Both Trump and Clinton Is Record-Breaking," *Five-Thirty-Eight*, May 5, 2016, http://fivethirtyeight.com/features/americans-distaste-for-both-trump-and-clinton-is-record-breaking/.

89.   John Atcheson, "Four Myths Keeping Hillary Clinton Afloat," *Common Dreams*, April 12, 2016, http://www.commondreams.org/views/2016/04/12/four-myths-keeping-clinton-afloat

90.   C. Eugene Emory Jr., "Spot check of Hillary's Senate record fails to support bipartisan claim," *Politifact*, January 20, 2016, 12:10 p.m. http://www.politifact.com/truth-o-meter/statements/2016/jan/20/hillary-clinton/spot-check-hillary-clintons-senate-record-immolate/

91.   GovTrack, Sen. Hillary Clinton. See: https://www.govtrack.us/congress/members/hillary_clinton/300022

92.   See: Michael Sainato, "Wikileaks Proves Primary Was Rigged: DNC Undermines Democracy," Opinion, *The Observer*, July 26, 2016, http://observer.com/2016/07/wikileaks-proves-primary-was-rigged-dnc-undermined-democracy/.

93. Margaret Sullivan, "Were Changes to Sanders Article 'Stealth Editing'," Public Editor's Journal; *New York Times*, March 17, 2016, http://publiceditor.blogs.nytimes.com/2016/03/17/new-york-times-bernie-sanders-coverage-public-editor/.

94. Charles Blow, "A Bernie Blackout?," Opinion, *New York Times*, March 16, 2016, http://www.nytimes.com/2016/03/17/opinion/campaign-stops/a-bernie-blackout.html?_r=0.

95. Ibid.

96. See: http://television.gdeltproject.org/cgi-bin/iatv_campaign2016/iatv_campaign2016.

97. Adam Johnson, "Washington Post Runs 16 Negative Stories on Bernie Sanders in 16 Hours," Fairness and Accuracy in Reporting, March 8, 2016, http://www.commondreams.org/views/2016/03/08/washington-post-ran-16-negative-stories-bernie-sanders-16-hours.

98. "Millions of New Yorkers Disenfranchised from Primaries Thanks to State's Restrictive Voting Laws," *Democracy Now*, April 19, 2016, http://www.democr" acynow.org/2016/4/19/millions_of_new_yorkers_disenfranchised_from.

99. Nate Silver, "The Hidden Importance of the Sanders Voter," *Five-Thirty-Eight*, May 19, 2016, http://fivethirtyeight.com/features/the-hidden-importance-of-the-bernie-sanders-voter/.

100. John Meyers, "California's registered voters hit record high ahead of Tuesday presidential primary," *Los Angeles Times*, June 30, 2016, 5:48 PM. See: http://www.latimes.com/politics/la-pol-sac-essential-politics-california-new-voters-voter-registration-primary-html-story.html

101. Jessie Hellmann, "Poll: Sanders Edging Clinton out in California," *The Hill*, June 2, 2016.

102. Dennis Romero, "Bernie Sanders Could Actually Beat Clinton in California," *LA Weekly*, June 3, 2016, 6:02 AM, http://www.laweekly.com/news/bernie-sanders-could-actually-beat-clinton-in-california-6993355

103. Neal Gabler, "Did the Press Take Down Bernie Sanders?" *Moyers and Company*, June 10, 2016. See: http://billmoyers.com/story/press-take-bernie-sanders/

104. On October 7, 2016, WikiLeaks released e-mails hacked from the Clinton campaign chairman John Podesta's account that show Clinton's views on Wall Street, trade, and the XL pipeline to be distinctly different from her public positions and those of most Democrats, and even quoted her as saying there was a need to have a private position on issues that differed from the public one. See: https://wikileaks.org/podesta-emails/emailid/927.

Chapter 9

105. Jefferson provided the original draft of the Declaration, and although he was a Minister to France during the Constitutional Convention in Philadelphia in 1787, his ideas were extremely influential—his draft for the Virginia Constitution (which he also missed), and his mentorship and communication with Madison helped shape the Constitution's ultimate framework.

106. See: Ben Heineman Jr., "The Origins of Today's Bitter Partisanship: The Founding Fathers," *The Atlantic*, September 9, 2011, http://www.theatlantic.com/national/archive/2011/09/the-origins-of-todays-bitter-partisanship-the-founding-fathers/244839/.

107. See: "The Two Parties Emerge," http://www.ushistory.org/us/19c. asp.

Chapter 10

108. See: http://mentalfloss.com/article/12487/adams-vs-jefferson-birth-negative-campaigning-us.

109. Alexander Reed Kelly, "North Carolina Lawmakers Legislate Sea Level Rise," *Truthout*, June 13, 2012. See: http://www.truth-dig.com/eartotheground/item/north_carolina_lawmakers_legislate_sea_level_rise_20120613

110. Seth Cline, "Global Warming Text Was Removed from Virginia Report on Rising Sea Levels," *US News,*June 13, 2012, 4:47 PM. See: https://www.usnews.com/news/articles/2012/06/13/global-warm-ing-text-was-removed-from-virginia-bill-on-rising-sea-levels-

111. Karen Valentine, "Florida Officials Ban the Term Climate Change," *Think Progress*, May 8, 2015, https://thinkprogress.org/florida-offi-cials-ban-the-term-climate-change-4188d53e5290#.yocl18q8t.

112. Peter U. Clark, Jeremy D. Shakum, Shaun A. Marcott, et al., "Consequences of Twenty-First Century Policy for Multi-Millennial Climate and Sea Level Change," *Nature Climate Change*, February 2016, http://www.nature.com/articles/nclimate2923. epdf?referrer_access_token=dbRqIHS6vuBhm1oWXT1Td9RgN 0jAjWel9jnR3ZoTv0P7bBCydl3XkC-iEMeXdnEdD0CDGSU B4J_y6QudGd2kHIYi-Fz4RKzEbLtdoaoMjNMxDkLLyOgeR-TWP6jdyYvAin9vLrnDc8psQ5IgSkAB59UiAqi2lM5cPtJc1a5E-nfYg1UAU6G8fAv7ZWmpg6ekQJy5mgf6rHVGl28tNpq2SyH0u-WpLj99b6m0rLux0_onilo8XBK4P7UkIRSsJ3S9nYNR9aXZYu-

pOS38fQjeB30TxGl32zfW0jRc0Gd5EqsBNcc%3D&tracking_referrer=www.theguardian.com.

113. How Stupid Are Americans? LOOK and see...don't we all wish it wasn't so. See: https://www.youtube.com/watch?v=QpDEu8KmNj0. *Idiocracy* is a movie that takes place in the distant future at a time when the intellectual capacity of Americans has diminished.

114. Michael Snyder, "It's Official: Americans R Stupid," *The Economic Collapse*, March 16, 2015, http://www.globalresearch.ca/its-official-americans-r-stupid/5437181.

CHAPTER 11

115. Max Fisher, "US Ranks Near Bottom on Income Distribution," *The Atlantic*, September 19, 2011. See: https://www.theatlantic. com/international/archive/2011/09/map-us-ranks-near-bottom-on-income-inequality/245315/ The CIA, which is the source for this statistic, changed their rankings when the press began referencing their data, but nothing changed to make the US more favorable.

116. "The Terrorist Statistics Every American Needs to Hear," Center for Research on Globalization, May 19, 2014, http://www.glob-alresearch.ca/the-terrorism-statistics-every-american-needs-to-hear/5382818. The figure of thirty-eight deaths includes the San Bernardino attack.

117. Ibid.

118. "U.S. "War on Terror Has INCREASED Terrorism," Center for Research on Globalization, October 23, 2013, http://www.globalre-search.ca/u-s-war-on-terror-has-increased-terrorism/5355073.

119. Michael Shermer, "The Five Myths of Terrorism—Including That It Works: Why Terror Doesn't Work," *Scientific American*, August 1, 2013, http://www.scientificamerican.com/article/five-myths-of-terrorism-including-that-it-works/.

CHAPTER 12

120. See Facts and Figures about Our TV Habit at: http://www.letsgo.org/wp-content/uploads/3-S-2-Facts-and-Figures-About-Our-TV-Habit-Tab-1-DOUBLE-SIDED.pdf.

121. Jane Wakefield," Children Spend Six or More Hours a Day on Screens," *BBC News*, Technology, March 27, 2015, http://www.bbc.com/news/technology-32067158.

122. Robert D. Putnam, *Bowling Alone* (New York: Simon and Schuster, 2000).

123. "Please consume mass quantities," was a catch phrase of the Coneheads on *Saturday Night Live*, popularized in the late 1970s, as our shift from producers to consumers was beginning to accelerate. It was a masterpiece of satire aimed at the existentially empty transformation that was underway.

124. Thomas Frank, in <u>*Listen Liberal*</u> does an extremely good expose on the role of the Innovator in the Democratic Party's embrace of the elite, and how it serves the interests of the corporate interests within the party.

125. See: https://en.wikipedia.org/wiki/Original_affluent_society. For another discussion of this topic, see: http://hunter-gatherers.org/facts-and-theories.html.

CHAPTER 13

126. Garret Hardin, "The Tragedy of the Commons," *Science* 162, no. 3859 (December 13, 1968): 1243-48, http://science.sciencemag.org/content/162/3859/1243.full.

127. See: https://wikileaks.org/podesta-emails/emailid/11011 for a sample of what Ms. Clinton said to Wall Street in her paid speeches.

CHAPTER 14

128. Dani Rodrik, "Goodbye Washington Consensus, Hello Washington Confusion: A Review of the World Bank's Economic Growth in the 1990s: Learning from a Decade of Reform," *Journal of Economic Literature*, Vol. XLIV (December 2006), pp. 973–987. See: http://www.aae.wisc.edu/coxhead/courses/731/PDF/Rodrik%20Goodbye%20Washington%20Consensus%20JEL%202006.pdf

129. See Dr. Stiglitz lecture, The Purpose of the Economy at the Paradigm Lost Conference in Berlin, Germany, sponsored by the Institute for New Economic Thinking, April 12-15, 2012. See: https://www.youtube.com/watch?v=jNqe-pn8xq8

130. "World Footprint," http://www.footprintnetwork.org/our-work/ecological-footprint/#worldfootprint.

131. Ned Rozwell, "When Reindeer Paradise turned into Purgatory," Geophysical Institute, University of Alaska Fairbanks, article 2127, August 9, 2012, http://www.gi.alaska.edu/alaska-science-forum/when-reindeer-paradise-turned-purgatory.

132. Robert Repetto, "Forest for the Trees: Government Policies and the Misuse of Forest Resources," World Resources Institute,

May 1988, http://www.wri.org/publication/forest-trees-government-policies-and-misuse-forest-resources.

133. See: UN FAO Water: Hot Issues at: http://www.fao.org/nr/water/issues/scarcity.html.

134. See, John Peet, *Energy and The Ecological Economics of Sustainability* (Washington, DC: Island Press; 1992).

135. "How Climate Change Is Increasing Forest Fires Around the World," Environment, DW Made for Minds Series, http://www.dw.com/en/how-climate-change-is-increasing-forest-fires-around-the-world/a-19465490.

136. "One Billion People Dependent Upon Sea Food as Their Primary Protein Source," Small Planet Institute, Fast Facts, May 27, 2015, http://smallplanet.org/content/one-billion-people-depend-seafood-their-primary-protein-source.

137. "Failing Phytoplankton, Failing Oxygen: Global Warming Disaster Could Suffocate Life on Planet Earth," *Science Daily*, December 1, 2015, https://www.sciencedaily.com/releases/2015/12/151201094120.htm.

138. Mae-Won Ho, "O_2 Dropping Faster than CO_2 Rising," Institute for Science in Society, September 19, 2009, http://www.i-sis.org.uk/O2DroppingFasterThanCO2Rising.php.

139. See: http://www.huffingtonpost.com/entry/coral-bleaching-third-year_us_57687fa9e4b015db1bca6578.

140. Chris Asenault, "Only 60 Years of Farming Left if Soil Degradation Continues," *Scientific American*, https://www.scientificamerican.

com/article/only-60-years-of-farming-left-if-soil-degradation-continues/ .

141. From "Plastic Garbage," Eco360, http://www.sustainablecommunication.org/eco360/what-is-eco360s-causes/plastic-garbage.

142. Karl Zimmer, "Putting a Price Tag on Nature's Defenses," *New York Times*, June 5, 2014, http://www.nytimes.com/2014/06/05/science/earth/putting-a-price-tag-on-natures-defenses.html.

143. J. B. Maverick, "How Big Is the Derivatives Market?," *Investopedia*, May 27, 2015, http://www.investopedia.com/ask/answers/052715/how-big-derivatives-market.asp.

CHAPTER 15

144. See Merchants of Doubt by Naomi Oreskes and Erik Conway for an excellent summary of the tactics and methods used to stall action on climate change and the players who used them.

145. Joseph Romm, "TV coverage of climate fell 66 percent during a record-setting year for global warming," Think Progress, March 24, 2017. See: https://thinkprogress.org/medias-coverage-of-climate-change-collapsed-in-2016-just-when-we-needed-it-most-2fb793847e69

146. Kevin Anderson, "Duality in Climate Science," *Nature Geoscience* 8 (October 12, 2015): 898–900, doi:10.1038/ngeo2559, http://www.nature.com/ngeo/journal/v8/n12/full/ngeo2559.html.

147. "Two Degrees: The History of Climate Change's Speed Limit," Carbon Brief, August 12, 2014, https://www.carbonbrief.org/two-degrees-the-history-of-climate-changes-speed-limit.

148. You can see Dr. Anderson's critique of the Paris Agreement here: http://www.web.cemus.se/2016/09/05/watch-the-lecture-with-kevin-anderson-from-aug-31/.

149. "Domino Effect: The Jellyfish Example," Slow Fish. See: http://slowfood.com/slowfish/pagine/eng/pagina.lasso?-id_pg=172

150. James Hansen, et. al., "Ice melt, sea level rise and superstorms: evidence from paleoclimate data, climate modeling, and modern observations that 2 °C global warming could be dangerous," Atmos. Chem. Phys., 16, 3761-3812, 2016 See: http://www.atmos-chem-phys.net/16/3761/2016/acp-16-3761-2016-discussion.html

151. Robert M. DeConto and David Pollard, "Contribution of Antarctic to Past and Future Sea-level Rise," *Nature* 531 (March 31, 2016): 591.

152. "Climate Scoreboard: UN Climate Pledge Analysis," Climate Interactive, https://www.climateinteractive.org/programs/scoreboard/.

153. Daniel Grossman, "Paris Climate Agreement: Between the Lines," Yale Climate Connections, December 17, 2015, http://www.yaleclimateconnections.org/2015/12/paris-climate-agreement-between-the-lines/ .

154. David Spratt and Ian Dunlop, "Dangerous Warming: Myth, Reality and Risk Management;" and Raupach (2013, unpublished), based on M. R. Raupach, I. N. Harman, and J. G. Canadell, "Global Climate Goals for Temperature, Concentrations, Emissions and Cumulative Emissions," accessed via http://www.cecoalition.org/carbon_budget.

155. Theo Stein, "Record annual increase of carbon dioxide recorded at Mauna Loa for 2015," National Oceanic and Atmospheric

Administration, March 9, 2016. See: http://www.noaa.gov/news/record-annual-increase-of-carbon-dioxide-observed-at-mauna-loa-for-2015

156. International Energy Agency, "Decoupling of global emissions and economic growth confirmed," March 16, 2016. See: http://www.iea.org/newsroom/news/2016/march/decoupling-of-global-emissions-and-economic-growth-confirmed.html

157. Jospeh Romm, "Ocean Acidification May Amplify Global Warming This Century Up To 0.9°F," *Think Progress*, August 26, 2013. See: https://thinkprogress.org/ocean-acidification-may-amplify-global-warming-this-century-up-to-0-9-f-f9501adb6a46

158. Markus Reichstein, et. al., "Climate extremes and the carbon cycle," *Nature*, V 500, pp 287-295, August 15, 2013.

159. See for example, "Humans Hard-Wired for Optimism, Study Finds," Technology and Science: CBS News, October 24, 2007, http://www.cbc.ca/news/technology/humans-hard-wired-for-optimism-study-finds-1.653385. This finding has been widely confirmed using a variety of testing techniques—humans see the glass half full.

160. Joe Romm, "Chart of the Year: 'Incredible' Price Drops Jumpstart Clean Energy Revolution, *Think Progress*, September 29, 2016, https://thinkprogress.org/clean-energy-revolution-now-81a8e61134c7#.idiog9dge.

161. Eric Wesoff, "How Soon Can Tesla Get Battery Cell Costs Below $100 per Kilowatt-hour?," *Green Tech Media*, March, 15, 2016, https://www.greentechmedia.com/articles/read/How-Soon-Can-Tesla-Get-Battery-Cell-Cost-Below-100-per-Kilowatt-Hour.

162. Joe Romm, "Why Used Electric Car Batteries Could Be Crucial to a Clean Energy Future," *Think Progress*, May 9, 2016, https://think-progress.org/why-used-electric-car-batteries-could-be-crucial-to-a-clean-energy-future-6ab9a2308cdb#.2mve9widc.

163. Our Children's Trust—See: https://www.ourchildrenstrust.org/us/federal-lawsuit/.

164. Peter Niel, "Our Children's Trust and the Public Trust Doctrine," *Huffington Post*, April 19, 2016, http://www.huffingtonpost.com/peter-neill/our-childrens-trust-and-t_b_9734058.html.

165. Ben Adler, "Sanders and Clinton Teams Clash Over Climate Language in Democratic Platform," *Grist*, June 28, 2016, http://grist.org/election-2016/sanders-and-clinton-teams-fight-over-climate-language-in-democratic-platform/.

Chapter 16

166. For example, in April of 2015, Nate Silver, Micah Cohen and Harry Enten of Five Thirty Eight rated the odds of eight Democrats for getting the nomination and Sanders tied for last with Cuomo, who was embroiled in a controversy at the time. Both were given a zero percent chance.

167. John Atcheson, "Poll Driven Spin Doctors in the Age of Big Money Elections," *Common Dreams*, July 11, 2015. See: https://www.commondreams.org/views/2015/07/28/poll-driven-spin-doctors-age-big-money-elections

168. Rick Claypool, "Corporate Interests Infect Trump Transition at Federal Agencies," *Public Citizen*, November 29, 2016, https://

medium.com/public-citizen/corporate-interests-infest-trump-transition-at-federal-agencies-c42d32cb5ec1#.ek51e7u19.

169. Julianna Goldman, "Donald Trump's Cabinet Richest in U. S. History, Historians Say," *CBS News*, December 20, 2016, http://www.cbsnews.com/news/donald-trump-cabinet-richest-in-us-history-historians-say/.

170. Ryan Grimm and Daniel Marans, "New Pre-election Poll Suggests Sanders Could Have Trounced Trump," *Huffington Post*, November 11, 2011, http://www.huffingtonpost.com/entry/2016-election-poll-bernie-sanders- http://www.huffingtonpost.com/entry/2016-election-poll-bernie-sanders-trump_us_58260f7ee4b0c4b63b0c6928.

171. Zach Carter and Daniel Marans, "DNC Contenders Are Not Interested in Your Populist Moment: Rank-and-File Voters Are Angry, But No One Told the Candidates," *Huffington Post*, January 19, 2017, http://www.huffingtonpost.com/entry/dnc-debate-courage-opposition_us_58803552e4b02c1837e9bf7f.

Chapter 17

172. Arthur S. Brisbane, "Should the Times Be a Truth Vigilante," *New York Times*, January 12, 2012, https://publiceditor.blogs.nytimes.com/2012/01/12/should-the-times-be-a-truth-vigilante/?_r=0.

173. Van Jones, Fareed Zakaria, Brian Williams and several others noted the "moment" when Trump became presidential – once again, proving the power of low expectations.

174. "Indivisible: A Practical Guide for Resisting the Trump Agenda," https://static1.squarespace.com/static/5855a354cd0f68bab2089b40/

t/5867cd26be65940ffdeeac1e/1483197741124/IndivisibleGuide_2016-12-31_v1.pdf.

175. John Atcheson, "The People's Budget vs. The Plutocracy," *Common Dreams*, July 21, 2011, http://www.commondreams.org/views/2011/07/21/peoples-budget-vs-plutocracy.

176. Rebecca Savransky, "Poll: Majority of Americans Support Universal Health Care," *The Hill*, May 16, 2016, http://thehill.com/blogs/blog-briefing-room/news/279991-poll-majority-of-americans-support-federally-funded-healthcare.

Chapter 18

177. Gallup Daily: US Consumer Spending. See: http://www.gallup.com/poll/112723/gallup-daily-us-consumer-spending.aspx

178. Nick Thornton, "Total retirement assets near $25 trillion mark," *Benefits Pro*, June 20, 2015. See: http://www.benefitspro.com/2015/06/30/total-retirement-assets-near-25-trillion-mark?slreturn=1498691405

179. John Atcheson, "Making 'Our Revolution' Ours," *CommonDreams*, September 2, 2016. https://www.commondreams.org/views/2016/09/02/making-our-revolution-ours

180. Thom Udall's proposed Constitutional Amendment to overturn Citizens United was voted on by the Senate on September 11, 2014 and received fifty-four votes, but it needed sixty-six to move forward.

181. "American's Views on Money in Politics," *New York Times/CBS News*, June 2, 2015, http://www.nytimes.com/interactive/2015/06/02/us/politics/money-in-politics-poll.html.

CHAPTER 19

182. Cornell West, "Goodbye American neoliberalism. A new era is here," *The Guardian,*November 17, 2016, 6:00 AM. See: https://www.theguardian.com/commentisfree/2016/nov/17/american-neoliberalism-cornel-west-2016-election

183. Polling by Gravis Marketing, a non-partisan research firm, on November 6, showed Sanders beating Trump by 12 percent. http://big.assets.huffingtonpost.com/Gravis_Sanders_Election_Poll.pdf.

184. Gerry Mullany, "World's Richest 8 Have as Much Wealth as Bottom Half, Oxfam Says," *New York Times,* January 16, 2017, https://www.nytimes.com/2017/01/16/world/eight-richest-wealth-oxfam.html?_r=0.

CHAPTER 20

185. "Santa Clara County v. Southern Pacific Railroad Co," *Wikipedia,* https://en.wikipedia.org/wiki/Santa_Clara_County_v._Southern_Pacific_Railroad_Co.

186. Jeffery Tobin, "MONEY UNLIMITED: How Chief Justice John Roberts Orchestrated the Citizens United Decision," Annals of Law, *The New Yorker,* May 21, 2012, http://www.newyorker.com/magazine/2012/05/21/money-unlimited.

CHAPTER 21

187. Thomas E. Mann and Norman J. Orenstein, "Let's Just Say It: The Republican Party Is the Problem," *The New Republic,* April 27, 2012, https://www.washingtonpost.com/opinions/lets-just-say-it-the-republicans-are-the-problem/2012/04/27/gIQAxCVUIT_story.html?utm_term=.765279aa80eb.

188. Ryan McMaken, "If You Want Bigger Government, Vote Republican," February 09, 2016, MISES Wire, MISES Institute, https://mises. org/blog/if-you-want-bigger-government-vote-republican.

CHAPTER 22

189. Jamess, "Media Consolidation—Brought to you by Reagan and Clinton," *The Daily Koss*, Januarly 8, 2008, 5:19 PM, PST, http:// www.dailykos.com/story/2008/1/18/439135/-

190. Andrew Seifter, "Politifact Equates Sanders' Broadly Accurate Climate-Terror Comment with Blatantly False Climate Denial," *Media Matters*, November 18, 2015.

191. Scott Horsely, "Fact Check: Once Again, Politicians Are Stretching the Facts on Obamacare," NPR politics blog, January 4, 2017, http:// www.npr.org/2017/01/04/508242215/fact-check-once-again-law-makers-are-stretching-the-facts-of-obamacare.

192. Arthur S, Brisbane, "Should the Times Be a Truth Vigilante," *New York Times*, January 12, 2012, https://publiceditor.blogs.nytimes. com/2012/01/12/should-the-times-be-a-truth-vigilante/.

CHAPTER 23

193. John Nichols, "The Senate Tried to Overturn Citizens United Today: Guess What Stopped Them: But this Fight Is Far from Over," *The Nation*, September 11, 2104.

194. Greg Stohr, "Bloomberg Poll: Americans Want Supreme Court to Turn Off Political Spending Spigot," September 28, 2015, https://www. bloomberg.com/politics/articles/2015-09-28/bloomberg-poll-amer-icans-want-supreme-court-to-turn-off-political-spending-spigot.

195. Chris Nolter, "TV Political Ad Spending Will Break Records in 2016, and These Broadcasters Will Cash In," *The Street*, June 8, 2016, https://www.thestreet.com/story/13594342/1/tv-political-ad-spending-will-break-records-in-2016-and-these-broadcasters-will-cash-in.html.

196. Lynda Saad, "Half in US Support Publically Funded Campaigns," *Gallup*, June 24, 2012, http://www.gallup.com/poll/163208/half-support-publicly-financed-federal-campaigns.aspx.

197. Jeffrey M. Jones, "Americans' Desire for a Third Party Persists this Election Year," *Gallup*, September 30, 2016, http://www.gallup.com/poll/195920/americans-desire-third-party-persists-election-year.aspx?g_source=Election%20 2016&g_medium=newsfeed&g_campaign=tiles.

198. Lee Fang, "Gerrymadering Rigged the 2014 Election for GOP Advantage," *Moyers and Co.*, November 5, 2014, http://billmoyers.com/2014/11/05/gerrymandering-rigged-2014-elections-republican-advantage/.

199. Elizabeth Kolburt, "Drawing the Line: How Redistricting Turned America from Blue to Red," Books, *New Yorker*, June 27, 2016.

200. Christopher Ingraham, "This Computer Programmer Solved Gerrymandering in His Spare Time," Wonkblog, *Washington Post*, June 3, 2014, https://www.washingtonpost.com/news/wonk/wp/2014/06/03/this-computer-programmer-solved-gerrymandering-in-his-spare-time/?utm_term=.54de6fa8bebf.

201. Chris Kirk, "How Powerful Is Your Vote: When It Comes to Voting not All States Are Created Equal," *Slate*, November 3, 2012, http://www.slate.com/articles/news_and_politics/map_of_the_week/

2012/11/presidential_election_a_map_showing_the_vote_power_of_all_50_states.html.

202. Jason Easely, "Study Finds Worse States to Live in Are Controlled by Republicans," *PoliticusUSA*, October 8, 2014, http://www.politi-cususa.com/2014/10/08/study-finds-majority-worst-states-live-con-trolled-republicans.html. http://www.cnn.com/2015/01/13/politics/gop-governors-economic-records/.

203. Alexandra Jaffe, "Republicans will have to spin struggling state econ-omies in 2016," CNN Politics, January 13, 2015, 8:11PM, http://www.cnn.com/2015/01/13/politics/gop-governors-economic-records/

204. See: https://diy.rootsaction.org/petitions/support-and-improve-our-revolution

205. John Atcheson, "There's a Reason the Big Banks Aren't Mad with Hillary," *CommonDreams*, March 30, 2015.

Chapter 24

206. John Atcheson, "Backing Hillary in 2016; Bad for Progressives and Bad Politics, Too," *CommonDreams*, November 29, 2014. https://www.commondreams.org/views/2014/11/29/backing-hillary-2016-bad-progressives-and-bad-politics-too

207. Lisdey Espinoza and Markus Heinrich, "Water Scarcity: Cooperation or Conflict in the Mideast and North Africa," *Foreign Policy Journal*, September 2, 2016, http://www.foreignpolicyjournal.com/2016/09/02/water-scarcity-cooperation-or-conflict-in-the-middle-east-and-north-africa/.

Made in the USA
Middletown, DE
17 August 2017